Canadian Red Cross

First Aid
The Vital Link

Second Edition

Canadian Red Cross

First Aid
The Vital Link

Second Edition

StayWell

StayWell

Printed in Canada

Composition by Jansom
Color separation by Eclipse Colour Inc.
Printing/binding by Printcrafters

The StayWell Health Company Ltd.
780 Township Line Road
Yardley, PA 19067-4200

ISBN 1-58480-080-1

05 06 07 08 / 6 5

The Basic Life Support skills outlined in this publication are consistent with the Guidelines 2000 for Cardiopulmonary Resuscitation and Emergency Cardiovascular Care.

Acknowledgements

The original version of this manual was developed and produced through a joint effort of the American Red Cross Society and Mosby-Year Book, Inc. Our sister Society kindly authorized us to use their materials and shared with us the success they had with Mosby-Year Book, Inc. The Canadian Red Cross Society wishes to express our appreciation to the volunteers and staff of the American Red Cross Health and Safety Department who made this project possible. The Society also wishes to acknowledge the efforts of the many volunteers and staff involved in the Canadian development of this manual. The growth and development of *First Aid: The Vital Link* is a result of the work and dedication of hundreds of Canadians from across the country. Their commitment to excellence made this training program and its resources possible.

A very special thank you to the volunteer members of the Society's Development Team who were responsible for the textbook: Marj Busse, Jeff Calibaba, Diane Girard, Marilyn Hoffman, Linda Hutchins, Anita LeBlanc, Sheri McDougall, Dr. Jean Mireault, and Dr. Brian Wietzman.

Revision was supplied by:
Brian Weitzman, M.D.C.M., F.R.C.P.(C.), C.C.F.P.(E.M.)
S.H. Knox, M.D., C.M.

The Mosby-Year Book production team included David T. Culverwell, Publisher; Claire Merrick, Executive Editor; Christi Mangold, Developmental Editor; Gayle May Morris, Project Manager; Donna Walls, Senior Production Editor; Kay Michael Kramer, Art and Design Director; and Susan Lane, Senior Designer. Thanks go to Steve O'Hearn, Alan Orr, and John Hirst of Times Mirror Professional Publishing.

Special thanks go to Tom Lochhaas, Ed.D., Developmental Editor; Rick Brady, Photographer; and Fearless Designs, who produced the cover collage with photographs by White Cat Studio.

External review and guidance were provided by the following individuals:
Jill Courtemanche
Unit Administrator
Ontario Regional Poison Information Centre
Children's Hospital of Eastern Ontario
Dr. Robert Conn
Canadian Injury Prevention Foundation
Toronto, Ontario

Revisions 2000

With gratitude we thank the Canadian Red Cross volunteers and employees who participated in the review of the *First Aid: The Vital Link* Program.

Kathrin Andersen
Ismael Aquino
Dana Banke
Tracey Braun
Marjorie Busse
Ian Fitzpatrick
Sébastien Gagnon
Diane Girard
Kevin Holder
Anne LaCroix
Ovil Mazzerolle
Michèle Mercier
Tannis Nostedt
Elizabeth Ramlogan
Carolyn Tees
Louis-Philippe Tétrault
Line Vermette
Louise Waldner
Wendy Wilson
Mark Young

We also want to thank Caroline Gagnon and Margaret Zimmerman who coordinated the review and Suzanne Gasseau, translator, who translated the changes of this revised edition into French.

> **This manual is a reference for the Canadian Red Cross First Aid courses, Standard First Aid and Emergency First Aid, and should not be considered a substitute for an up-to-date first aid training course.**

Contents

9   The Secondary Survey

10   Head and Spine Injuries

11   Musculoskeletal Injuries

15 Healthy Lifestyles

APPENDICES

A First Aid Supplies

B Sample Examination Questions

C Sample Examination Answers

The Red Cross

What the Red Cross Emblem Really Stands For

The twin spectres of conflict and disaster continue to haunt the international community, and every day Red Cross workers are in the forefront bringing aid and comfort to victims all over the world. In such trying circumstances both workers and victims often endure situations of hardship and extreme personal danger.

Red Cross workers carry no arms; their only shield is the universally recognized Red Cross emblem, which serves as a symbol of protection and neutrality. The emblem conveys the sense of humanity and impartiality that is embodied in the worldwide Red Cross and Red Crescent Movement.

In every hazardous situation it is essential that the Red Cross emblem be readily recognized and respected by all parties as a trusted symbol of protection and humanitarian assistance. Any adoption of the emblem for commercial use not only dilutes the impact of this symbol at home and abroad, it is against the law.

Contrary to popular belief, the Red Cross emblem is not approved as a universal symbol of first aid or any other program activity of the Red Cross and Red Crescent Movement. When you think "Red Cross," don't only think "first aid" or other Red Cross program. Take time to consider what the Red Cross emblem really embodies in its exacting function as an international symbol of protection and neutrality.

Apart from purposes of identification and protection in the field already noted, the Red Cross emblem is jealously guarded within the Red Cross and Red Crescent Movement. In this first aid text, it is used specifically to identify the training material as that developed and used by The Canadian Red Cross Society.

The Fundamental Principles

Individuals live by a set of principles, which expresses to others the values they believe in. Organizations abide by certain principles as well, which become formulated into guidelines for following appropriate actions.

Look at the fundamental principles on the inside cover of this book and read them to yourself. What is your initial impression? Do they make sense? What values do you see in the Fundamental Principles that you can identify with personally and as a first aid provider? Your instructor will be pleased to assist you in answering these questions.

These fundamental principles have evolved over time and were not fully developed and officially accepted throughout the International Red Cross and Red Crescent Movement until the middle of the 1960s. The Fundamental Principles emerged from accepted practices that had evolved long before they were ever officially written down and accepted.

The Fundamental Principles work together and should be seen as mutually supportive; how-ever, they are arranged in a hierarchy as shown in the diagram.

The two principles that have been at the core of Red Cross since its inception in 1859 at the Battle of Solferino are **humanity** and **impartiality**. They are the **substantive principles**. This means that they are the "core" values, the essence of the Red Cross and Red Crescent Movement.

Neutrality and **independence** are the **derived principles**, which are necessary to put the substantive principles into action.

Voluntary service, unity, and **universality** are the **organizational principles**, describing the practical and operational nature of the Red Cross and Red Crescent movement. Together, all seven principles form a worldwide system of beliefs and serve as a guide for Red Cross and Red Crescent National Societies in over 175 countries.

Emergency Response: The Organizational Context

One of the keys to understanding The Canadian Red Cross Society, its volunteers and staff, and the Red Cross programs is to know how the Society responds to emergencies and how it trains people in "emergency response."

So what's an emergency? In Red Cross terms, an emergency is any real or potential situation that is, or has the possibility to become, life threatening. An emergency may involve only one person or millions of people. It can range from a heart attack to a severe drought in Africa or to an armed conflict producing civilian casualties and refugees, prisoners of war, and wounded soldiers.

Obviously, Red Cross is not the only organization to respond to emergencies. Government, the police, fire departments, and other rescue organizations play the most significant roles in securing public safety. Red Cross, however, is the largest voluntary, nonprofit organization in Canada and complements the civil authorities by playing a major role in "emergency response" and safety education.

**The seven Fundamental Principles
that Red Cross follows**

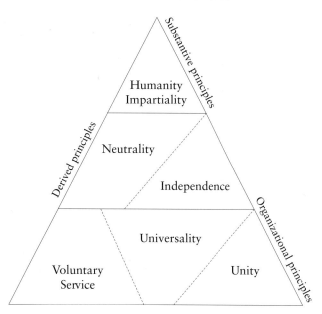

People need knowledge and skills for emergency response and Red Cross offers first aid programs and other types of training for precisely this reason. By taking a Red Cross First Aid course you are honing your emergency response skills. First you acquire **diagnostic skills** (what's wrong?) and then **treatment skills** (what to do about it). Your priorities are to first save life and then to prevent further injury. Red Cross trains you to be an "accident manager" so that those requiring help have the best possible chance to survive and recover. This means you are an extension of Red Cross, doing its work whenever you render first aid, regardless of why you are taking this course.

The emergency response ethic is present in all Red Cross programs: International Services, Water Safety Services, Emergency Services, Abuse Prevention Services, and, of course, First Aid Services. If you are interested in these programs in your community, please contact your local Red Cross office for details and volunteering possibilities. Your instructor will be happy to provide more information.

Henry Dunant: A Moment in Time
What If He Just Turned Around and Went Home?

Imagine this happening today: you are travelling alone down the highway and come across an accident. You see several people injured, many others immobile (are they dead?). This is a horrifying experience, all too common on Canada's roads. You approach the situation safely and do your best to give first aid and get help quickly. This is what your Red Cross Fist Aid course has trained you to do.

Now imagine this just a few years ago: you come to a railway crossing where two trains have collided. The wreckage resembles a scene from a bad movie. Flames and acrid smoke fill the air. Cries for help come from inside the trains, bodies are everywhere, and people are walking around stunned and covered in blood. Again you respond and assist the police and fire department to help

the injured. Your Red Cross First Aid training is invaluable. This really happened in 1986 at Hinton, Alberta, where a train wreck killed 21 people and seriously injured another 78.

Now visualize yourself much further back in time. You walk over the crest of a hill, and in the valley below you see not a few casualties, but as many as 40,000 dead and wounded soldiers. They are abandoned, left to live or die as luck would have it. A human disaster of this magnitude seems impossible for one person alone to cope with, even with the finest first aid training available.

This scene was precisely what Henry Dunant, the founder of the Red Cross and Red Crescent Movement, saw in June 1859 at the Battle of Solferino in Italy, where French and Austrian armies clashed in the bloodiest battle of the 19th century in Europe. A struggling grain merchant from Geneva, Dunant was trying to secure a contract with the French Army, whom he had followed all over Italy and had finally caught up with at Solferino.

A great deal depended on Dunant; this was the crucial moment of his life and the seminal moment for the Red Cross and Red Crescent Movement. If he turned away and returned to Switzerland, no one could or would blame him; the scene was too staggering. If he stayed and helped the soldiers around him, he would earn a brief footnote in a battle report and perhaps a medal, and he could go home with a sense of satisfaction in having done something.

What did he really do? What would you have done in his place? His first action was to organize local villagers into first aid teams to help as many of the wounded as possible. In this way, thousands of lives were saved. After some sense of order was established, Dunant analyzed the situation. Why should scenes of such horror be repeated over and over in battles? Was there no way to make sure that soldiers who were "hors de combat" would stand a better chance of survival? At this moment Dunant envisaged a neutral organization, respected and protected by both sides in conflicts, that would care for the wounded and prisoners. The symbol of respect and protection he eventually would choose was a Red Cross emblem on a white background, the reverse of the Swiss flag. Dunant spent the rest of his life lobbying governments, organizing National Red Cross Societies, and speaking in public so that the suffering war causes would be reduced.

Dunant was honoured in 1901 as a co-winner of the first Nobel Peace Prize. He died in 1910, after having lived much of his latter years in poverty. We owe him our gratitude and thanks for having founded the International Red Cross and Red Crescent Movement. Millions of people over the years also owe him their lives.

Preparing to Respond

2

Objectives

After reading this chapter, you should be able to:

1. State the most important action you can take in a life-threatening emergency.

2. Describe the five common barriers to action that may prevent people from acting in emergencies.

3. List the emergency action principles of first aid.

4. Discuss the four conditions that must occur for a person to contract an infectious disease.

5. Identify the four different routes through which infectious diseases are transmitted from one person to another.

6. Describe what you can do to prevent emergencies from occurring.

7. Explain four ways in which you can prepare effectively for emergencies.

8. Describe how Good Samaritan laws protect you when you give first aid.

9. Describe actions to take to prevent becoming infected when giving first aid.

10. Identify effective ways to cope with a traumatic event.

11. Define the key terms for this chapter.

Key Terms

bystander A lay person who recognizes an emergency and decides to help.

casualty Someone needing emergency medical care because of an injury or a sudden serious illness.

emergency A situation requiring immediate action.

emergency medical services (EMS) system A network of community resources and personnel organized to give emergency care in cases of injury or sudden illness.

first aid Immediate care given to a casualty until more advanced care can be obtained.

Good Samaritan laws Laws that protect bystanders acting in good faith when giving first aid to ill or injured casualties of an emergency.

infection A condition caused by microorganisms such as viruses and bacteria.

injury Damage to the body from an external force such as a blow, a fall, a fire, or a collision.

medical emergency A sudden illness requiring immediate medical attention.

shaken baby syndrome A type or combination of injuries a baby receives from being shaken.

universal precautions Safety measures taken to prevent occupational-risk exposure to blood or other body fluids containing visible blood.

5

You are driving home after a ball game. While stopped at an intersection, you see a car hit another car head-on. To your horror, one of the drivers crashes against the windshield. Glass is everywhere, and the injured driver slumps over the steering wheel, motionless.

On a Saturday afternoon you walk into your garage and find your father lying on the floor. He barely seems conscious and is clutching at his chest.

In each case, what would you do? What help can you give?

As a *bystander* trained in *first aid*, you may be in a position to give first aid to a *casualty* in an *emergency* situation. This book describes the emergency action principles, which are the basic principles of first aid to follow in any emergency. Your response may help save a life.

Emergency Action Principles of First Aid

First aid is usually not as complicated as many people think. In any emergency always follow these emergency action principles (EAPs):

1. Survey the emergency scene to be sure no danger exists before you approach the casualty.
2. Check the casualty for unresponsiveness. If the person does not respond, call EMS.
3. Do a primary survey. Check that the casualty has an open airway and is breathing, the heart is beating, and there is no severe bleeding. Give first aid immediately for any of these life-threatening problems, and call EMS.
4. Do a secondary survey to check the casualty for other problems, and give other first aid as needed.
5. Keep monitoring the casualty's breathing and circulation until EMS arrives.
6. Help the casualty rest in the most comfortable position and give reassurance.

These principles are discussed more fully in Chapter 5. Because you always follow these same steps in any emergency, remembering what to do when you see that an emergency has occurred is easy. Knowing these basic principles is the first step in being prepared for emergencies.

The First Aider's Role

Your goal in learning first aid is to give care to someone suffering from an injury or medical emergency until trained medical help can arrive.

A bystander is someone like you who recognizes an emergency and decides to help (Figure 2–1). Ideally, everyone should know what to do in an emergency. Everyone should know first aid. First aid is the immediate care given to a victim of injury or sudden illness until more advanced care is obtained.

You must first recognize that the illness or injury that has occurred is an emergency. Calling *emergency medical services (EMS)* professionals is the most important action you and other bystanders can take. The next chapter describes the emergency medical services system that provides emergency medical care throughout Canada. Early arrival of EMS personnel increases the casualty's chances of surviving a life-threatening emergency. In addition, a bystander trained in first aid can provide help that may save a life in the first few minutes of an emergency.

Becoming involved in emergency situations, where you may be the only one who can help, is very important. Don't worry that you might do something wrong; you can always help in some way, even if it's only calling for help.

First aid *can* make the difference between life and death. Often it *does* make the difference between complete recovery and permanent disability. Your role includes four basic steps:

1. Recognize that an emergency exists.
2. Decide to act.
3. Call EMS.
4. Give first aid until EMS arrives.

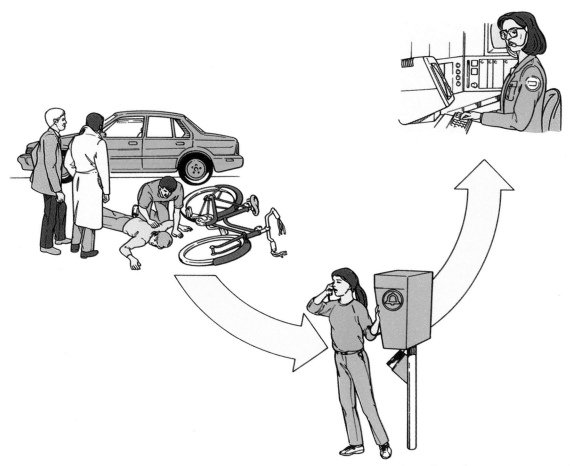

Figure 2–1   Deciding to help means taking action. Deciding to help includes calling the emergency number for an ambulance and giving first aid care at the scene.

The first two steps are described in the following sections. Chapter 3 discusses when and how to call EMS, and later chapters then describe appropriate first aid to give for injuries and sudden illness while waiting for EMS to arrive.

Recognizing Emergencies

Recognizing an emergency is the first step in responding. A *medical emergency* is a sudden illness that requires immediate medical attention, such as a heart attack. An *injury* is damage to the body, such as a broken arm, that results from a violent force. Some injuries can be serious enough to be considered emergencies. In the next chapter you will learn what situations should always be considered an emergency. If in doubt, call EMS and let the professionals decide how to respond.

Decide to Act

Bystanders need to get involved in emergency situations, and many lives are saved because people like you do get involved. Every year countless bystanders recognize and respond to emergencies. Some phone for help, some comfort the casualty or family members, some give first aid to casualties, and still others help to keep order at the emergency scene. There are many things you can do once you decide to act (Table 2–1).

Barriers to Action

Sometimes in an emergency people are reluctant to act, for various reasons. These reasons are called barriers to action. The five common reasons people give for not acting are as follows:

- Presence of other people
- Uncertainty about the casualty
- Nature of the injury or illness
- Fear of disease transmission
- Fear of doing something wrong

Thinking about these things now and mentally preparing yourself for an emergency will help you overcome these barriers.

Presence of other people

The presence of other people can cause confusion at an emergency scene. Do not assume that, just because there is a crowd, someone is giving first aid. Do not feel embarrassed in front of strangers.

Table 2–1	You Can Always Do Something to Help In Any Emergency
What to do	*How to do it*
Take appropriate safety precaution.	Ensure the safety of the casualty, yourself, and bystanders. Be alert to possible dangers at the scene.
Activate the EMS system.	Telephone your local emergency number.
Communicate effectively.	Reassure the casualty and others at the scene. Gather information from the casualty, family, friends, and bystanders. Provide necessary information to EMS personnel.
Manage bystanders.	Organize bystanders to— Call the local emergency number. Meet and direct the ambulance to the scene. Help give care. Comfort the casualty and other bystanders. Help obtain supplies. Keep the area free of unnecessary traffic. Help protect the casualty from possible dangers.

Even if someone else is already giving care, offer your help. You may help keep the crowd back, send someone to call for an ambulance, retrieve blankets or other supplies, or help comfort the casualty and others at the scene.

Uncertainty about the casualty

The person needing your first aid may be a stranger, someone much older or much younger than you, or someone of a different gender or race. Regardless of who the casualty is, put such concerns aside to give first aid. If the person acts offensively because of stress, emotions, or even intoxication, do not take offense. If for some reason you cannot give first aid directly, you can still help by calling EMS and assisting in crowd management.

Nature of the injury or illness

An injury or illness can be very unpleasant because of blood, vomit, unpleasant odors, or torn or burned skin. If necessary, turn away for a moment and take a few deep breaths. Then do your best. Remember this situation is an emergency. Your help can save a life. Try to do for the casualty what you would want someone to do for you.

Fear of disease transmission

Some people hesitate to act because they fear they may catch some disease from the casualty. This risk is actually very small. Although many diseases can be passed from one person to another, you can greatly reduce the risk by taking precautions when giving first aid.

Germs can be contracted from people, objects, food, animals, or insects. Your body will react to the germs; it may or may not be able to fight off the infection caused by the germs. Infection may lead to disease. This manual will help you recognize situations in which disease might be transmitted. You will also learn how to protect yourself and others from infectious disease at home, at school, in the workplace, and in other public and recreational settings.

What Is an Infection?

A disease is a result of an infection caused by germs, also called *microorganisms* or *pathogens,* in the body.

What Causes an Infection?

An infection, or infectious disease, results when germs enter the body and affect one or more organs. Bacteria and viruses are the most common germs and cause most infectious diseases.

Germs are present everywhere: in the air, in our homes and offices, and in our mouths and digestive tracts. Many germs either do not cause disease or are killed by the body's immune system upon entering the body. Infectious diseases range from the common cold—a relatively mild infection—to fatal diseases such as HIV infection. Bacteria cause infections such as strep throat, tuberculosis, and meningitis (Figure 2–2, *A* to *C*). Antibiotics can help the body fight a bacterial infection, but medications are not very effective against viruses. The body's immune system is our primary weapon against viruses.

The Body's Natural Defences

The skin is the body's first line of defence against germs. Germs can enter the body only through one of the body's natural orifices (e.g., nose or mouth), unless there is a break in the skin. Sexually transmitted germs enter the body through the orifices of the genitalia or rectum.

Once a germ is in the body, the only natural defence is the body's immune system. Leukocytes attack the germ. When the body is healthy and the immune system is strong, it can overcome and destroy most germs. We often feel feverish and fatigued when our immune system is battling an infection. We may also have other symptoms, such as muscular weakness, joint pain, cough, vomiting or nausea, and headache, caused by a specific type of germ. In the young, the elderly, the ill, or oth-

ers with weak immune systems, a germ may multiply faster than the immune system can fight it; this can lead to a serious infection or death.

When Do Infectious Diseases Occur?

For a person to contract an infectious disease, four conditions must occur:

1. Germs are present in the surrounding environment.
2. The germs enter the body.
3. The individual has no or weak natural defence.
4. Enough germs are present in the body to cause disease.

If any one of these conditions is missing, an infection cannot occur. For example, germs present on your skin cannot harm you if they cannot enter your body. Also, if you are immune to a particular disease because you have received a vaccination, your immune system will kill the germs in your body that cause the particular disease before you become infected.

Knowing how germs are transmitted and how they enter the body helps us understand how we can prevent infection.

Infectious Diseases

Infectious diseases vary considerably in seriousness. An infection, such as the flu, that may cause only discomfort in one person can prove fatal to an elderly or ill person.

Knowing how diseases are transmitted can help you understand how to prevent them. The following serious diseases are described in more detail in Appendix A of the Red Cross *Yes You Can Prevent Disease Transmission* Manual.

- Chickenpox
- Diphtheria
- *Escherichia coli* infection
- Giardiasis
- HIV
- Hepatitis

- Herpes
- Influenza
- Lyme disease
- Measles
- Meningitis
- Mononucleosis
- Mumps
- Rubella
- Salmonellosis
- Tetanus
- Tuberculosis

How Is an Infection Transmitted from One Person to Another?

Infectious diseases can be transmitted from one person to another through four different routes:

- Direct contact
- Indirect contact
- Airborne transmission
- Vector transmission

Some diseases are transmitted through only one of these routes, but others may be transmitted through two or more routes.

Direct Contact

A disease is transmitted by direct contact when a person touches body fluids that contain a germ from an infected person. Body fluids include blood, vomit, secretions, and saliva. Different germs are sometimes present in different body fluids.

Diseases spread by direct contact include giardiasis, AIDS, hepatitis B and C, herpes, meningitis, mononucleosis, mumps, and salmonella.

To prevent disease transmission by direct contact, you must eliminate or reduce the chance of direct contact with the infectious material. Infectious material includes all body fluids. The risk of disease from direct contact depends on these factors:

- The type of body fluid contacted (although some diseases may be transmitted through some body fluids and not others, consider all body fluids as potentially infectious).
- The concentration of virus in the body fluid.
- The amount of body fluid with which contact is made.
- The body opening exposed to infectious material (such as mucous membrane, broken skin, mouth).
- The length of the exposure.

Specific ways to reduce direct contact with infectious material vary from one setting to the next. However, the universal precautions remain the same in all situations, such as handwashing and wearing gloves whenever giving first aid. See

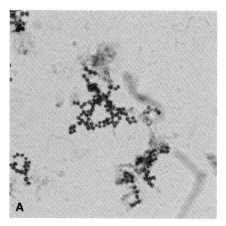
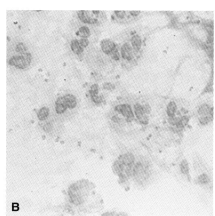
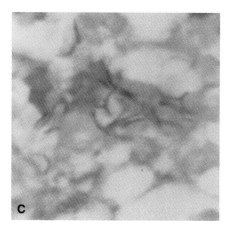

Figure 2–2   Germs are bacteria and viruses that can enter the body and cause infections. Examples of such germs are *A*, streptococcus Group A; *B*, Neisseria meningitis; and *C*, tuberculosis. (From Murray PR and others: *Medical microbiology*, ed 2, 1993, St Louis, Mosby.)

the "Precautions to Prevent Disease Transmission" on p. 13–18 for a complete list of precautions used to prevent disease transmission through direct contact.

Indirect Contact

Some diseases are transmitted by indirect contact with germs on an object that has been in contact with an infected person's body fluids. Many germs can live a short (or long) time outside the human body on almost any object. For example, blood, fecal material, or vomit on a piece of equipment can infect someone who later handles the equipment if the germ enters the person's body. Objects such as intravenous needles are particularly dangerous because they can penetrate the skin of another person and easily deposit germs inside that person's body. Even soiled clothing or tissues can transmit infection through indirect contact (Figure 2–3).

Diseases that spread through indirect contact include diphtheria, *E. coli* infection, giardiasis, hepatitis A, and mononucleosis.

To prevent transmission by indirect contact you must avoid contact with items that have been in direct contact with body fluids. These items include dressings, equipment, and work surfaces. Precautions to prevent indirect contact transmission include using proper disposal containers and using proper equipment when handling contaminated materials. See the "Precautions to Prevent Disease Transmission" on p. 13–18 for a complete list of precautions to prevent disease transmission through indirect contact.

Airborne Transmission

An airborne disease is transmitted when someone breathes out germs and you breathe them in. Usually the germs are present in tiny droplets that an infected person coughs or sneezes out from up to 3 feet from your face. Some germs, such as tuberculosis bacteria, may live a relatively long time in the air, requiring the infected person to be isolated until treatment is completed. It also may

Figure 2–3 Some diseases are transmitted by indirect contact. Intravenous needles, equipment, tissues, bandages, and other contaminated objects can transmit infection through indirect contact.

be necessary to maintain an adequate ventilation system to prevent airborne transmission to others in the building.

Diseases spread by airborne transmission include chickenpox, influenza, and tuberculosis.

Taking precautions against airborne diseases can be more difficult than with other forms of transmission. You can avoid touching certain objects but you cannot stop breathing. Special breathing apparatus may not be practical in most circumstances. However, you can still take important precautions against airborne diseases by reducing the number of germs in the air and making sure ventilation is adequate. See the "Precautions to Prevent Disease Transmission" on p. 13–18 for a complete list of precautions to prevent infection through airborne transmission.

Vector Transmission

Some diseases can be transmitted if an animal, insect, or even a human bites or stings a person and transmits a pathogen into the person's body (Figure 2–4). The animal, insect, or person is called a *vector* and has to be carrying the germs already. Malaria, rabies, and Lyme disease are transmitted by vectors.

To prevent transmission of vector-borne diseases, you must eliminate or lower the risk of

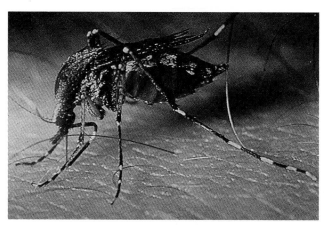

Figure 2–4   Vectors are animals, insects, or humans that transfer an infective agent from one host to another. The Latin translation of vector is *one who carries*. (From the American Mosquito Control Association.)

exposure to the vector. Vaccinations are available against some of these infections.

Recommended precautions vary greatly depending on the risk for exposure, which in turn depends on the types and numbers of animals or insects in the area and the risk of human bites. In addition to the following precautions, see the Precautions to Prevent Disease Transmission" on p. 13–18 for a complete list of precautions to prevent transmission.

The best way to prevent a vector-borne disease is to lower the risk of being bitten or stung. The following precautions are recommended:

- Wear repellent, protective clothing and shoes to prevent bites and stings. Use proper containers for garbage to keep animals out and to discourage insects.
- If you cannot control the natural environment, be aware of the risks and avoid them. Do not disturb wild animals in their homes. Post warning signs where humans are likely to encounter wild animals, such as in parks.
- If you are bitten or stung, try to remain calm, and treat the bite or sting with the appropriate first aid.
- After being bitten or stung, clean the entry site as soon as possible. With a wild or a

domestic animal that has not had immunization, seek medical assistance, and notify appropriate authorities (i.e., Public Health Animal Control Centre).

- Use soap and water to clean the entry site, and apply a bandage to keep out airborne germs. You may also apply ice to slow the blood flow to the injured site.
- Consider what other changes you can make in the environment to prevent other people from being bitten or stung.

General Guidelines to Prevent Disease Transmission

Infectious disease transmission can usually be prevented. Many guidelines have been developed to prevent disease by killing or reducing the number of germs in the environment or blocking the transmission route. Listed in this section are general guidelines that should be followed in all settings and locations to help prevent disease transmission. Later sections list additional guidelines for specific settings, such as schools, workplaces, daycare centres, and health care institutions.

The following guidelines are called *universal precautions* because you should use them at all times in all places—whether you think a person is infected or not. *How* you apply the precautions may vary with each individual location, but not the use of the precautions themselves. For example, when helping a coworker bandage a cut finger, you should wear gloves and avoid contact with the person's blood, even though you may feel certain that he or she does not have an infectious disease. Many people with diseases like HIV or some forms of hepatitis are not aware that they are infected. You could acquire a life-threatening infection through blood contact with only one momentary mistake. You should view the body fluids of all people as potentially infectious.

The guidelines in this manual are organized in three categories:

1. Personal precautions.
2. Equipment precautions.
3. Environmental precautions.

Personal precautions are actions that individuals or groups can take to reduce the risk of disease transmission. Personal hygiene, such as washing your hands, often is a good example. Other examples include educating others about precautions such as infection prevention methods and safe sexual practices.

Equipment precautions involve items used to protect people from direct contact with contaminated objects (Figure 2–5). They usually put a barrier between you and objects that may be contaminated with germs. These items include protective clothing and equipment that prevent contact with blood or other body fluids, such as gloves, resuscitation devices, and proper disposal containers. Always wash your hands after you remove your gloves.

Environmental precautions involve the set up of an area that reduces exposure and encourages proper use of personal and equipment precautions. Environmental controls can minimize the risk of contact with germs by isolating or removing hazards from contact with people and changing the way tasks are performed.

In most settings, there are risks of infectious disease that require following all three types of

> **NOTE**
> **Attention to personal precautions can be the most effective means of preventing exposure.** Taking personal precaution also means being aware of potential hazards and how to prevent them. Other precautions are useless if personal precautions are not applied properly.

precautions. Yet in different settings, some are more important than others. For example, more equipment and environmental precautions are generally required in a public place than in the home. Some precautions, like handwashing, are important in all settings. Other precautions listed here are relevant only when providing first aid or patient care in a health care institution. Nonetheless, remember that these are universal precautions—the only way to be completely safe is to follow these guidelines at all times.

When you administer first aid, even for a minor scrape or cut, you may come into contact with another person's body fluids. Regardless of how healthy that person may seem, universal precautions should always be followed to lower the risk of infection transmission through direct or indirect contact with body fluids.

Precautions To Prevent Disease Transmission

Personal Precautions

- Wash your hands frequently and thoroughly (see p. 14). This is the single most important precaution you can take to prevent disease transmission. Wash your hands often at home, at work, in school, and in all settings where you are around others—not only when you know someone in the area is sick.
- If you contact body fluids with your hands or other body areas, avoid transmitting possible

Figure 2–5   Gloves and masks help protect people from contamination.

HANDWASHING

Handwashing is an important precaution in all settings and helps prevent transmission of germs that can cause many infectious diseases. Following are public health guidelines for effective handwashing technique. The guidelines given are for use in public settings. In the home, you can adapt these guidelines regarding the use of paper towels, leaving the water running when drying hands, and touching the faucet handles.

1. Always use warm running water and a mild soap (preferably liquid). Antibacterial soaps may be used but are not required. Premoistened cleansing towelettes do not effectively clean hands and do not take the place of handwashing.
2. Wet the hands and apply a small amount (dime to quarter size) of soap to hands (Figure 2–6, A and B).
3. Rub hands together vigorously until a soapy lather appears and continue for at least 15 seconds. Be sure to scrub between fingers, under fingernails, and around the tops and palms of the hands (Fig. 2–6, C).
4. Rinse hands under warm running water. Leave the water running when drying hands (Fig. 2–6, D).
5. Dry hands with a clean, disposable (or single-use) towel, being careful not to touch the faucet handles or towel holder with your clean hands (Fig. 2–6, E).
6. Turn the faucet off using the towel as a barrier between your hands and the faucet handle (Fig. 2–6, F).
7. Discard the used towel in a trash can lined with a plastic bag. Trash cans with foot-pedal operated lids are best.
8. Consider using hand lotion to prevent chapping of hands. If using lotions, use liquids or tubes that can be squirted so that the hands do not have direct contact with the container's spout. Direct contact with the spout could contaminate the lotion inside the container.

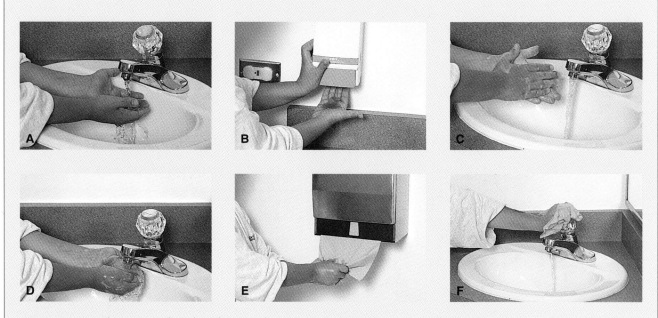

Figure 2–6 The proper handwashing technique is an important step of preventing transmission of germs. *A,* Wet the hands. *B,* Lather. *C,* Scrub. *D,* Rinse. *E,* Leave the water running while you dry your hands with clean, disposable (or single-use) towels. *F,* Turn the faucet off using the towel as a barrier between your hands and the faucet handle.

germs to other areas of your body. Do not touch other parts of your body, especially those areas such as eyes, nose, and mouth, which are more vulnerable to germs.

- After any exposure to potentially infectious material, thoroughly wash your hands and any other affected parts of the body as soon as possible with soap and water.
- Handle all blood and other body fluids as infectious materials.
- Always wash your hands after removing gloves.
- Administer first aid in a way that reduces exposure to blood and other body fluids.
- If you think you have been exposed to an infectious disease, ask your doctor about possible appropriate treatment.
- To help prevent airborne disease transmission when you are ill, cover your mouth and nose when you cough or sneeze.
- Since airborne germs are often present and unavoidable in many settings, be on the defensive by helping your immune system combat disease through adequate nutrition, exercise, and rest.
- If a building has poor air circulation, take breaks to go outside or go somewhere with better air quality.
- If you have a cold or the flu, avoid shaking hands with others.
- Smoking makes one more susceptible to some respiratory infections; stopping smoking will help prevent infections.
- Cover any cuts, scrapes, or skin irritations you may have with protective clothing and/or bandages.
- In an area where you might accidentally directly or indirectly contact infectious materials, do not eat or drink anything or touch your mouth, eyes, or nose with your hands.

Equipment Precautions

- Always use some type of barrier between you and any potentially infectious material. The type of equipment used varies depending on the situation. For example, use tissues to pick up a dry object that may have germs on it, but use tweezers or other equipment to pick up and dispose of a bloody bandage.
- Use dressings and tissues to minimize direct contact with blood, other body fluids, and wounds. If possible, have the casualty wash the wound first and assist you, such as by holding a dressing in place or putting pressure on a wound to stop bleeding.
- Soap and water, paper towels, disinfectant, and cleaning materials should be present in bathrooms.
- Ensure that first aid kits are readily accessible to everyone (Figure 2–7).
- Ensure that all first aid kits are fully stocked with several pairs of disposable gloves, pocket masks or face shields, and antibacterial hand cleanser.
- Remember to restock items used from the first aid kit (Figure 2–8).
- Maintain all protective equipment in good working order. Immediately dispose of any protective equipment that is peeling, discoloured, torn, or punctured.
- Proper disposal containers are needed for any items that contact body fluids. These can be containers with regular garbage bags or designated biohazard containers.

Figure 2–7 First aid kits should be placed so that they are easy to find and use.

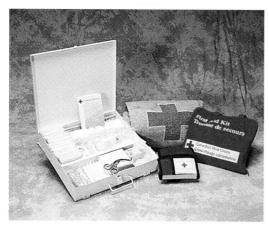

Figure 2–8   First aid kits should be kept well stocked.

- Tissues are the most common tool to help prevent exposure to airborne disease. In some cases, more sophisticated masks may be required. This may range from simple masks, which reduce but do not eliminate exposure to airborne particles, to very sophisticated equipment, which eliminates all exposure to air-borne diseases.

- Put on well-fitting, high-quality gloves in any situation where you may encounter a person's body fluids either directly or indirectly. Remember that in addition to infection by direct contact with a person, you could be infected by indirect contact with many materials handled by an infected person.

- To remove latex gloves, peel them off from the wrist, turning them inside out as they roll down the hand. To remove the second glove, grasp it at the inside of the wrist and peel it back from the inside, not touching the soiled outer surface (Figure 2–9).

- Remove and dispose of any gloves that are peeling, discoloured, or no longer intact.

- Never reuse disposable gloves.

- Do not touch anything with soiled gloves except items you plan to dispose of or wash and disinfect.

- Put on a new pair of gloves before contacting a second person.

- Use breathing devices, such as disposable resuscitation masks and airway devices.

These items should be readily available in settings where the need for resuscitation can be anticipated but the risk of infection is so slight that no one should hesitate to give mouth-to-mouth resuscitation if such equipment is not available.

- After providing care, wash your hands thoroughly with soap and water in a utility or bathroom sink, not a sink in a food preparation area.

Environmental Precautions

- Environmental precautions work along with personal and equipment precautions. If gloves are in the first aid kit, but the first aid kit is not accessible, they cannot be used. Environmental precautions also include ensuring the safety of the area. What procedures and tools are in place to prevent exposures?

- For body fluids, additional equipment can be used to prevent contact and to reduce potential exposure by containing body fluids. In some environments, special spill-containment material may be present.

- Ensure that other people are not exposed to spilled infectious material. This could mean keeping them away from the scene or sending

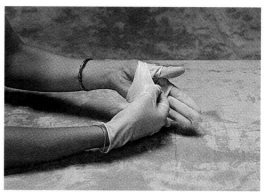

Figure 2–9   The correct technique for removing latex gloves is to peel them off from the wrist, turning them inside out as they roll down the hand. To remove the second glove, grasp it at the inside of the wrist and peel it back from the inside, not touching the soiled outer surface.

ALLERGIC REACTIONS TO LATEX GLOVES

Well-fitting, high-quality gloves are an important tool used to help prevent infection. Latex gloves have been used by more people over the past decade, and as a result more people have had allergic reactions to latex. Up to 10% of the general population are estimated to have some reaction to a latex protein present in this kind of rubber. Typically, such a reaction is mild, but in some cases of allergy the reaction has been very severe, causing the medical emergency known as *anaphylactic shock*.

A mild reaction may occur as a skin irritation called *contact dermatitis*. The skin may have an itching or burning sensation and may look red and swollen (Figure 2–10, *A*). The reaction occurs only in the skin contacted by the gloves and may go away during periods when no gloves are worn (e.g., when on vacation). It may also be caused by the powder used to make the glove easier to put on and remove. Treatment involves trying other brands of gloves and using anti-inflammatory creams.

More serious hypersensitivity reactions also may occur, either immediately or soon after putting on the gloves or delayed up to 48 hours later. Itching may progress to pain with a skin rash developing up the arm beyond the contact area or elsewhere on the body. Other body tissues may swell, including the eyelids, lips, face, and airway (Figure 2–10, *B*).

A serious systemic hypersensitivity reaction can be like other life-threatening allergic reactions. The person may experience hives on the body, difficulty breathing, nausea, a rapid heart rate, and anaphylactic shock. This condition is an emergency situation, and the person requires immediate medical help.

If you have any symptoms that you suspect may result from latex hypersensitivity, see your family physician. You may be advised to switch to a non-latex glove or a special low-protein allergen latex glove. *In no case, however, should you stop using gloves; they are an essential barrier to help prevent infectious disease.*

Latex hypersensitivity may be present from birth in some people, but there is evidence that some people who wear latex gloves often may become hypersensitive over time. You are never free of the risk of developing a reaction.

Note that other people not actually wearing latex gloves may also be affected if they have latex hypersensitivity. A person can have a reaction when touched by *your* gloves. If you work in a health care institution or in any other capacity in which you are likely to be providing care to patients, check for your institution's policy and protocol regarding latex gloves. Know what to assess when a patient may be having a latex reaction. When providing first aid in any setting, always look for a Medic Alert® bracelet that may indicate the person's allergy. Once a patient is known to be latex sensitive, a special protocol should be followed to prevent a reaction. New guidelines have been issued for the use of latex in health care facilities.

Latex is also present in many products used in the home and community, such as balloons, kitchen supplies and utensils, rubber bands, and many other objects.

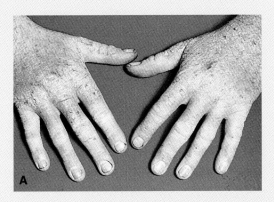 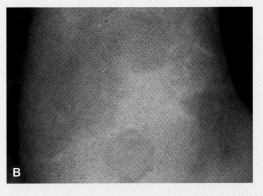

Figure 2–10   Some people develop an allergic reaction to Latex. Reactions include *A*, contact dermatitis and *B*, hives. (*A*, From McKee PH: *Pathology of the skin with clinical correlations*, ed 2, 1996, London, Mosby-Wolfe.

them to get more equipment. If possible, move objects to prevent contact with body fluids. Post warning signs if necessary during the area clean-up.

- Immediately disposing of contaminated material greatly reduces the risk of indirect contact. Wear gloves if you need to dispose of anything that has been in contact with other people's body fluids. This includes wearing gloves to empty garbage cans that may contain contaminated material or clean areas such as washrooms where body fluids may still be on surfaces.
- Put disposal containers where they are easy to use.
- Ensure separation between areas where body fluids are common (e.g., use of separate washrooms in work and kitchen areas). Ensure that people do not use the same sink for hygiene and food preparation.
- Ensure that there is an adequate supply of clean air, and avoid recirculating contaminated air.
- In all cases, if a precaution is not working properly, re-examine the precautions that were used so that they can be improved. If people are developing diseases transmitted by air, for example, reduce the recirculation of air to other parts of the building and increase the amount of cleaner air.
- After an exposure, consider what changes are needed to prevent this type of re-exposure. Does the first aid kit need to be moved? Do procedures need to be changed?

Immunization

Most people have been immunized against common childhood diseases, such as measles and mumps. Immunization introduces a substance into the body that allows the immune system to build up resistance to a specific infection.

Talk to your doctor about your immunizations. If you are frequently around ill people,

your doctor may recommend immunizations for the following diseases and others:

- DPT (diphtheria, pertussis, tetanus)
- Polio
- Hepatitis B (HBV)
- MMR (measles, mumps, rubella)
- Influenza

Children generally receive immunizations because they are required by school or extracurricular activities, but adults may lack immunizations. Talk to your doctor or local community health nurse about your immunizations.

If you are planning a trip outside of the country, check which immunizations you may need for countries you will visit. Allow several weeks for this procedure, as some vaccines cannot be given the same day, and others must be given in stages.

Additional Guidelines to Prevent Infection in Specific Settings

> **NOTE**
> Because the risk of disease varies greatly from place to place, it is impossible to cover all possible hazards in all locations. Therefore, for comprehensive guidelines specific to your particular situation, please contact your community public health centre.

Legal Issues in First Aid

Sometimes people worry that they may be legally liable when giving first aid. As long as you act reasonably and prudently when you give first aid, you need not worry about being sued. In fact, most of the provinces explicitly encourage bystanders to give first aid with laws called *Good Samaritan laws*. These laws protect citizens and medical professionals who act in good faith to give emergency assistance to ill or injured persons at the scene of an emergency.

The law provides that when you act reasonably and prudently under the conditions of the emergency, you cannot be held responsible for the person's injury. According to experts in the field of first aid, the following are reasonable actions:

- Move a casualty only if the person's life is endangered.
- Call EMS for professional help.
- Check the casualty's airway, breathing, and circulation before providing further care.
- Continue to care for any life-threatening conditions until EMS personnel arrive.
- Note that you must receive a conscious person's permission before giving care. An exception can be made in the case of a minor when a parent or guardian is not present. If one is present, you must have the consent of the parent or guardian.

Use common sense and the skills you have learned and do not *try* to do something beyond your training. You are not expected to perform miracles or endanger your own life. When you act with reasonable skill, care, and prudence, the courts will not hold you negligent even if your efforts are unsuccessful. But this does not mean that no one can ever be sued. In some cases, courts have ruled that an individual rescuer was liable because of grossly or willfully negligent or reckless conduct or because of abandoning the casualty after starting care. Once you start to give first aid, you absolutely must continue it until EMS personnel arrive.

Just as you should act reasonably when giving first aid to the casualty, you should be reasonable in not endangering your own life. Always be sure the scene is safe before approaching the casualty and starting to give care. Protect yourself from the risk of disease.

Preparing for Emergencies

Being prepared for emergencies helps ensure that a casualty gets help as soon as possible. First aid training gives you a plan of action for any emergency. Knowing what to do also helps overcome barriers to action.

Since many emergencies occur in the home, you can prepare yourself and your family by doing the following things *now*:

- Keep important information about you and your family in a handy place, such as on the refrigerator door and in your automobile glove compartment (Figure 2–11). Include your address, everyone's date of birth, medical conditions, allergies, and prescriptions and dosages. List physicians' names and phone numbers.
- Keep medical records up to date.
- Find out the emergency telephone numbers in your community. Post the numbers for police, fire department, EMS, and poison centre near every phone in your home. With these emergency numbers also post your address and telephone number. Be sure to keep these telephone numbers current. Teach children how to call for help as soon as they can use the telephone.
- Keep a first aid kit handy in your home, automobile, work place, and recreation area (see

Figure 2–11 Important information should be readily available.

Figure 2–8). Store each kit in a dry place and restock used or outdated contents. Appendix A lists what you should keep in your first aid kit.

- Learn and practice first aid skills such as cardiopulmonary resuscitation (CPR).
- Make sure your house or apartment number is easy to see in case EMS is called. Report any missing street signs to the proper authorities.
- You and family members should wear a Medic Alert tag if you have a potentially serious medical condition such as epilepsy, diabetes, heart disease, or allergies (Figure 2–12). A Medic Alert tag on a necklace or bracelet gives important medical information to medical professionals if needed.

After learning first aid, stay prepared for emergencies by practicing periodically. Think of emergencies that could occur where you live or work, and rehearse your response to them. Make sure your family and co-workers know what to do in all types of emergencies. Suggest that others take a first aid course also.

Preventing Emergencies

Trying to prevent emergencies from happening in the first place is the best attitude. Although some may still occur, you can do much in the way of prevention.

Injuries are the leading cause of death for people under the age of 44 (Figure 2–13). In fact, injuries kill more young children than all other causes of death combined. But that is just the tip of the iceberg. For every person in Canada who dies from an injury, there will be 40 people admitted to a hospital for treatment and another 1300 who visit emergency departments. The number of people who visit doctors' offices or clinics to be treated for injuries is unknown.

Why don't most Canadians know this? It is because many people believe there is little they can do to prevent *accidents*. The good news is

Figure 2–12   Medical alert tags can provide important medical information about the casualty.

that injuries are not accidents—over 90 percent of all injuries can be prevented.

Life is about taking risks—and for the most part, risk-taking behaviour is fun. It is important, however, to take smart risks. After all, the worst thing about not taking smart risks is you may never be able to take risks again.

To prevent emergencies, first consider potential risks in your own life. Then take precautions to conserve your health and safety and that of your family and friends. Chapters throughout this book include information on preventing emergencies.

Coping with a Traumatic Event

Being involved in an emergency can be very stressful. People respond to traumatic events in different ways, and it is important to cope with the psychological reaction after the emergency.

How we respond depends on individual factors such as our personality, our current stress levels, and our past experience with traumatic events. There is no right or wrong way to react. Some people have an immediate, intense reaction, while for others the reaction may occur hours or days later. One may have a strong physical reaction, including crying, shaking, tension, nausea, and/or weakness in the limbs.

The psychological reaction too can be very intense, especially if the casualty does not survive the injury or sudden illness. You need to realize that not every casualty we try to save will survive. Many times circumstances beyond our control lead to the final outcome. One's psychological reaction may include a sense of disbelief, anger, fear, and /or feelings of guilt. One may also relive the sights and sounds of the event or have nightmares.

To cope with the effects of a traumatic event:

- Avoid being alone after responding to an upsetting emergency.
- Remind yourself that a strong reaction is natural and normal but also varies from person to person.

- Share your thoughts and feelings with someone close to you. Talk with your family physician if necessary.
- Be gentle and patient with yourself. Consider how you would comfort a frightened child, and do the same for yourself.
- Go easy on yourself for a few days; do not demand much of yourself.
- Try to find some activity or diversion to help you forget about the event temporarily.

Follow these principles to help a family member or friend cope with their reaction to a traumatic event:

- Your caring for a family member or friend after a traumatic event is especially beneficial. Encourage the person to talk with you and share his or her feelings. Listen sympathetically and do not try to talk the person out of the feelings.

Deaths Resulting from Unintentional Injury, Distribution by Major Category, Canada 1994*

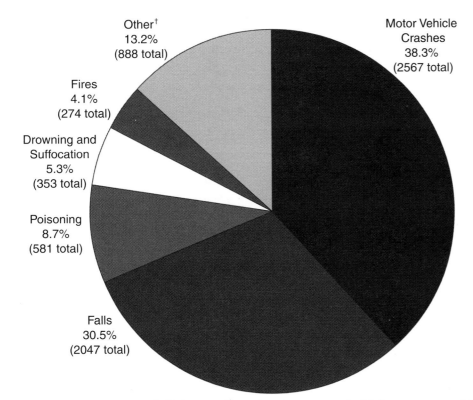

Other†
13.2%
(888 total)

Fires
4.1%
(274 total)

Drowning and
Suffocation
5.3%
(353 total)

Poisoning
8.7%
(581 total)

Falls
30.5%
(2047 total)

Motor Vehicle
Crashes
38.3%
(2567 total)

*Data limitations: Mortality data taken from 1994 Vital Statistics (the most recent available) lack data from British Columbia because that province's mortality data are collected in a different way from the rest of Canada. Also, the morbidity data taken from the Canadian Institute for Health Information (CIHI) hospital discharge abstracts for 1995–1996 lack data from Quebec. The CIHI does not gather these data because Quebec classifies their data differently from the other Canadian provinces.

†Other includes the following categories: railway, motor vehicle non-traffic, pedal cycle, water transport, air and space, natural and environmental, recreational and other incidents.

Note: percentages might not sum up due to rounding.

Figure 2–13   Injuries kill thousands each year, many of which are preventable.

- Be sensitive and responsive to the person's needs and requests. Be patient if the person demands more of your time or attention with his or her thoughts and feelings about the event.
- Try to reduce other stresses that may affect the person.
- Be alert for any unusual behaviour that does not improve over time or worsens. If necessary, encourage the person to seek professional advice from his or her physician.

Crisis Intervention

Regardless of the nature of the incident, caring for someone experiencing an emotional crisis involves offering emotional support, as well as care for any specific injury. The most important initial step you can take is to communicate with the casualty in an open manner. Communication can be both verbal and nonverbal.

Nonverbal communication refers to your body actions. Avoid physical contact and positioning your arms across your chest, or hands on your hips. As you begin to communicate verbally, remember that communication involves stimulating **discussion** and **active listening** as much as talking.

Casualties of emotional crisis may be withdrawn or hysterical. Some may be entirely dependent on you to help. Avoid being judgmental. Do not place blame on the casualty. The casualty needs to be cared for gently and with respect. If care is needed for a minor injury, try to get the casualty to help you. By encouraging the casualty to participate, you may help the casualty to regain a sense of control that he or she had lost.

Do not be fooled into thinking that you can manage a situation involving emotional crisis yourself. A suicidal person or rape casualty needs professional counselling. Summon for more advanced personnel. While waiting for others to arrive, continue to talk with the casualty. Never leave a casualty alone unless there is a threat to your safety.

Shaken Baby Syndrome (SBS)*

Shaken Baby Syndrome is a type or combination of injuries that First Aiders need to be aware of.

When does this happen?
SBS happens when people cannot control their anger and frustration when trying to calm a crying and upset baby.

Why does this happen?
SBS happens because the offender believes that shaking helps quiet the baby or out of pure will.

Who are the victims?
Studies have shown that:
- Victims are children between the ages of 0 to 5 years old. The majority of victims are under the age of 6 months.
- Older children are more likely to die than younger children. Sixty to 82% of victims are boys.

Who are the perpetrators?
Studies have shown that:
- 37 to 47% are the biological fathers
- 21 to 41% are the mother's boyfriends
- less than 12% are the mothers and female child caregivers

What are the symptoms of SBS?
- Skull, rib, and long bone fractures
- Bruising, usually on the face or mid-body area
- Brain swelling and lack of oxygen to the brain
- Subdural (the layer between your skull and brain) hemorrhaging
- Optic nerve sheath (the nerve between your retina and brain) hemorrhaging

What can a parent or caregiver do?
Stay calm. A frustrated or angry parent or caregiver will have a hard time getting a baby to set-

tle down. If feeding, changing, walking, rocking, and cuddling have not worked, the baby should be gently placed in a safe place and allowed to "cry it out" for a few minutes. The parent or caregiver can use the time to relax and calm down before making another attempt to console the baby. A babysitter should also know that if the above does not work, then they should contact the parents of the child.

How long does it take for symptoms to occur?

* Life-threatening injuries take just a few minutes to develop.
* It takes an average of 2 to 3 hours for an infant to develop "not so serious" symptoms.

Outcomes of SBS:

* 13 to 28% of SBS victims die.
* Babies that do not die can suffer from a wide variety of systemic diseases and disorders.

---

*Source: Showers, Jacy EdDd. Director, SBS Prevention Plus for the National Association and Related Institutions. *Never, Never, Never Shake a Baby*.

Summary

The following are four basic steps to take in an emergency:

* Recognize that an emergency has occurred.
* Decide to act.
* Call EMS.
* Give first aid until help arrives.

* Being mentally prepared for emergencies helps one overcome the barriers to action.

* The general principles of first aid are to survey the scene before approaching to be sure no danger exists; to check the casualty for unresponsiveness and call EMS if unresponsive; to do a primary survey to check the casualty's airway, breathing, and circulation and give first aid for life-threatening problems first; to do a secondary survey to check the casualty for other problems and give first aid as needed; to monitor breathing and circulation until EMS arrives; and to help the casualty rest comfortably and give reassurance.

* Preparation for emergencies includes having a first aid kit and emergency telephone numbers ready.

* Many emergencies can be prevented with safety precautions and a healthy lifestyle.

* The law protects bystanders who do their best in giving first aid.

* By taking precautions you can greatly reduce the risk of infection when giving first aid.

The Emergency Medical System

Objectives

After reading this chapter, you should be able to:

1. Explain how the emergency medical services (EMS) system works.

2. Describe your role as a bystander in the EMS system.

3. List what information to give the EMS dispatcher when calling for help.

4. List at least four situations in which an emergency move of a casualty is necessary.

5. Describe how to perform five common rescue moves.

6. Describe the reaching assist method of rescuing a near-drowning casualty.

7. Define the key terms for this chapter.

After reading this chapter and completing the class activities, you should be able to:

1. Decide what to do in an example of an emergency situation in which someone may need to be moved.

Key Terms

dispatcher   The emergency medical services person, usually in a communications centre, who answers the emergency telephone number and decides which EMS professionals to send to the scene and who may give advice regarding first aid to be given until EMS professionals arrive.

emergency medical attendant (EMA)   Someone trained in a province-approved Emergency Medical Attendant program. There are several different levels of EMAs, including ambulance attendants and paramedics.

emergency medical services (EMS) professionals   Trained and equipped personnel, including police, firefighters, and ambulance personnel, who are dispatched through a local emergency number to give emergency care for ill or injured casualties.

poison centre   A centre staffed by medical professionals to give information about first aid in cases of poisoning. Poison centre phone numbers are on the inside first page of the telephone directory.

In Chapter 2 you learned how as a bystander trained in first aid, you are the first link in the *emergency medical services (EMS) system*. As this first link, you may need to give first aid to a casualty until trained personnel arrive. The sooner you or someone calls the EMS system, the sooner emergency medical help will arrive.

The EMS System

The EMS is a coordinated system that exists throughout the country to get emergency assistance to casualties with injury or sudden illness and to transport them to a hospital. The EMS has different parts linked together like a chain (Figure 3–1). You are the first link when you call the local emergency number. The *dispatcher* who answers is the second link. The *EMS professionals* who come to the scene, such as police, firefighters, and EMAs, are the third link. The hospital emergency department professionals are the fourth link. This chain begins with your telephone call.

The EMS system varies somewhat from community to community. Many areas have a 9-1-1 system, and others have a different local number. Although the level of training of the ambulance attendants and EMAs may also vary somewhat, the overall system and the principles of calling EMS are the same in all provinces.

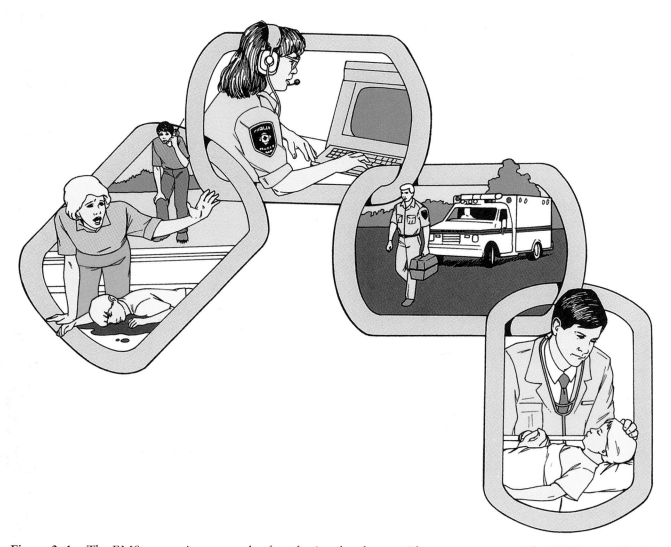

Figure 3–1   The EMS system is a network of professionals who provide emergency care. The EMS system begins with people like you.

When to Call EMS

Chapter 5 describes the emergency action principles for first aid in any emergency. When you are sure the scene is safe, you quickly check the injured or ill person to see if he or she is unresponsive. If so, the next step is to call EMS.

Sometimes you may not be sure if you should call EMS. The injured or ill person may tell you not to call an ambulance because he or she is embarrassed about creating a scene. Perhaps you may be unsure if the casualty's condition is serious enough to require going to a hospital. As a general rule, call EMS personnel for any of the following conditions:

- Unconsciousness or altered level of consciousness
- Breathing problems (difficulty breathing or no breathing)
- Persistent chest pain or pressure
- No signs of circulation
- Severe bleeding
- Vomiting blood or passing blood
- Poisoning
- Convulsions, severe headache, or slurred speech
- Injuries to head, neck, or back
- Possible broken bones

Also always call EMS if the casualty is involved with any of the following:

- Fire or explosion
- Poisonous gas
- Downed electrical wires
- Swift-moving water
- Motor vehicle collisions
- A casualty who cannot be moved easily

In other cases, trust your instincts. If you think that an emergency exists, it probably does. Do not lose time calling friends or family members. Call EMS for professional help immediately. It is better for these professionals to come and find out they are not needed than not come in an emergency when they were needed.

How to Call EMS

Sending someone else to call the emergency number is better because it enables you to stay with the casualty and keep giving first aid.

The dispatcher in a communications centre will answer the local emergency number. This person quickly decides which professionals to send to the scene and may give the caller instructions on how to give first aid until the help arrives. For a casualty of poisoning the dispatcher may also connect you to the nearest poison centre for instructions on what first aid to give. Therefore, you or the caller first must have the right information to give the dispatcher.

When you tell someone to call for help, do the following:

1. Send a bystander, or possibly two, to make the call.
2. Give the caller(s) the EMS telephone number to call. This number is 9-1-1 in many places. Tell the caller(s) to dial 0 for the Operator only if you do not know the local emergency number. Sometimes the emergency number is listed on the inside front cover of the telephone book or displayed on the pay phone.
3. Tell the caller(s) what to tell the dispatcher. Most dispatchers will ask for the following important facts:
a. Where the emergency is located. Give the exact address or location and the name of the city or town. Give the names of nearby intersecting streets (cross streets or roads), landmarks, the name of the building, the floor, and the room number. If the casualty is being moved, give that location. (If there is any risk that arriving EMS personnel may not locate you immediately, give additional information about how to reach you and if needed have someone meet them when they arrive.)
b. Telephone number from which the call is being made. Give any other available phone number for a call back.

c. Caller's name. Note: give these first three pieces of information first so that the dispatcher can still act even if the call is cut off.
d. What has happened—for example, a motor vehicle collision, fall, or fire.
e. How many people are involved.
f. Condition of the casualty—for example, chest pain, trouble breathing, no signs of circulation, bleeding. The dispatcher will ask if the person is conscious and breathing and the person's approximate age.
g. The first aid being given.
4. Tell the caller(s) not to hang up until the dispatcher hangs up. Be sure the dispatcher has all the information needed to send the right help to the scene.
5. Tell the caller(s) to report to you after making the call and tell you what the dispatcher said.

If you are alone with the casualty, call out loudly for help. Shouting may attract someone who can help you by making this call. If no one comes, get to a phone as fast as you can to call EMS. Then return to the casualty to keep giving help.

EMS Personnel

The third link in the system is composed of firefighters, police, and the ambulance. Often police or firefighters arrive first. They are often close to the scene and have the supplies, equipment, and training to give a higher level of care. Usually they will take over whatever care you are giving, such as continuing to give CPR, and start other care.

The emergency medical attendant (EMA) is more highly trained. EMAs may arrive first on the scene or may take over from police or others who have arrived first. The EMA can give more advanced first aid and may use life-support techniques. Most ambulance personnel are certified at least at the basic EMA level.

Paramedics are highly specialized EMAs who can also give medications and intravenous fluids, give advanced airway care, and assess abnormal heart rhythms.

Hospital Care Providers

The first three links of the EMS system give the best possible prehospital medical care in emergencies. The fourth link begins once the casualty arrives at a hospital or medical facility and the emergency department takes over. Many different professionals, such as emergency doctors and nurses, then become involved. The casualty may be discharged home after being treated in the emergency department or may be admitted to the hospital for further medical care and nursing.

Your Role in the EMS System

Once you recognize the emergency, calling EMS is the most important thing you and other bystanders can do. Early arrival of EMS personnel increases the casualty's chances of surviving a life-threatening emergency. Without the help of bystanders, the EMS system could not function effectively. All emergency first aid you will learn in this book is directed to helping the casualty until these professionals arrive.

Rescue and Emergency Moves

Usually in emergencies you give first aid in the same place you find the casualty. Moving a casualty needlessly can lead to further injury. However, in some cases the situation is dangerous, and the casualty must be moved or rescued before you can give first aid (see page 29).

Assisting a Near-Drowning Casualty with a Reaching Assist

When trying to rescue someone from the water, **always remember not to endanger yourself.** Rescues that require swimming out to a casualty

BEFORE PROVIDING CARE

Move an injured casualty only if—
- The scene is becoming unsafe.
- You have to reach another casualty who may have a more serious injury or illness.
- You need to provide proper care (for example, someone has collapsed on a stairway, does not have signs of circulation, and needs CPR. CPR needs to be performed on a firm, flat surface).

Clothes Drag
To move a casualty that may have a head, neck, or back injury—
1. Gather the casualty's clothing behind the casualty's neck.
2. Pull the casualty to safety.
3. While moving the casualty, cradle the head with the casualty's clothes and your hands.

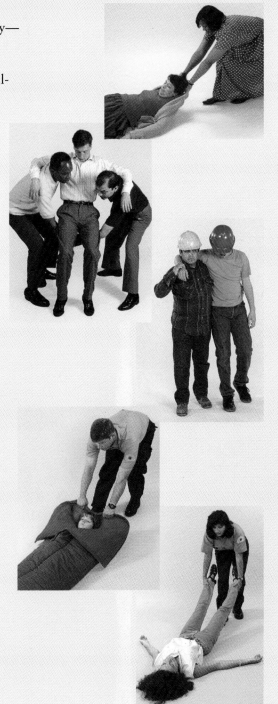

Two-Person Seat Carry
To carry a casualty who cannot walk and has no suspected head, neck, or back injury—
1. Put one arm under the casualty's thighs and the other across the casualty's back.
2. Interlock your arms with those of a second rescuer under the casualty's legs and across the casualty's back.
3. Move the casualty to safety.

Walking Assist
To help a casualty who needs assistance walking to safety—
1. Place the casualty's arm across your shoulders and hold it in place with one hand.
2. Support the casualty with your other hand around the casualty's waist.
3. Move the casualty to safety.

Blanket Drag
To move a casualty in an emergency situation when equipment is limited—
1. Keep the casualty between you and the blanket.
2. Gather half the blanket and place it against the casualty's side.
3. Roll the casualty as a unit toward you.
4. Reach over and place the blanket so that it will be positioned under the casualty.
5. Roll the casualty onto the blanket.
6. Gather the blanket at the head and move the casualty.

Foot Drag
To move a casualty too large to carry or move otherwise—
1. Firmly grasp the casualty's ankles and move backwards.
2. Pull the casualty in a straight line, and be careful not to bump the casualty's head.

require special training. If you try it without this training, you are not likely to save the casualty but only put yourself in danger.

For someone far out in the water, call for a lifeguard or other trained person. For someone nearby in the water, try a reaching assist while you stay in a safe position. First, lie down and firmly brace yourself. Extend your reach with any object that will reach the casualty, such as a pole, oar or paddle, tree branch, shirt, belt, or towel.

Emergency Cardiac Care

Of the many types of emergencies needing the EMS system, heart attacks are one of the most important. Each year 50,000 Canadians die of heart attacks. As a bystander trained in first aid, one of the most important things you can do is be prepared to give emergency cardiac care. This consists of the following:

- Healthy lifestyles
- Recognizing the signs and symptoms of heart attack
- Promptly calling EMS
- Starting basic life support immediately (including CPR if needed)
- Early defibrillation
- EMAs giving advanced cardiac life support as soon as possible
- Transporting the casualty to the hospital
- Early rehabilitation

In the following chapters you will learn how to recognize a heart attack, how to perform CPR, and give other first aid. The key to survival for such a casualty is quick activation of the EMS system.

Summary

- The EMS system provides emergency care at the scene and transports the casualty to the hospital, where medical care is given.

- Call EMS when faced with any serious illness or injury that seems a possible emergency.

- The links of the EMS system include the bystander who gives first aid and calls the EMS dispatcher, the EMS dispatcher, professionals who come to the scene to give care and transport the casualty, and hospital personnel.

- Give the EMS dispatcher full information about your location, the casualty, and the care being given.

- Never move a casualty from the scene unless an immediate danger exists, and then move the person only if you can do so safely.

- Unless you have specialized training, do not swim out to try to rescue a drowning person; call trained professionals or use a reaching assist.

Body Systems

4

Objectives

After reading this chapter, you should be able to:

1. Identify the major structures of the body that may be involved in emergency situations.

2. Describe what can happen to the body if a problem occurs in one or more of the body systems.

3. Define the key terms for this chapter.

Key Terms

airway   The pathway for air from the mouth and nose to the lungs.

arteries   Large blood vessels that carry oxygen-rich blood from the heart to all parts of the body.

bone   The dense, hard tissue that forms the skeleton.

brain   The centre of the nervous system that controls all body functions.

cells   The basic units of all living tissue.

exhale   To breathe air out of the lungs.

heart   The muscular organ that pumps blood throughout the body.

infection   A condition caused by disease-producing microorganisms in the body.

inhale   To breathe air into the lungs.

lungs   The two organs that take oxygen in and remove carbon dioxide during breathing.

muscle   A fibrous tissue that lengthens and shortens to move body parts.

nerve   A part of the nervous system that carries impulses to and from the brain and all body parts.

pulse   The beat felt in arteries near the skin with each contraction of the heart.

respiration   The breathing process whereby oxygen is taken in and carbon dioxide is eliminated.

shock   A serious condition that occurs when the circulatory system cannot get enough oxygen-rich blood to all parts of the body, such as with severe blood loss or allergic reaction.

skin   The membrane that covers the entire surface of the body.

spinal cord   The bundle of nerves from the brain to the lower back that runs through the spinal column.

tissue   A group of similar cells that work together for specific functions.

trachea   The tube from the upper airway to the lungs; also called the *windpipe*.

veins   Blood vessels that carry oxygen-poor blood from all parts of the body back to the heart.

The human body is made up of billions of microscopic *cells*. A cell is the basic unit of all living *tissues*. Different cells and tissues working together make up organs with special functions. For example, the *heart* is an organ whose function is to pump blood throughout the body. The *brain*, heart, and *lungs* are essential for life and are thus called vital organs.

A body system is a group of organs and structures that work together to carry out a function needed for life. For example, the heart, blood, and blood vessels make up the circulatory system, which provides oxygen to all parts of the body.

For the body to work properly, all the different systems must be working well. This chapter describes these important body systems:

- Respiratory
- Circulatory
- Nervous
- Musculoskeletal
- Integumentary

You do not need to be an expert about body systems to give first aid, but knowing how the body works will help you understand when something is wrong. The different body systems work together when one is healthy, and an injury or illness that affects one body system can affect others. For instance, a head injury may affect the brain and nervous system in a way that causes breathing to stop.

Respiratory System

All body tissues constantly need oxygen. The respiratory system supplies the body with oxygen through the breathing of air. The air we breathe is about 21% oxygen. When you *inhale*, air fills the lungs and oxygen enters the blood. This oxygen-rich blood is carried back to the heart and then pumped to all parts of the body. Carbon dioxide is removed from the blood in the lungs and breathed out when you *exhale*. This breathing process is called *respiration*.

The body uses only about one fourth of the oxygen we breathe in. Exhaled air is about 16% oxygen, which is enough to give oxygen to a non-breathing casualty when you give rescue breathing (Chapter 7).

The respiratory system includes the *airway* and lungs (Figure 4–1). Air passes through the nose and mouth and then through the *trachea*, also called the *windpipe*. A flap of tissue called the *epiglottis* covers the trachea when you swallow to keep food and liquids out of the lungs.

Air enters the lungs from the trachea through two tubes called bronchi. These branch into smaller and smaller tubes like tree branches (Figure 4–2, *A*). The branches end in millions of tiny air sacs called *alveoli* (Figure 4–2, *B*). Oxygen and carbon dioxide pass into and out of the blood through the thin walls of the alveoli and capillaries.

Air enters the lungs when you inhale and leaves the lungs when you exhale. When you inhale, the chest *muscles* and the diaphragm expand the chest and draw air into the lungs.

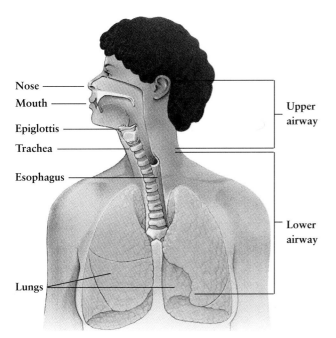

Nose
Mouth
Epiglottis
Trachea
Esophagus
Lungs

Upper airway
Lower airway

Figure 4–1   The respiratory system.

When you exhale, the chest muscles and diaphragm relax and let air exit the lungs (Figure 4–3). An adult breathes about half a litre of air in each breath. The average adult at rest breathes 10 to 20 times per minute. Breathing is controlled by the nervous system and the brain.

Respiratory Problems That Require First Aid

Because the body constantly needs oxygen, you need to recognize breathing emergencies and give first aid immediately. Breathing difficulties, called *respiratory distress*, can be caused by asthma, allergies, chest injuries, or physical obstructions such as food.

A person in respiratory distress may be breathing noisily or gasping. The casualty may be unconscious. A conscious person may be anxious, excited, or feel short of breath. The *skin* of the lips and under the nails may look blue. This colouration occurs when tissues do not receive enough oxygen.

A person who stops breathing is in respiratory arrest, a life-threatening emergency. Without oxygen, other body systems cannot function. For example, if the brain does not get oxygen, a person will become unconscious in less than 1 minute.

Respiratory problems require immediate attention. Making sure the airway is open and clear is an important first aid step. You may have to breathe for the nonbreathing casualty or help

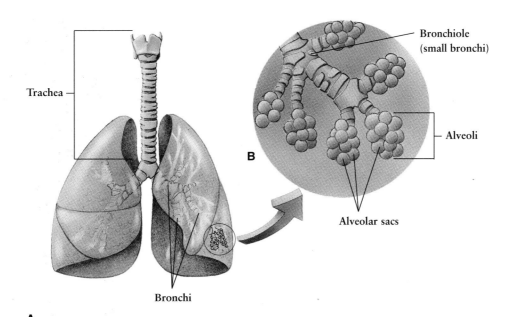

Trachea
Bronchiole (small bronchi)
Alveoli
Alveolar sacs
Bronchi

A

B

Figure 4–2   *A,* The bronchi branch into many small tubes. *B,* Oxygen and carbon dioxide pass into and out of the blood through the cell walls of the alveoli.

clear the airway of someone who is choking. Breathing for the casualty, called *rescue breathing*, is discussed in Chapter 7.

Circulatory System

The circulatory system works with the respiratory system to carry oxygen to all body parts. It also carries nutrients to the body and removes wastes. The circulatory system includes the heart, blood, and blood vessels (Figure 4–4). The heart is a muscular organ behind the sternum, or breastbone. The heart circulates blood around the whole body via **arteries** and **veins**, at a rate of about 5 litres per minute. Arteries are the vessels that carry oxygen-rich blood from the heart to the rest of the body. The coronary arteries carry blood to the heart tissue itself. The arteries branch into smaller vessels and become tiny capillaries that allow oxygen and carbon dioxide exchange in the cells. The veins then carry the oxygen-poor blood back to the heart. The heart pumps it to the lungs to pick up more oxygen, before pumping it back to the rest of the body. This process is called the circulatory cycle. Figure 4–5 shows how blood moves through the heart in this cycle.

The pumping actions of the heart are called *contractions*. The heart's electrical system makes the heart beat regularly at 60 to 100 beats per minute in an adult. The beat you feel in arteries

INHALATION

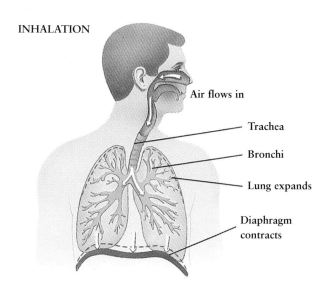

Air flows in

Trachea

Bronchi

Lung expands

Diaphragm contracts

EXHALATION

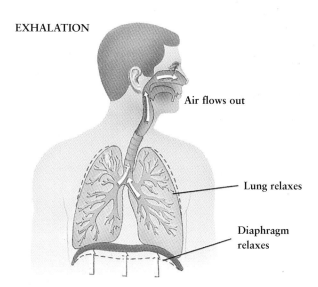

Air flows out

Lung relaxes

Diaphragm relaxes

Figure 4–3   During breathing the diaphragm and chest muscles contract and relax for inhalation and exhalation.

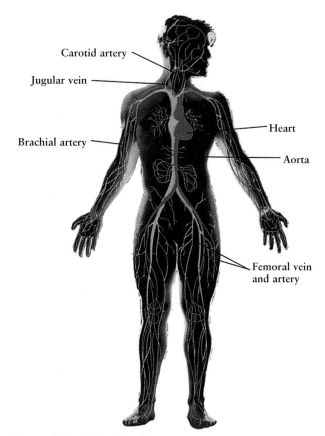

Carotid artery

Jugular vein

Brachial artery

Heart

Aorta

Femoral vein and artery

Figure 4–4   The circulatory system.

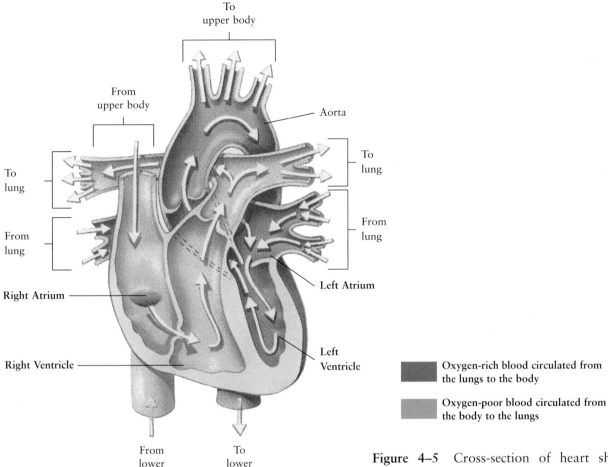

To
upper body

From
upper body

Aorta

To
lung

To
lung

From
lung

From
lung

Right Atrium

Left Atrium

Right Ventricle

Left
Ventricle

Oxygen-rich blood circulated from
the lungs to the body

Oxygen-poor blood circulated from
the body to the lungs

From
lower
body

To
lower
body

Figure 4–5 Cross-section of heart showing pathway of blood.

close to the skin with each heart contraction is called the *pulse*. The heart must beat steadily to get oxygen to body cells for all body functions to continue. During exercise the heart pumps as much as 25 litres of blood per minute.

If a casualty stops breathing, the heart continues to beat for a few minutes and carries the oxygen still in the blood to the body. For this reason, rescue breathing given quickly to someone who has stopped breathing can keep the heart from stopping (see Chapter 7). However, once the heart does not receive enough oxygen, it stops, and the rescuer also has to give chest compressions to help the blood circulate.

Circulatory Problems That Require First Aid

The following problems may keep the body from getting enough oxygen through the blood:

1. Severe bleeding
2. Shock
3. Impaired circulation, for example, from a blood clot
4. The heart not pumping well, as in the case of a heart attack

Severe bleeding causes a loss of blood from the circulatory system. If this loss is severe enough, *shock* will develop. Shock occurs when the tissues do not receive adequate oxygen.

Body tissues that do not get oxygen die. If an artery to the brain is blocked, brain tissue dies and the person may have a stroke. If a coronary artery supplying the heart with blood is blocked, heart muscle tissue dies and the person may have a heart attack.

The heart may stop after a heart attack; then breathing will also stop. The heart stopping, called *cardiac arrest*, requires first aid immediately. The circulation must be maintained artificially with cardiopulmonary resuscitation (CPR): combined chest compressions and rescue breathing. You will learn how to perform CPR in Chapter 8.

Nervous System

The brain, the centre of the nervous system, is the master organ of the body. It controls all body functions, including the respiratory and circulatory systems. The brain has three kinds of functions:

- Sensory functions, allowing one to see, hear, feel, taste, and smell.
- Motor functions, controlling how the body moves.
- Integrated functions, those controlling other body systems as well as consciousness, memory, language, and emotions.

The brain receives and sends information through the *nerves*. The *spinal cord,* a large bundle of nerves, extends from the brain through the spinal column, or backbone. Nerves from the brain and spinal cord reach every part of the body.

Nerves transmit information from the body to the brain and from the brain to the body. Sensory nerves from the eyes and ears, for example, are responsible for sight and hearing. Other nerves transmit orders from the brain to the muscles to move arms and legs.

The integrated functions of the brain are more complex. Normally, when you are awake or conscious, you are oriented. Being oriented means that you know who you are, where you are, the approximate date and time, and what is happening around you. There are, however, different levels of consciousness. For example, someone with a head injury might be awake but may be confused about who he or she is or what has happened.

Nervous System Problems That Require First Aid

Unlike other body parts, the brain cannot grow new cells. Once brain cells die from disease or injury, they are gone forever. If a part of the brain is injured, its functions may be lost. For example, if a part of the brain that controls a body part is damaged, that body part may never regain its function.

Consciousness may be affected by illness or injury. Illness or injury affecting the brain can also alter memory, emotions, and speech.

A head injury can make the casualty confused or even unconscious. Medical professionals should evaluate any injury causing confusion or unconsciousness. Such an injury can cause bleeding within the skull, putting pressure on the brain and keeping oxygen from reaching brain cells.

Injury to the spinal cord or a nerve can cause paralysis, a loss of feeling and movement. For example, a lower back injury can cause paralyzed legs. A broken *bone* or a deep wound can also cause nerve damage. In Chapter 10 you will learn about first aid techniques for head and spine injuries.

Musculoskeletal System

The musculoskeletal system consists of the bones, muscles, ligaments, and tendons working together for several functions:

- Supporting the body
- Protecting internal organs
- Allowing movement
- Storing minerals and producing blood cells
- Producing heat

Bones and Ligaments

The body has over 200 bones. Bone is hard, dense tissue that forms the skeleton and supports the body (Figure 4–6). Two or more bones come together at joints. Figure 4–7 shows a typical joint. Ligaments hold bones together at a joint.

The skull bones protect the brain. The spine bones, called *vertebrae*, protect the spinal cord. The ribs, attached to the spine and the breastbone, protect vital organs such as the heart and lungs.

Bones also make movement possible. The bones of the arms and legs allow movements for walking, lifting, and other functions. The small bones of the hand and fingers allow for fine movements like writing. The small foot bones allow walking.

Bones also store minerals and help produce blood cells in the bone marrow within the bone.

Muscles and Tendons

Muscle tissue lengthens and shortens to make body movements. Tendons attach muscles to the bones. When muscles work, they produce heat. Muscles also help protect the bones, nerves, and blood vessels they cover.

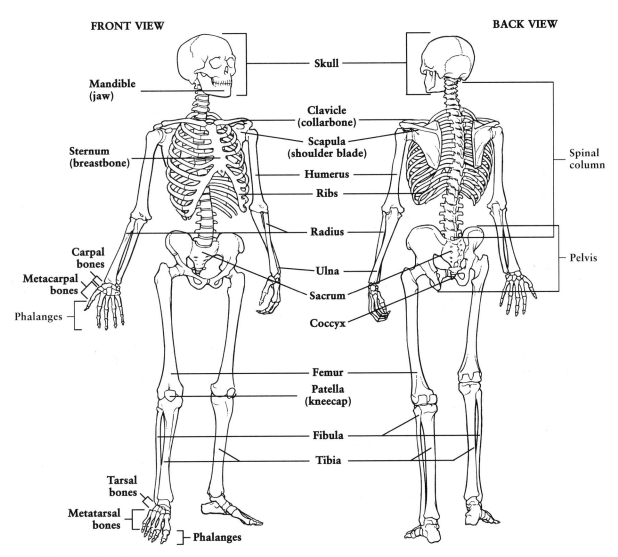

Figure 4–6   The skeleton.

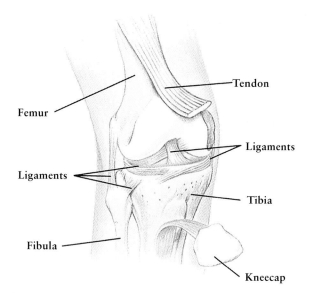

Figure 4–7   A typical joint consists of two or more bones held together by ligaments.

The brain directs the muscles to move by sending messages through the nerves. Muscle actions may be involuntary or voluntary. The brain automatically controls involuntary muscles, such as those in the heart, diaphragm, and intestines. For example, the heart beats 60 to 100 beats per minute without a person directing it. Voluntary muscles, such as leg and arm muscles, are under one's conscious control. Figure 4–8 shows the muscular system.

Musculoskeletal Problems That Require First Aid

Musculoskeletal injuries include fractures, dislocations, and strains and sprains of muscles, ten-

FRONT VIEW   BACK VIEW

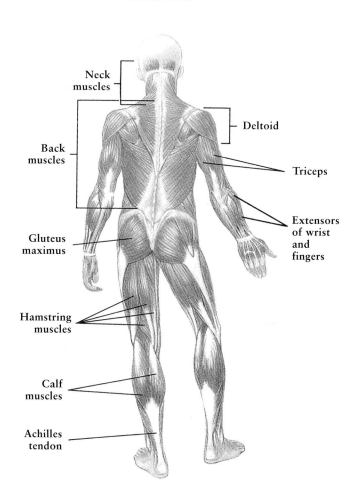

Figure 4–8   The muscular system.

dons, and ligaments. Although injuries to bones and muscles may not at first seem emergencies, the injury may damage nearby nerves, blood vessels, or organs and become a serious injury. The injury may cause a lifelong disability or even threaten the casualty's life. For example, broken ribs can puncture the lungs and impair breathing.

When you give first aid, remember that injuries to muscles and bones may cause other injuries. You will learn first aid for musculoskeletal injuries in Chapter 11.

Integumentary System

The integumentary system is the skin, hair, and nails. The skin is most important because it protects the body and helps keep fluids in. It helps prevent *infection* by keeping disease-producing microorganisms out. The skin also helps make vitamin D and stores minerals.

Sweat glands and pores in the skin help control body temperature. The nervous system monitors the body's temperature and causes sweating if the temperature rises even slightly, and the evaporation of sweat cools the body.

The colour of skin in light-skinned people helps one detect the person's condition. When blood circulates close to the skin's surface, the skin looks flushed, or red, and feels warm. But when there is not as much blood close to the surface, such as when a casualty is going into shock, the skin looks pale and feels cool. You may not be able to recognize this colour difference in people with darker skin.

Integumentary System Problems That Require First Aid

Although the skin is tough, it can be injured. It can be punctured or torn by objects, burned by heat or the sun, and frozen by extreme cold. Injuries that cause bleeding let vital fluids escape from the body. Microbes may enter the body through breaks in the skin and cause potentially serious infections.

In later chapters you will learn how to care for wounds, burns, and heat and cold emergencies.

Summary

- All body systems must work together for the body to function properly (Table 4–1).

- The brain controls all body functions and the respiratory, circulatory, musculoskeletal, and integumentary systems.

- An injury that affects any body system can produce problems that need first aid.

- Understanding how a body system works in an injury or illness can help you realize the importance of first aid.

Table 4–1	Body Systems		
System	**Major structures**	**Primary functions**	**How the system works with other body systems**
Respiratory system	Airway and lungs	Supplies the body with the oxygen it needs through breathing	Works with the circulatory system to provide oxygen to cells; is under the control of the nervous system
Circulatory system	Heart, blood vessels, and blood	Transports nutrients and oxygen to body cells and removes waste products	Works with the respiratory system to provide oxygen to cells; works in conjunction with urinary and digestive systems to remove waste products; helps give skin colour; is under the control of the nervous system
Nervous system	Brain, spinal cord, and nerves	One of two primary regulatory systems in the body; transmits messages to and from the brain	The brain regulates all body systems through network of nerves
Musculoskeletal system	Bones, ligaments, muscles, and tendons	Provides body's framework; protects internal organs and other underlying structures; allows movement; produces heat; manufactures blood components	Muscles and bones provide protection to organs and structures of other body systems; muscle action is controlled by the nervous system
Integumentary system	Skin, hair, and nails	Skin is an important part of the body's communication network; prevents infection and dehydration; assists with temperature regulation; aids in production of certain vitamins	Skin helps to protect the body from disease-producing organisms; together with the circulatory system, helps to regulate body temperature under the control of the nervous system; communicates sensation to the brain by way of the nerves

The Emergency Action Principles

5

Objectives

After reading this chapter, you should be able to:

1. List the six emergency action principles (steps to take in every emergency).
2. Explain why you should follow the emergency action principles in any emergency.
3. List four important questions when you survey the emergency scene.
4. Explain what you should do if you cannot reach the casualty because the scene is not safe.
5. List three statements you must make before getting consent to care for an ill or injured person.
6. Explain why you should do a primary survey in every emergency situation.
7. Describe how to do a primary survey.
8. List the facts you should have ready for the EMS dispatcher when you call for help.
9. Describe when you should continue from the primary survey to a secondary survey.
10. Explain how to proceed in the event of an incident with more casualties than rescuers.
11. Define the key terms for this chapter.

Key Terms

carotid arteries   Major blood vessels bringing blood to the head and neck.

consent   Permission to provide care, given by the casualty to the rescuer.

emergency action principles (EAPs)   Six steps to guide your actions in any emergency.

primary survey   A check for conditions that are an immediate threat to a casualty's life.

secondary survey   A head-to-toe check for injuries or conditions that require attention and could become life- or limb-threatening problems if not cared for.

sign   An objective signal of injury or illness, which can be seen, felt, or heard.

symptom   A subjective signal of injury or illness, which the casualty tells you he or she feels.

triage   The process of sorting and providing care to multiple victims according to the severity of their injuries or illnesses.

After reading this chapter and completing the class activities, you should be able to:

1. Demonstrate a primary survey.

2. Decide what care to give when doing a primary survey in an emergency situation.

3. Demonstrate how to put a casualty in the recovery position.

As someone trained in first aid, you can make a difference in an emergency— you may even save a life. In an emergency you can always do something to help.

In this chapter you will learn an action plan for any emergency. When an emergency occurs, stay calm and think before you act. Ask yourself, "What do I need to do? How can I help most effectively?" The six *emergency action principles (EAPs)* guide your action and are your plan for any emergency. In this chapter you will learn about these principles and how to do a primary survey and care for life-threatening problems. In Chapter 9 you will learn how to do a secondary survey and give first aid for other problems.

Emergency Action Principles

There are six emergency action principles to follow in order:

1. Survey the scene.
2. Check the casualty for unresponsiveness. If the person does not respond, call EMS.
3. Do a **primary survey** and care for life-threatening problems.
4. Do a **secondary survey**, when appropriate, and care for additional problems.
5. Keep monitoring the casualty's condition for life-threatening problems while waiting for EMS to arrive.
6. Help the casualty rest in the most comfortable position and give reassurance.

These steps help keep you, the casualty, and other bystanders safe and increase the casualty's chance of survival.

Step One: Survey the Scene

Once you recognize an emergency and get ready to help, make sure the scene is safe for you and others. Take time to look around and ask these questions:

1. Is the scene safe?
2. What happened?
3. How many casualties are there?
4. Can others help?

When you survey the scene, look for anything that may threaten your safety and others'. Look for downed power lines, falling rocks, traffic, fire, smoke, dangerous fumes, extreme weather, and deep or fast water (Figure 5–1). If any kind of danger is threatening, do not approach the casualty. Call EMS right away for professional help.

Never risk your own safety. You could become a second casualty yourself. Leave dangerous situations for EMS professionals with training and equipment to handle.

Try to determine what has happened. The *Mechanism of Injury* can alert you to the possibility that certain types of injuries may be present. For example, serious head or neck injuries are usually caused from motor vehicle collisions and falls. Remember that there may be a number of obvious and hidden injuries. Determining what happened is

Figure 5–1   Survey the scene.

especially important if the casualty is unconscious and no one else is present (Figure 5–2).

Also look for other casualties. You may not spot everyone at first. In a car crash, an open door may be a clue that a second person left or was thrown from the car. If one casualty is bleeding or screaming, you might not notice another casualty who is unconscious. It is easy to overlook an infant or small child. Always look for other casualties and, if needed, ask other bystanders to help you care for them.

Other people at the scene may be able to tell you what happened or help in other ways. Someone who knows the casualty may know about any medical problems or allergies. You can ask someone to call EMS for help, to meet and direct the ambulance to your location, to keep people and traffic out of the way, and to help you provide care. If no one is around, shout for help.

Multiple casualties

In later chapters, you will learn how to conduct a primary and secondary survey. This will enable

Figure 5–2   If the casualty is unconscious, nearby objects may be your only clue to what has happened.

you to care for life-threatening emergencies before minor injuries. If you take the time to conduct these surveys completely, your entire time could be spent with only one casualty. A casualty who is unconscious and not breathing, simply because the tongue is blocking the airway, could be overlooked and get worse while your attention is given to caring for someone with a less severe injury, such as a broken arm.

In a multiple casualty incident, you must modify your technique for checking casualties. This requires you to understand your priorities. It also requires that you accept death and dying, because some casualties, such as those in cardiac arrest who would normally receive CPR and be a high priority, will be beyond your ability to help in this situation.

To identify which casualties require urgent care in a multiple casualty incident, you use a process known as triage. **Triage** is an old French term that was first used to refer to the sorting and treatment of those injured in battle. Today, the triage process is used any time there are more casualties than rescuers.

The general principle to follow is to do what is best for the most. For example, if one casualty has minor bleeding and another has more severe bleeding, you would help the serious bleeding because EMS professionals would arrive before the minor bleeding becomes serious. The severe bleeding could be life threatening **right now**. If you are ever in a situation where triage is needed, trust your own judgment to do what is best for the most casualties.

Once you reach the casualty

Once you reach the casualty, make sure the scene is still safe. Look for other dangers, clues to what happened, or casualties you did not notice before.

Do not move a casualty unless an immediate danger, such as a fire or poisonous fumes, exists. If you must move the casualty, do so as quickly as possible using the methods described in Chapter 3. Otherwise, tell the casualty not to move.

Figure 5–3 When talking to the casualty, stay close to the casualty's eye level and speak calmly and reassuringly.

The purpose of the primary survey is to determine quickly if the casualty has any life-threatening problems and give immediate first aid for them. Follow the guidelines below for informing the casualty who you are and obtaining consent to give first aid, but do not delay in moving forward to the primary survey.

Tell the casualty you are trained in first aid. Try to keep the person calm and stay at the casualty's eye level (Figure 5–3). Speak calmly. Explain you have first aid training and ask if you can help.

Get permission to provide care. You need the person's permission before you can give care; this permission is called *consent*. A conscious casualty has the right to refuse your care. To get consent you *must* tell the casualty three things:

1. Who you are.
2. That you are trained in first aid.
3. What you are going to do.

Then the casualty can give you permission to give care. With an infant or child, ask the supervising adult for consent. If a person refuses your help, do not try to give help but stay nearby if possible and have someone call EMS. The EMS professionals who arrive will deal with the situation.

For a casualty who is unconscious or unable to respond because of the illness or injury, you can assume consent. The same is true for an infant or child alone.

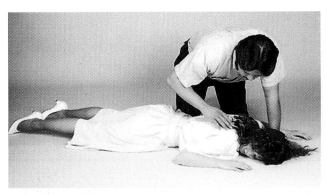

Figure 5–4 Determine if the person is conscious by gently tapping and asking, "Are you okay?"

Step Two: Check the Casualty for Unresponsiveness and Call EMS

Start by checking if the casualty is conscious. Gently tap the person and ask, "Are you okay?" (Figure 5–4). Do not jostle or move the casualty. A casualty who does not respond may be unconscious. Unconsciousness may mean the person's life is threatened. When a person is unconscious, the tongue relaxes and may fall to the back of the throat and block the airway. Then breathing stops and soon the heart stops.

Call 9-1-1 or your local emergency number for EMS. If possible, send someone else to call while you give care to the casualty (Figure 5–5). If you are alone and the casualty is unconscious, shout

Figure 5–5 Sending someone else to call EMS lets you stay with the casualty to give care.

for help. If no one else can call EMS, you must call EMS yourself.

In Chapter 3 you learned about the emergency medical system (EMS) and why and when to call for help. When you are about to call or send someone else to make the call, be sure to have the right information ready:

1. The exact location of the emergency. Give the address or location and the name of the city or town. Give the names of nearby intersecting streets (cross streets or roads), landmarks, the name of the building, the floor, and the room number.
2. Telephone number you are calling from.
3. Your name.
4. How the emergency happened (for example, car crash or fire).
5. The number of casualties.
6. The condition of casualties (for example, chest pain, trouble breathing, no signs of circulation, or bleeding).
7. First aid being given.

If you send someone else to make this call, tell the person to stay on the line and do whatever the EMS dispatcher says. The dispatcher may tell the caller how to care for the casualty until help arrives. Ask the caller to come back and tell you what the dispatcher said.

Step Three: Do a Primary Survey For Life-Threatening Conditions

In any emergency you must determine if any conditions threaten the casualty's life; this is called the *primary survey*. After you have surveyed the scene, checked the casualty for unresponsiveness, and called EMS if unresponsive, do a primary survey to check and care for these life-threatening conditions: altered level of consciousness, airway obstruction, absence of or difficulties with breathing, loss of heartbeat, severe bleeding, and shock. While doing the primary survey, you may have to stop at any point to call EMS.

In the primary survey you check the casualty's airway, breathing, and circulation. It is easy to remember these steps because they are called the *ABCs* of the primary survey:

| A = *A*irway |
| B = *B*reathing |
| C = *C*irculation |

Try to check the ABCs without moving the casualty. Only if necessary should you roll the casualty gently onto his or her back, keeping the head and spine in as straight a line as possible (Figure 5–6).

The steps of the ABCs are described more fully in the next three chapters. The following is an overview.

A—Check the airway

Be sure the casualty has an open airway. The airway is the pathway from the mouth and nose to the lungs. Any person who can speak or cry is conscious and has an open airway.

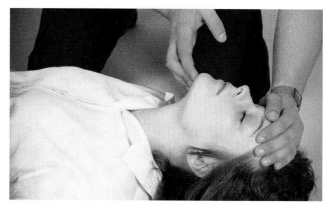

Figure 5–7   If you do not suspect a head or neck injury, tilt the head and lift the chin to open the airway.

If the person is unconscious, you must ensure the airway is open. To do this you tilt the head back and lift the chin (Figure 5–7). This action moves the tongue away from the back of the throat and lets air reach the lungs. If you think the casualty may have a neck injury, you use a different method, called the jaw thrust, to open the airway.

Jaw Thrust

Another way to open the airway is the *jaw thrust*. Always use this method if you suspect a neck or back injury. You should suspect such an injury in those casualties who experienced a violent force, such as in a motor vehicle crash, a fall, or a diving or sports injury. In such cases use the jaw thrust method instead of the head-tilt/chin-lift method to minimize movement of the head and neck.

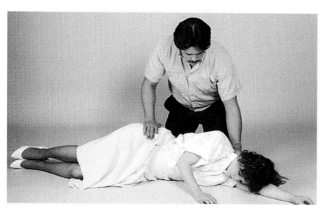

Figure 5–6   If the casualty's position keeps you from checking the ABCs, roll the casualty gently onto his or her back while supporting the head and neck.

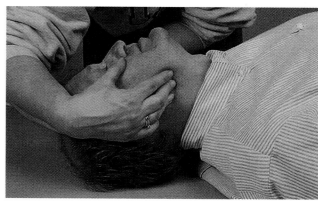

Figure 5–8   Use the jaw thrust method for opening the airway if the casualty has a neck or back injury or if the head-tilt/chin-lift method does not succeed.

Grasp the angles of the jaw with the fingers of both hands and lift the jaw forward (Figure 5–8). Since both hands are used to hold the jaw, you will need to seal the casualty's nose with your cheek when you blow in the two breaths.

When the person's airway is blocked by food or some object, you need to remove the blockage first. Chapter 6 describes first aid for an obstructed airway.

B—Check breathing

Next check for breathing. Someone who can speak or cry is breathing. Watch an unconscious person carefully for signs of breathing. The chest should rise and fall, but you must also listen and feel for breathing. Put your face close so you can hear and feel air coming out the nose and mouth while you watch the rise and fall of the chest. Look, listen, and feel for breathing for no more than 10 seconds (Figure 5–9). A person is considered to be not breathing when no breathing is observed or attempts to breathe appear to be ineffective.

If the casualty is not breathing, you must help the person to breathe. To do this, you breathe air into the casualty's mouth. Pinch the nostrils and start with two full breaths. This aid is called *rescue breathing*. You will learn how to do this in Chapter 7.

C—Check circulation

The last step in the primary survey is to check the circulation. This step involves checking for signs of circulation and looking for severe bleeding and signs of shock.

If the person is breathing effectively, more than an occasional gasp, the heart is beating and you do not need to check the pulse. If the person is not breathing effectively, you must check for other signs of circulation. To check circulation, look for movement of the casualty, effective breathing (more than an occasional gasp), coughing, appropriate colour of the skin, and presence of a carotid

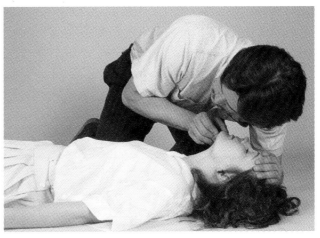

Figure 5–9   To check for breathing, look, listen, and feel for breathing for no more than 10 seconds.

pulse. To check for the carotid pulse, feel for the pulse in the *carotid artery* in the neck on the side closest to you (Figure 5–10). To find the pulse, find the Adam's apple and slide your fingers into the groove at the side of the neck. The pulse may be hard to find if it is slow or weak. If at first you do not find a pulse, start again at the Adam's apple and slide your fingers into place. When you think you are in the right spot, keep feeling for up to 10 seconds. Make sure you do not take more than 10 seconds checking for signs of circulation.

If you do not observe the presence of the signs of circulation or are unsure, do not hesitate; begin *cardiopulmonary resuscitation* (CPR). In Chapter 8 you will learn how to do CPR.

Figure 5–10   To determine if the heart is beating check for signs of circulation including movement of the casualty, effective breathing, coughing, appropriate colour of the skin, and presence of a carotid pulse.

This step in the ABCs also means looking for severe bleeding. Look for severe bleeding by looking at the casualty from head to toe (Figure 5–11). Severe bleeding must be controlled as soon as possible. You will learn how to do this in Chapter 8.

Sometimes an injured person may be bleeding inside the body. A casualty who is bleeding either externally or internally may go into shock. Shock is a serious condition when the body has lost a lot of blood. If the person is in shock, the skin may look pale and feel cool to your touch. In Chapter 8 you will learn how to care for shock.

If you find that an unconscious casualty is breathing effectively, do not leave the person lying on his or her back. Unless you suspect a neck or back injury, roll the casualty onto the side to keep the airway open.

Recovery Position

The recovery position, also called the *drainage position*, is used for unconscious casualties (1) who have an open airway, (2) who are breathing, (3) who have signs of circulation and no serious bleeding, (4) who are not thought to have neck or back injury. These casualties are positioned on their side to keep the airway open and to allow drainage from the mouth if the casualty vomits or is bleeding. Use the recovery position for these casualties even if you first used the chin or jaw lift to open

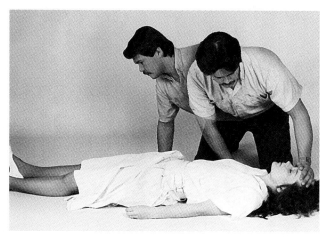

Figure 5–11 Check for severe bleeding by checking the casualty from head to toe.

the airway, because the airway will stay open without you having to hold the chin in position.

Follow these steps to move the unconscious casualty into the recovery position from a position on the back:

1. Raise the arm closest to you over the casualty's head.
2. Raise the knee of the leg further away from you.
3. Support the head and neck with one hand as you pull the person toward you with your other hand on the raised knee (Figure 5–12, A).
4. Position the casualty on his or her side with knee out in front and hip at right angle to prevent the person from rolling onto his or her face (Figure 5–12, B).
5. Move the casualty's other arm into a position of comfort in front of the body.
6. With the casualty's head resting on the extended arm, tilt the head and open the mouth to clear the way for drainage (Figure 5–12, C).

Signs and symptoms

In both the primary survey and secondary survey you are checking the casualty for health problems caused by injury or sudden illness. The terms *signs* and *symptoms* are used throughout this book for the evidence of injury or illness that you find. A **sign** is an objective signal of injury or illness—something you can see, feel, or hear. A **symptom** is a subjective signal of injury or illness, which the casualty tells you he or she feels. Both signs and symptoms will help you know what problem the casualty has that requires first aid.

Step Four: Do a Secondary Survey

After you have called EMS and only if you are sure that the casualty has no life-threatening problems that require continued care, should you move on to the next step.

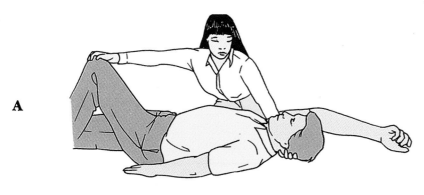

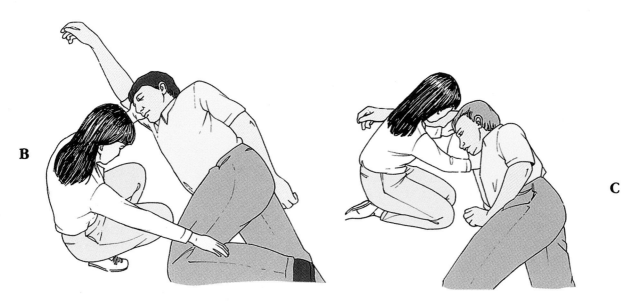

Figure 5–12 Positioning an unconscious casualty in the recovery position. See text for descriptions of steps.

The *secondary survey* is a way to look for other problems that may need first aid. Again ask the casualty and others present about what has happened. When a child is the casualty, ask parents or adults at the scene. Then check the casualty's vital signs, and examine the casualty from head to toe. The vital signs are pulse rate, breathing rate, and level of consciousness. The secondary survey is important because even problems that do not threaten life directly can become serious if first aid is not given.

Chapter 9 describes the secondary survey in detail. In later chapters you will learn how to give first aid for problems you find in the secondary survey.

Step Five: Keep Monitoring the Casualty's ABCs

If you have completed the secondary survey of the casualty and have given first aid for any injuries or illness, continue to monitor the ABCs while you wait for EMS to arrive. The person's condition can gradually worsen or a life-threatening condition such as respiratory or cardiac arrest can occur suddenly. Do not assume that the person is out of danger just because there were no serious problems at first.

Step Six: Help the Casualty Rest Comfortably and Provide Reassurance

While waiting for EMS to arrive, help the casualty stay calm and as comfortable as possible while waiting. Tell the person help is on the way and try to relieve the person's anxiety. Anxiety can actually make a person's condition worse.

Summary

- In any emergency follow the six emergency action principles (EAPs) to guide your actions, ensure everyone's safety, and give care for life-threatening emergencies or less serious injuries or illness.

- First, survey the scene to make sure no dangers are present.

- Second, check for unresponsiveness and call EMS or send someone else to call, giving the correct information to the dispatcher.

- Third, do a primary survey of the casualty by checking the airway, breathing, or circulation (ABCs) and care for any life-threatening problems right away.

- Fourth, if you find no life-threatening conditions, do a secondary survey to find and care for any other injuries or illness.

- Fifth, keep monitoring the casualty's airway, breathing, and circulation until help arrives, in case a life-threatening condition develops for which you may have to give first aid.

- Sixth, help the casualty rest in the most comfortable position and give reassurance.

- In the following chapters, apply the EAPs with each injury or illness, because these principles are the basis of first aid in any emergency (Figure 5–13).

Survey the scene
- Is it safe?
- What happened?

Assess unresponsiveness and phone EMS
If person is unresponsive:
- Send someone to call EMS.
- If alone call EMS before beginning a primary survey "CALL FIRST."

Begin a primary survey
- Is the casualty conscious?
- Does the casualty have an open airway?
- Is the casualty breathing?
- Are there signs of circulation—major bleeding?
- Is the person in shock?

Do a secondary survey
- Interview the casualty.
- Check vital signs.
- Perform a head-to-toe survey.

Monitor casualty's condition
- Continue checking vital signs.

Rest and reassure the casualty
- Treat for shock.
- Help casualty rest in the most comfortable position and give reassurance.

Figure 5–13 Use the EAPs to make care decisions in an emergency.

Airway Emergencies

6

Objectives

After reading this chapter, you should be able to:

1. List at least three causes of choking.
2. Describe how choking can be prevented.
3. Describe first aid for a conscious and an unconscious adult, child, and infant with a partly or completely obstructed airway.
4. Explain how first aid is modified for large or pregnant casualties.
5. Define the key terms for this chapter.

After reading this chapter and completing the class activities, you should be able to:

1. Demonstrate first aid for a conscious adult, child, and infant with an obstructed airway.
2. Demonstrate first aid for an unconscious adult, child, and infant with an obstructed airway.
3. Make appropriate decisions for the first aid to be given in an example of a choking emergency.

Key Terms

abdominal thrusts   Method to dislodge a foreign object from the airway; also called the *Heimlich manoeuvre.*

airway obstruction   Blockage of the airway that prevents air from reaching a person's lungs.

choking   The condition when the person's airway is partly or completely blocked by a foreign object.

finger sweep   Technique used to remove foreign material from a casualty's upper airway.

head-tilt/chin-lift   Technique for opening the airway in an unconscious adult or child.

jaw thrust   Alternative method of opening the airway.

In the previous chapter you learned the emergency action principles (EAPs) for any emergency. Once you are sure the scene is safe, check the casualty for unresponsiveness and call EMS if necessary. Begin a primary survey of the casualty to detect any life-threatening conditions. Check the ABCs:

- *Airway*
- *Breathing*
- *Circulation*

This chapter concerns the first of these, the airway. The airway is the passage through which air moves from the nose and mouth to the lungs. If anything blocks the airway, the person chokes and cannot get enough oxygen, and life is threatened. This is an emergency, and you must give first aid to remove whatever is obstructing the airway.

Anatomy and Physiology of the Airway

Figure 4–3 in Chapter 4 shows how the air passes from the nose and mouth to the lungs. Air moves into the trachea (windpipe) to the bronchi, which branch into smaller passages in the lungs. A flap of tissue called the epiglottis covers the opening from the back of the mouth to the trachea to prevent food and liquid from entering the lungs during swallowing.

Causes of Airway Obstruction

An *airway obstruction* can occur if the tongue or swollen tissues of the mouth and throat block the airway. This blockage may occur after an injury or because of a severe allergic reaction. The most common cause in an unconscious person is the tongue, which has dropped to the back of the

throat and blocked the airway. A person cannot "swallow" the tongue, as in the common saying.

The airway can also be blocked by a foreign object, such as a piece of food; a small toy; or fluids like vomit, blood, mucus, or saliva. This is called *choking*. The foreign object can be lodged in the airway at any point from the throat to the lungs.

Common causes of choking include the following:

- Trying to swallow large pieces of food without chewing them adequately.
- Drinking alcohol in excess before or during meals. Alcohol dulls the gag reflex, which aids swallowing, making choking on food more likely.
- Wearing dentures. Dentures make it difficult to sense whether food is fully chewed before swallowing.
- Eating while talking excitedly or laughing, or eating too quickly.
- Walking, playing, or running with food or objects in the mouth.

PREVENTION

Choking

Choking can usually be prevented, if you are careful when eating. Follow these guidelines:

- Chew food well before swallowing; eat slowly and calmly. Be especially careful if you have dentures. Avoid talking or laughing with food in your mouth.
- Minimize alcohol consumption before and during meals.
- Avoid walking or other physical activity with food in your mouth.
- Keep other objects out of the mouth. For example, do not hold a pen cap or nails in your mouth when your hands are busy.

Infants and young children are particularly at risk for choking. Parents and other supervisors should follow these guidelines:

- Feed children only when they are seated in a high chair or a secure seat. Do not let young children move about with food in their hands or mouth.
- Feed an infant or young child appropriate soft foods in small pieces. Constantly watch the child when eating.
- Check the environment and all toys to be sure no small objects or parts are present that the infant or young child may put in the mouth.
- Keep young children away from balloons, which can burst into small pieces that can be easily inhaled.

Signs and Symptoms of Choking

A person who is choking may have either a complete or a partial airway obstruction. A casualty with a complete airway obstruction is not able to breathe at all. With a partial airway obstruction, the casualty may be able to get some air into the lungs.

Signs and Symptoms of Partial Airway Obstruction

A person with a partial airway obstruction can often get enough air into the lungs to try to dislodge the object by coughing. The person may also be able to speak. The following are signs and symptoms of a partial obstruction:

- High-pitched or wheezing sounds (stridor) when trying to breathe in
- Coughing
- Clutching at the throat with one or both hands, the universal distress signal for choking (Figure 6–1)

Signs and Symptoms of Complete Airway Obstruction

- May be conscious or unconscious
- Unable to breathe
- Unable to speak
- Unable to cough
- Face may appear bluish

A conscious adult can usually indicate that he or she is choking. With an infant or small child who is conscious but suddenly not able to breathe, assume the person is choking on something and give first aid as described in the next sections.

If you find a casualty unconscious and not breathing, you may not realize at first whether the person is choking; you do not have to know this to give first aid. First aid starts in the same way for any unconscious person who is not breathing. You will quickly discover that the casualty has an obstructed airway when you attempt rescue breathing and air does not go in and the chest does not rise, as described later in this chapter.

FIRST AID

Choking

For a casualty with a partial airway obstruction, do not interfere with attempts to cough up the object.

Figure 6–1 Clutching the throat with one or both hands is the universal distress signal for choking.

A person who can cough or speak is getting enough air to breathe. Stay with the casualty and encourage continued coughing. If coughing persists, call EMS for help. If the person is barely able to breathe, the cough is very weak, and he or she cannot speak at all, treat this as a complete airway obstruction.

When someone is choking on a foreign object, your goal is to open the airway as quickly as possible. First aid is based on *abdominal thrusts*, also called the *Heimlich manoeuvre*, which force air from the lungs to push the object out, like a cork from a bottle of champagne (Figure 6–2). The method you use depends on whether the casualty is conscious or unconscious and is an adult, child, or infant. Variations are used for large adults and pregnant women who are unconscious.

First Aid for a Conscious Choking Adult with Complete Airway Obstruction

In order to determine if the person is choking, ask "Are you choking?" If the person is choking, summon someone who can help you. Then attempt abdominal thrusts for a conscious choking child or adult with complete airway obstruction. Stand behind the person and wrap your arms around the waist. Make a fist with one hand and place the thumb side of the fist on the middle of the abdomen slightly above the navel and well below the tip of the breastbone. Grasp your fist with the other hand and give quick, upward thrusts into the abdomen to dislodge the object. Repeat them until the casualty stops choking or becomes unconscious.

Chest Thrusts for a Conscious Choking Adult with Complete Airway Obstruction

In some cases, you should give chest thrusts instead of abdominal thrusts to choking adults. Use chest thrusts when you cannot reach far enough around the casualty or for women in late stages of pregnancy.

To give chest thrusts to a conscious casualty, stand behind the casualty; place your arms under the casualty's armpits and around the chest. As with abdominal thrusts, make a fist with one hand; place the thumb side against the centre of the casualty's breastbone. Be sure that your fist is centred on the breastbone, not on the ribs. Also make sure that your fist is not near the lower tip

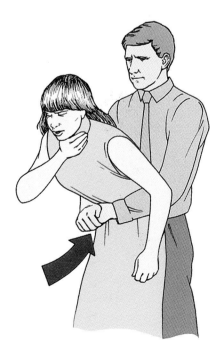

Figure 6–2 Abdominal thrusts simulate a cough, forcing air trapped in the lungs to push the object out of the airway.

Figure 6–3   Give chest thrusts if you cannot reach around the casualty to give abdominal thrusts or if the casualty is noticeably pregnant.

of the breastbone. Grab your fist with your other hand and thrust inward (Figure 6–3). Repeat these thrusts until the object is dislodged or the casualty becomes unconscious.

First aid for yourself choking

If you are alone and choking, you can give yourself abdominal thrusts in one of two ways. (1) Make a fist with one hand and place the thumb side on the middle of your abdomen slightly above your navel and well below the tip of your breastbone. Grasp your fist with your other hand and give a quick upward thrust. Or (2) you can lean forward and press your abdomen over any firm object such as the back of a chair, a railing, or a sink (Figure 6–4). Be careful not to lean over anything with a sharp edge or a corner that might injure you.

When to Stop Abdominal Thrusts, Chest Thrusts, and Back Blows

Stop giving thrusts immediately if the object is dislodged or if the person begins to breathe or cough. Make sure the object is cleared from the airway. Watch that the person is breathing freely again, since the person may still have breathing problems. Since abdominal thrusts and chest thrusts may cause internal injuries, the person

should be taken to the nearest hospital emergency department for follow-up care, even if he or she seems to be breathing without difficulty.

First Aid for Conscious Choking Children with Complete Airway Obstruction

First aid for a child over age 1 who is choking is similar to that for an adult. The only significant differences involve considering the child's size when you provide care. Obviously, you cannot use the same force when giving abdominal thrusts to expel the object. Otherwise, use the same methods as for an adult.

First Aid for Conscious Choking Infants with Complete Airway Obstruction

First determine if the infant is choking by observing if the infant can breathe, cough, or cry, or is coughing weakly or making high-pitched sounds. If the infant is choking, summon someone who can help and proceed to provide first aid.

First aid for an infant under age 1 who is choking includes a combination of back blows and chest thrusts. Do not use abdominal thrusts as with chil-

Figure 6–4   To give yourself abdominal thrusts, you can press your abdomen onto a firm object such as the back of a chair.

First Aid for Choking—*It Sure Saves Lives!*

It's remarkable the number of people who have written testimonial letters on how first aid for choking taught in Red Cross first aid courses has dramatically saved a life. The following extracts from these letters illustrate this point.

"I would like to thank the Red Cross for the 'Sauver une vie' program. What I learned from this program probably saved my husband's life. He is 61 years old, handicapped, and uses a motorized wheelchair. He choked on a piece of food, and his face turned very red and his lips started to turn blue. Even though this scared me very much and I had some difficulty due to my own handicap (affecting my legs and one arm), I used the abdominal thrust technique demonstrated in the program. Everything worked very well and my husband's face returned to its normal colour. Thank you for delivering this program, which I am sure will save many lives."

J.D. Quebec City

"Last summer our family travelled across Canada and included Newfoundland in our trip. On our return ferry trip from Argentia to Sydney on the ship *Joey and Clara Smallwood* the Red Cross offered a CPR course. Our two children, aged 12 and 16, and their cousins, aged 12, 16, and 17, all took the course. We were pleased that this very worthwhile course was offered during the voyage.

Four weeks later in Kelowna, B.C., just as we were completing our 9-week vacation, our 15-year-old son had the most remarkable opportunity to save a woman's life. While he was in a mall, a woman choking on food walked out of the restaurant unable to breathe. Our son did not hesitate to act. He immediately proceeded to perform the Heimlich manoeu-vre on her. He was able to dislodge the food and the woman sustained no injury.

It was a very emotional time for us all. We were grateful that he could do the manoeuvre, and very proud of him for his courage. We wish to thank you for offering the course. My son certainly saved the woman's life, and it gave my son a wonderful opportunity to do something very unique."

M.V. Osoyoos, B.C.

When 3-year-old Julie said "Mom, you hurt my stomach," her mother Anne just smiled and gave her a big hug. Anne had given her daughter a cough drop while she dried the youngster's hair when suddenly she realized something was wrong—Julie was silently choking but still conscious.

"Her lips were turning blue and she was obviously having difficulty breathing," Anne recalled. "I yelled at my husband to call an ambulance."

Initial panic was replaced by calm as Anne put into action the skills she had learned only a month earlier at a Red Cross CPR course. Twice she applied the Heimlich manoeuvre but Julie did not respond. The third time the cough drop popped out, and as the colour returned to Julie's cheeks, Anne and her husband breathed a sigh of relief.

Anne doesn't like to think about what might have happened if she hadn't taken the Red Cross course. "...imagine watching someone choke and not knowing what to do. Being trained in CPR and first aid has given me a sense of confidence I didn't have before, and I would never want to be without that training again, especially with children around."

From "New Brunswick Vision"

dren or adults. Turn the infant face down on your forearm with the head lower than the body, and with the heel of your hand give five forceful back blows between the infant's shoulder blades. Then turn the infant onto its back in your lap with head supported lower than the body. Give five chest thrusts with your middle and index fingers on the breastbone one finger width below the nipple line. Repeat back blows and chest thrusts until object is coughed up or infant becomes unconscious.

First Aid for a Conscious Choking Adult Who Becomes Unconscious

While giving abdominal thrusts to a conscious choking adult, be prepared for the person to become unconscious if the obstruction is not removed. If this occurs, lower the casualty to the floor on his or her back. Have someone call EMS immediately if this has not already been done. Open the airway and look in the mouth. If an object is seen, remove the object by sweeping it out with your finger. This is called a *finger sweep* (Figure 6–5). Use a hooking action to remove the object. Be careful not to push the object deeper into the airway. Next, try to open the airway using the head-tilt/chin-lift method (described in the next section) and assess for effective breathing for no more than 10 seconds. If the casualty is not breathing, attempt to ventilate. Often the throat muscles relax after the person becomes uncon-

scious, allowing air past the obstruction and into the lungs. If the air does not go into the lungs, retilt the head and attempt to ventilate again. If air still does not go into the lungs, assume that the airway is still obstructed and begin the CPR sequence (15 chest compressions).

After 15 chest compressions, open the airway and look in the mouth. If you see an object, remove it, then attempt to ventilate. Remember, if necessary, to reposition the head to adjust the airway. If you are still not able to get air into the casualty's lungs, continue the CPR sequence, always looking into the mouth prior to the ventilation attempt. If you see any change in the person's condition, stop CPR and reassess the ABCs.

Once you can breathe air into the casualty's lungs, give 2 slow breaths. Then complete the primary survey by checking the casualty for signs of circulation and checking and caring for severe bleeding. If there are no signs of circulation, begin CPR (see Chapter 8). If the casualty has signs of circulation but is not breathing on his or her own, continue rescue breathing.

First Aid for an Unconscious Choking Adult

To determine if an unconscious person is breathing, open the airway and place your ear close to the person's mouth; then look, listen, and feel for signs of breathing for no more than 10 seconds:

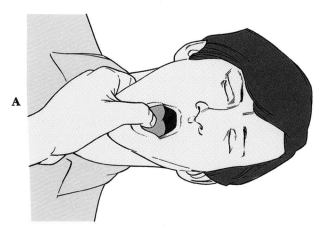
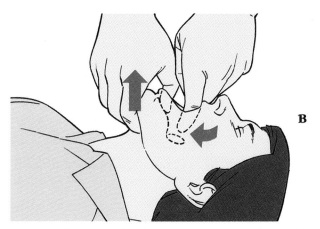

Figure 6–5   *A,* To do a finger sweep, first lift the lower jaw, and *B,* then use a hooking action to sweep the object out of the airway.

- Look at chest and abdomen for movement.
- Listen for breathing sounds.
- Feel for exhaled breath on your cheek.

If none of these signs are present, the person is not breathing.

If the casualty is unconscious and not breathing, use the head-tilt/chin-lift method to open the airway and attempt to ventilate. If air will not go in, retilt the head and attempt to ventilate again. If air still does not go in, begin the CPR sequence. One addition is made to the regular CPR sequence. Between chest compressions and ventilations the rescuer should look in the casualty's mouth for an obstruction. If one is seen it should be carefully removed but not discarded.

If your first attempts to clear the airway do not succeed, *do not stop*. The longer the person goes without oxygen, the more the muscles will relax, making it easier to clear the airway.

Once you can breathe air into the casualty's lungs, give 2 full breaths. Then complete the primary survey by checking the casualty for signs of circulation and checking and caring for severe bleeding. If there are no signs of circulation, begin CPR (see Chapter 8). If the casualty has signs of circulation but is not breathing on his or her own, continue rescue breathing.

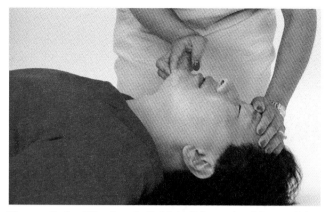

Figure 6–6   The head-tilt/chin-lift method is used for opening the airway.

If the casualty starts breathing on his or her own, monitor breathing and circulation until EMS arrives and takes over. Maintain an open airway, confirm the person is breathing, and keep checking the signs of circulation. Put the casualty into the recovery position, as described in Chaper 5.

First Aid for Unconscious Choking Children or Infants

First aid for an unconscious casualty under age 8 who is choking is similar to that for an adult. The difference is in the CPR sequence. Rather than 15 compressions, perform 5 compressions.

Table 6–1	Obstructed Airway Emergencies	
Problem	*Signals*	*Care*
Choking—conscious casualty, partial obstruction	Coughing forcefully Can speak and breathe Wheezing	Encourage casualty to continue coughing If coughing persists, call EMS
Choking—conscious casualty, complete obstruction	Coughing weakly Cannot speak or breathe	Shout for help Begin abdominal thrusts (back blows and chest thrusts for infants)
Choking—unconscious casualty complete obstruction	No breathing Breaths won't go in	Call EMS Begin CPR Look in the casualty's mouth for an obstruction after each cycle of compressions before attempting to ventilate

Head-Tilt/Chin-Lift

If an unconscious casualty's airway is blocked by the tongue, you can open the airway simply by tilting the head back and lifting the chin, using the head-tilt/chin-lift method. If the airway is blocked by swollen tissues, you may not be able to get the airway open and should call EMS immediately.

The *head-tilt/chin-lift* method positions the throat so that the tongue does not block the airway. If you suspect the casualty has other injuries, check for breathing before moving the person to avoid causing further harm. Then, if the casualty is not breathing, support the head and neck with one hand while rolling the person onto the back with the other. With the person lying flat on the back, tilt the head back with one hand on the casualty's forehead and raise the chin with your other hand (Figure 6–6). Pinch the nostrils closed, seal your mouth over the casualty's, and give two breaths. (Rescue breathing is described in more detail in Chapter 7.) If air goes in, the person does not have an obstructed airway. If air does not go in, retilt the head and attempt to ventilate again. If air still does not go in, the person has an airway obstruction and needs first aid for choking.

Summary

- Table 6–1 summarizes the signs and symptoms and care of different choking emergencies.

- Choking on a foreign object is a life-threatening emergency requiring immediate first aid.

- The goal of first aid for choking is to open the airway as quickly as possible with abdominal thrusts, chest thrusts, or back blows, as appropriate for the casualty.

- If an obstruction does not dislodge at first, continue first aid because relaxing muscles will make it easier to clear the object.

- Vary first aid for choking for conscious and unconscious casualties; adults, children, and infants; and large or pregnant casualties.

Breathing Emergencies

Objectives

After reading this chapter, you should be able to:

1. List the signs and symptoms of respiratory distress and respiratory arrest and the chest injuries that can cause them.

2. Describe the first aid for a casualty of respiratory distress.

3. Describe the first aid for a penetrating chest wound.

4. Describe when to provide rescue breathing.

5. Describe why and how to provide rescue breathing.

6. Describe the signs and symptoms of anaphylactic shock.

7. Describe the first aid for a casualty with anaphylactic shock.

8. Define the key terms for this chapter.

After reading this chapter and completing the class activities, you should be able to:

1. Demonstrate rescue breathing for an adult, child, and infant.

2. Decide what first aid to give in an example of an emergency in which a person is not breathing.

3. Describe the signs and symptoms of anaphylactic shock.

4. Describe the first aid for a casualty with anaphylactic shock.

Key Terms

allergic reaction   The response of the body to a substance to which the person has hypersensitivity. It can be mild or very severe.

anaphylactic reaction or shock   A form of shock caused by a very severe allergic reaction.

aspiration   Inhaling blood, vomit, saliva, or other foreign material into the lungs.

breathing emergency   Situation in which breathing is so impaired that life is threatened.

rescue breathing   The technique of breathing for a nonbreathing casualty.

respiratory arrest   Condition in which breathing has stopped or appears ineffective.

respiratory distress   Condition in which breathing is difficult.

In the previous chapter you learned how to help someone who is choking by giving first aid to clear the airway. In this chapter you will learn how to care for someone who is having other kinds of breathing difficulties, who has a penetrating chest wound affecting breathing, or who has stopped breathing altogether.

As always, follow the emergency action principles. Once you are sure the scene is safe, check for unresponsiveness. If the casualty is unresponsive, call EMS. Then check the ABCs:

- *Airway*
- *Breathing*
- *Circulation*

Ensure that the casualty has an open airway (Chapter 6) and is breathing. A *breathing emergency* exists if breathing is difficult or has stopped altogether. A person having difficulty breathing is in *respiratory distress*. A person who stops breathing or whose breathing appears ineffective is in *respiratory arrest*.

Anatomy and Physiology of Breathing

Breathing requires the respiratory, circulatory, nervous, and musculoskeletal systems to work together. Injuries or illnesses that affect any of these systems may impair breathing. For example, if the heart stops beating, the casualty will stop breathing. Injury or disease in certain areas of the brain may impair or stop breathing. Damage to muscles or bones of the chest and back can make breathing difficult or painful. All of these situations can be breathing emergencies.

The body requires a constant supply of oxygen for survival. When you breathe air into your lungs, the oxygen in the air is transferred to the blood. The blood then takes the oxygen to the brain, organs, muscles, and all parts of the body. The body needs oxygen to perform its many functions such as breathing, walking, talking, digesting food, and maintaining body temperature. Some functions require more energy and therefore more oxygen. For example, a person with a breathing problem may have just enough energy for sitting in a chair but not enough for climbing a flight of stairs.

In respiratory arrest, the body receives no oxygen to continue its functions. After a few minutes without oxygen, body systems begin to fail. A person loses consciousness within a minute and eventually the heart muscle stops. Other body systems then start to fail. Without oxygen, cells begin to die in 4 to 6 minutes (Figure 7–1). Some tissues, such as the brain, are very sensitive to oxygen deprivation. Unless the brain receives oxygen within minutes, brain damage or death will result.

Causes of Breathing Emergencies

Breathing emergencies include respiratory distress and respiratory arrest.

Common Causes of Respiratory Distress

Common conditions causing respiratory distress include:

- Asthma
- Medical illnesses
- Chest trauma
- Anaphylactic reaction

In an asthma attack, the air passages become narrowed and breathing is difficult. Asthma is more common in children and young adults. It may be triggered by stress, physical activity, or an allergic reaction to food, pollen, a drug, or an insect sting. Asthma is usually controlled with medication (Figure 7–2).

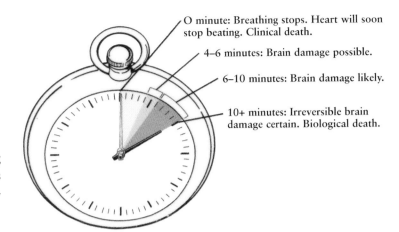

O minute: Breathing stops. Heart will soon stop beating. Clinical death.

4–6 minutes: Brain damage possible.

6–10 minutes: Brain damage likely.

10+ minutes: Irreversible brain damage certain. Biological death.

Figure 7–1 Time is critical in starting life-saving measures. Four to six minutes without oxygen generally causes irreversible brain damage.

Medical illnesses such as heart failure, pneumonia, emphysema, bronchitis, and high fever can cause respiratory distress. Rapid breathing or hyperventilation can be caused by fear, anxiety, or great excitement and occurs more frequently in tense or nervous people.

Anaphylaxis is a severe allergic reaction. Air passages may swell, making breathing difficult. Anaphylaxis may be caused by insect stings, food, or medications.

Chest injuries are a major cause of injury deaths. Chest injuries are caused by automobile collisions, falls, sports mishaps, and other crushing or penetrating forces. Chest injuries can cause a breathing emergency if the lungs are crushed by the ribs or punctured by a penetrating wound. A knife or bullet, for example, may cause a puncture wound. A forceful puncture penetrating the rib cage may allow air to enter the chest through the wound (Figure 7–3) and may result in serious internal bleeding.

Causes of Respiratory Arrest

Respiratory arrest may be caused by any of the following:

- An obstructed airway (choking)
- Illness (such as pneumonia)
- Respiratory conditions (such as emphysema or asthma)
- Electrocution
- Shock
- Drowning
- Heart attack or heart disease
- Injury to the head, chest, or lungs
- Severe allergic reaction to food or an insect sting
- Drugs and alcohol
- Poisoning, such as inhaling or ingesting toxic substances

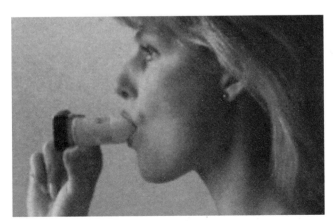

Figure 7–2 Medication used to treat asthma attacks is breathed in through an inhaler. Reprinted with permission of Astra Pharma Inc.

PREVENTION

Breathing Emergencies

Because breathing emergencies can result from so many different causes, prevention means that those at risk should take precautions in specific areas. Everyone should follow general safety

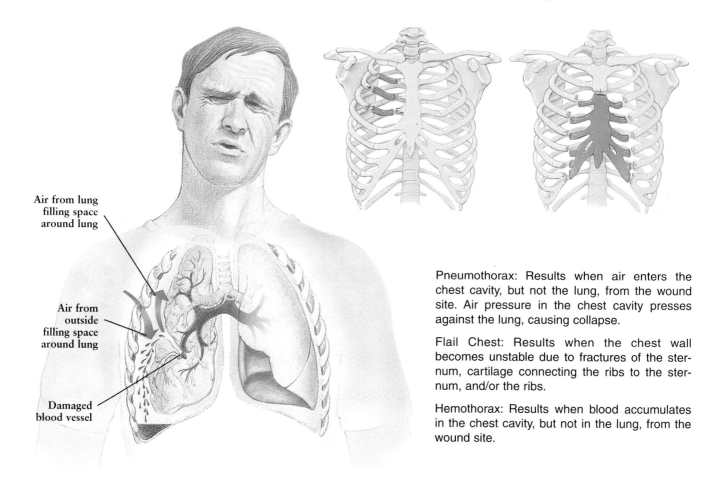

Pneumothorax: Results when air enters the chest cavity, but not the lung, from the wound site. Air pressure in the chest cavity presses against the lung, causing collapse.

Flail Chest: Results when the chest wall becomes unstable due to fractures of the sternum, cartilage connecting the ribs to the sternum, and/or the ribs.

Hemothorax: Results when blood accumulates in the chest cavity, but not in the lung, from the wound site.

Air from lung filling space around lung

Air from outside filling space around lung

Damaged blood vessel

Figure 7–3   A puncture wound penetrating the lung or chest cavity around the lung lets air go in and out of the cavity.

practices to prevent injuries that can cause breathing emergencies.

- People with asthma should always have their medication with them or nearby in case of an attack. Parents of asthmatic children should take all necessary steps to ensure that others who supervise their children know about the asthma and how to assist with medication.
- People who know they have severe allergies should be careful to avoid the substances or foods that cause the allergic reaction. If they have a severe allergic reaction to insect bites and stings, a condition called anaphylaxis, they should carry their medication with them whenever appropriate and wear a Medic-Alert bracelet. Parents of children with severe allergies must be especially careful.

- Chest injuries and other injuries that lead to respiratory arrest can often be prevented by good safety practices in all areas of life, including driving motor vehicles, sports and recreational activities, working around the home, and occupational activities. Follow the safety guidelines throughout this book for preventing injuries.
- Parents of infants and small children should take precautions to avoid anything that could cause suffocation.
- Store plastic bags and wrappings in a child-proof place.
- Remove the doors from old refrigerators and similar containers where a child could be trapped.
- Prevent drowning by closely supervising baths, keeping toilet lids closed or child-

proofed, using approved life jackets around water, and following safe water recreation practices.

- Prevent strangulation by removing from the children's environment any items with cords, belts, or other parts that could be wrapped around a child's neck.

Since breathing emergencies also result from some illnesses, one should always seek treatment before an illness becomes an emergency. Get regular checkups and always follow the doctor's advice for use of medications and self-care. Do not delay seeing a doctor whenever you have symptoms that might be warnings of impending respiratory difficulty.

Signs and Symptoms of Breathing Emergencies

Breathing emergencies are usually easily recognized because the signs and symptoms are clear. You do not need to know the cause of the emergency; you need only see that the person is having trouble breathing or has stopped breathing.

Signs and Symptoms of Respiratory Distress

- The casualty may seem unable to catch his or her breath or may be gasping for air.
- Breathing may be faster or slower than normal.
- Breathing may be unusually deep or shallow.
- The casualty may make unusual noises, such as wheezing or gurgling, or high-pitched sounds like crowing.
- The casualty's skin at first may be unusually moist and flushed, later appearing pale or bluish as the oxygen level in the blood falls.
- The casualty may feel dizzy or lightheaded.
- The casualty may feel pain in the chest or tingling in the hands and feet.
- The casualty may appear apprehensive, fearful, or very anxious.

Signs and Symptoms of Conditions Causing Respiratory Distress

Signs and symptoms of asthma

- Wheezing when exhaling

Signs and symptoms of hyperventilation caused by anxiety

- Shallow, rapid breathing
- Casualty says he or she cannot get enough air or is suffocating
- Casualty is fearful and apprehensive or confused
- Dizziness and numbness or tingling of fingers and toes

Signs and symptoms of allergic reaction

- Previous allergic episodes
- Rash, hives, itching
- A feeling of tightness in the chest and throat
- Swelling of the lips, face, ears, neck, and/or tongue
- Wheezing when exhaling, or high-pitched noises when inhaling
- Weakness, dizziness, or confusion
- Nausea, vomiting

Signs and symptoms of penetrating chest injury

- Difficulty breathing
- Bleeding from an open chest wound
- A sucking sound coming from the wound with each breath
- Severe pain at the site of the injury
- Obvious deformity, such as that caused by a fracture
- Coughing up blood

Signs and symptoms of respiratory arrest

- Unconsciousness
- Bluish appearance of the face
- Absence of chest and abdominal movement other than the occasional attempt to breathe
- Absence of breath sounds other than the occasional gasp or gurgle

To determine if the person is breathing, open the airway and place your ear close to the person's mouth. Look, listen, and feel for signs of breathing:

- Look at chest and abdomen for movement.
- Listen for breathing sounds.
- Feel for exhaled breath on your cheek.

If none of these signs is present, the person is not breathing and is in respiratory arrest.

FIRST AID

Breathing Emergencies

The first aid you give depends on whether the casualty is still breathing or is in respiratory arrest.

In all cases start with the emergency action principles:

1. Survey the scene to ensure no danger.
2. Check the casualty for unresponsiveness. If the person does not respond, call EMS.
3. Do a primary survey and care for life-threatening problems (ABCs). Call EMS for help if necessary.
4. Do a secondary survey, if needed, and care for other problems.
5. Keep monitoring the ABCs until EMS arrives.
6. Help the casualty rest in the most comfortable position and provide reassurance.

First Aid for Respiratory Distress

Immediate first aid for respiratory distress is often crucial in preventing a life-threatening emergency. Respiratory distress can lead to respiratory arrest, which, if not immediately cared for, will result in death.

In addition to the emergency action principles, follow these steps for first aid for respiratory distress:

1. Help the casualty take any prescribed medication for his or her condition. This may be oxygen, an inhaler for asthma, or medication in an allergy kit (Figure 7–4).

2. If the casualty is conscious but unable to speak, ask yes-or-no questions the casualty can answer by nodding. Try to reduce any anxiety that may contribute to the casualty's breathing difficulty.
3. Provide enough air by opening a window. Have bystanders move back.
4. Help the person maintain normal body temperature.

Anaphylactic Shock

Severe allergic reactions to poisons leading to anaphylactic shock are rare. When one occurs, however, it is truly a life-threatening medical emergency.

Causes of Anaphylactic Shock

Anaphylactic shock is a severe allergic reaction. It can be caused by an insect bite or sting or by contact with any drugs, medications, foods, or chemicals to which the individual is allergic.

PREVENTION

Anaphylactic Shock

People who know they are very allergic to a substance usually try to avoid it, but this is sometimes impossible. These people may carry a special kit, called an *epinephrine* or *epi-kit*, in case they have an allergic reaction (see Figure 7–4).

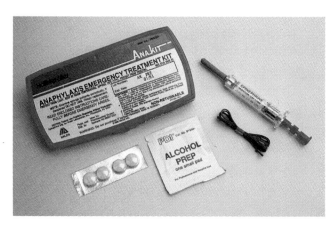

Figure 7–4   A sample allergy kit.

The kit contains the drug epinephrine that can be injected into the body to counteract the reaction.

Signs and Symptoms of Anaphylactic Shock

An allergic reaction often occurs suddenly after contact with the substance. The reaction can be mild or develop into anaphylactic shock. Milder reactions may have these signs and symptoms:

- Swelling and redness of the skin localized near the area of contact (Figure 7–5)
- Hives, itching, rash

More severe reactions leading to anaphylactic shock also have these signs and symptoms:
- Swelling of the lips, ears, hands, and/or feet
- Redness of the skin generalized over the body, such as a raised, itchy, blotchy rash (hives)
- Weakness, dizziness
- Nausea, vomiting
- Breathing difficulty, coughing, and wheezing that can progress to an obstructed airway as the tongue and throat swell

Death can occur from a severe reaction if the casualty's breathing is severely impaired.

FIRST AID

Anaphylactic Shock

Always start with the emergency action principles:

1. Survey the scene to ensure no danger.
2. Check the casualty for unresponsiveness. If the person does not respond, call EMS.
3. Do a primary survey and care for life-threatening problems (ABCs). Call EMS for help if necessary.
4. Do a secondary survey, if needed, and care for other problems.
5. Keep monitoring the ABCs until EMS arrives.
6. Help the casualty rest in the most comfortable position and give reassurance.

Watch the person carefully because any allergic reaction can become life threatening. Assess the person's airway and breathing. If the person has any breathing difficulty or complains that his or her throat is closing, call EMS immediately. Help him or her into the most comfortable position for breathing. Monitor the ABCs and offer reassurance. If the casualty has a known allergy and has an epinephrine kit, assist the casualty as needed in using it if breathing difficulty develops.

First Aid for Hyperventilation Caused by Anxiety

If the casualty's breathing is rapid and there are signs and symptoms of an injury or an underlying illness or condition, call EMS personnel immediately because this person needs advanced care. If the casualty's breathing is rapid and you are certain that it is caused by emotion, such as excitement, give the following first aid:

1. Tell him or her to relax and breathe slowly. Reassurance is often enough to correct hyperventilation.
2. Under no circumstances should you have the casualty breathe into a bag or other closed container.
3. If the condition does not correct itself within minutes or if the casualty becomes unconscious from hyperventilating, call EMS immediately.

Figure 7–5   In an allergic reaction the skin usually swells and turns red.

First Aid for a Penetrating Chest Wound

A casualty with a penetrating chest wound needs first aid and medical attention promptly because the condition will worsen. The affected lung or lungs will not work properly, breathing will become more difficult, and internal bleeding will worsen. After calling EMS follow these guidelines to care for a penetrating chest wound that is sucking air:

1. Cover the wound with a dressing that does not allow air to pass through it, such as a piece of plastic wrap or a plastic bag. If these are not available, use a folded cloth or an article of clothing.
2. Tape the dressing in place, except for one side that remains open (Figure 7–6). This method keeps air from entering the chest cavity through the wound during inhalation but allows it to escape during exhalation.

First Aid for Flail Chest

To stabilize the chest wall and enable the casualty to breath more effectively it is necessary to apply a bulky dressing, such as a towel, to the affected area. Secure the folded towel with tape or triangular bandages. This will allow the rib cage to move as one unit again. Remember that the fractured bone ends may puncture the lungs and cause further respiratory distress.

Monitor ABCs carefully while waiting for EMS to arrive.

First Aid for Respiratory Arrest

Rescue breathing for adults

Rescue breathing is a way of breathing air into someone to give the person the oxygen needed to survive. Rescue breathing is given to casualties who are not breathing but still have signs of circulation.

Rescue breathing works because the air you breathe into the casualty has enough oxygen to keep the person alive. The air has 21% oxygen, but your body uses only a small part of it. The air you breathe out has about 16% oxygen, which is more than enough to keep someone alive.

In the primary survey, after you have opened the airway if you cannot see, hear, or feel any signs of effective breathing, give 2 full breaths immediately to get air into the casualty's lungs.

To give breaths, keep the airway open with the head-tilt/chin-lift (see Chapter 6). Gently pinch the casualty's nose shut with the thumb and

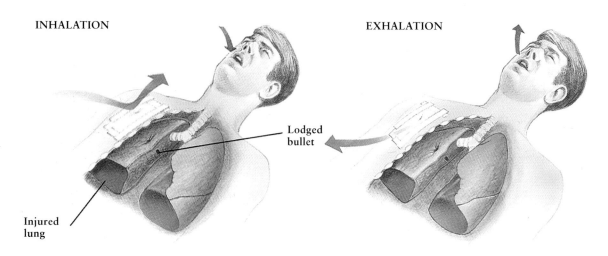

INHALATION   EXHALATION

Lodged bullet

Injured lung

Figure 7–6   A special dressing with one loose side keeps air from entering through the wound during inhalation but allows air to escape during exhalation.

index finger of the hand that is on the casualty's forehead. Next, take a deep breath and make a tight seal around the casualty's mouth with your mouth. Breathe slowly into the casualty until you see the casualty's chest rise (Figure 7–7). Each breath should last a full 2 seconds. Pause between breaths to allow you to take a breath and to let the air flow back out. Watch the casualty's chest rise each time you breathe in to ensure that your breaths are actually going in.

If you do not see the casualty's chest rise and fall as you breathe air into the casualty's lungs, you may not have the head tilted back correctly. Retilt the casualty's head and attempt to ventilate again. If air still does not go in, the casualty's airway is obstructed and you must clear it first (see Chapter 6).

When you have successfully delivered two breaths, check for signs of circulation. If the casualty has signs of circulation but is not breathing, continue rescue breathing by giving 1 breath every 5 seconds for an adult. A good way to time the breaths is to count, "one one-thousand, two one-thousand, three one-thousand. . ." Then take a breath yourself, and breathe *slowly* into the casualty. Each breath should last a full 2 seconds. After 1 minute of rescue breathing (about 12 breaths), recheck for signs of circulation to make sure the heart is still beating. If the casualty still has circulation but is not breathing, continue rescue breathing. Check for signs of circulation every few minutes. Do not stop rescue breathing unless one of the following occurs:

- Your personal safety is threatened.
- The casualty begins to breathe on his or her own.
- The casualty has no signs of circulation. Begin CPR (see Chapter 8).
- Another trained rescuer arrives on the scene and takes over.
- You are too exhausted to continue.

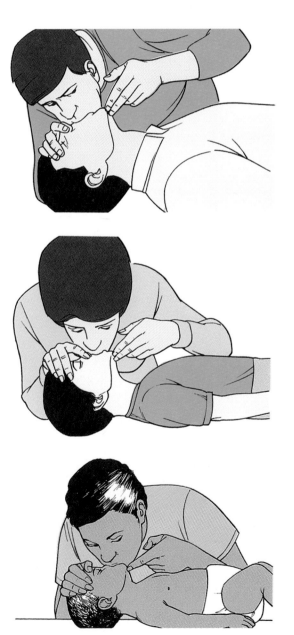

Figure 7–8   Rescue breathing for adults, children, and infants is basically the same.

Figure 7–7   To breathe for a nonbreathing casualty, pinch the nose shut, seal your mouth around the casualty's mouth, and breathe slowly into the casualty.

Rescue breathing for children and infants

Rescue breathing for children and infants follows the same general procedure as that for adults. The differences are based on the child's or infant's different physique and faster heartbeat and breathing rate (Figure 7–8). The following is a summary of the differences:

- Use the head-tilt/chin-lift position for an adult. Use a similar position for a child but move the

My Baby's Drowning

Connie Danson nearly collapsed when she saw her 18-month-old son in the pool. She pulled his limp, pale body from the water. Bubbles of water were coming out of his nose and mouth, and his eyes were open wide.

He had been in the living room when Connie left to put the laundry in the dryer. How had he gotten outside? One of the other children must have left the door open. Hysterical, Connie ran to call 9-1-1. "My baby's drowned," she sobbed into the phone. "I don't think he's breathing."

Dispatcher Anthony Carravaggio notified police and EMS personnel and then, speaking in a slow voice, he tried to calm Connie.

"Ma'am, there's an ambulance on the way," said the dispatcher. "Where is the child now?"

"He's right here on the floor," Connie said.

"Now tilt his head back gently and listen closely for any sounds," the dispatcher said.

"He's not making any sounds and he's not moving at all," Connie cried.

"Connie, you're going to have to breathe for him; do you know how?"

"I learned it in a CPR course, but I'm not sure I remember," Connie said.

"Listen to me. Pinch his nose shut. Put your mouth over his and give two slow breaths," the dispatcher said.

"OK."

Returning to the phone, Connie said, "OK, I did it."

"Now you have to see if he has any signs of circulation. Do you remember how to do that?" the dispatcher asked.

"Yes," Connie said, leaning over to recheck her son. "He has signs of circulation, but he's still not breathing."

"Connie, you need to keep breathing for him. Give him one breath, count to three, and breathe again. Do this for about a minute. I'll stay on the phone. I can hear you."

Connie listened as he explained the rescue breathing procedure. Over and over, she gave a rescue breath to her boy and watched for his chest to rise and fall.

Connie thought she heard him wheezing, but she wasn't sure. She leaned closer to his face and saw Andy's face redden and his body twitch. He began to cry.

Connie picked up the phone.

"Is that him?" the dispatcher asked.

"Yes," Connie said tearfully.

"He sounds good," the dispatcher said. "Are the paramedics there yet?"

"I hear the sirens outside," said Connie.

"OK. They will take care of him now."

It is difficult to stay calm in an emergency, even when you have learned first aid. With the help of a dispatcher, Connie overcame her panic and gave life-saving care to her son. If you feel yourself panicking in an emergency, remember 9-1-1 or your local emergency number; dispatchers can help you remember your first aid skills.

head very gently. For an infant use the neutral or "sniffing" position, and seal your mouth over both the infant's nose and mouth.

- For an adult give full breaths in rescue breathing. For a child use smaller breaths; for an infant use puffs of air. Breathe in only enough air to make the chest rise.

- Give rescue breathing to adults at the rate of one breath every 5 seconds (12 per minute), to children at the rate of one breath every 3 seconds (20 per minute), and to infants one puff every 3 seconds (20 per minute). Each breath or puff should last a full 2 seconds for adults and 1 to 1½ seconds for children and infants.

Continue to check for signs of circulation between ventilations (see Chapter 8).

Special Considerations for Rescue Breathing

Air in the stomach

In rescue breathing air normally enters the casualty's lungs. In some cases, however, air may enter the casualty's stomach instead. Do not over-inflate the lungs. Stop the breath when the chest has risen. Second, if the casualty's head is not tilted back far enough, the airway will not open completely and the chest may only rise slightly. This occurrence may cause you to breathe more forcefully, causing air to enter the stomach. Third, if breaths are given too quickly, increased pressure in the airway causes air to enter the stomach. Long, slow breaths minimize pressure in the air passages.

Air in the stomach is a problem because it can make the casualty vomit. When an unconscious person vomits, stomach contents may get into the lungs. This condition is called *aspiration*. Aspiration hampers rescue breathing and can be fatal.

Vomiting

When you give rescue breathing, the casualty may vomit, even without air in the stomach. If this

happens, turn the casualty's head and body together as a unit onto one side (Figure 7–9). This placement helps prevent vomit from entering the lungs. Quickly wipe the casualty's mouth clean, reposition the casualty on his or her back, and continue with rescue breathing.

Mouth-to-nose breathing

Sometimes you cannot seal your mouth well over the casualty's mouth to give rescue breathing. The person's jaw or mouth may be injured or shut too tightly to open, or your mouth may be too small to cover the casualty's. If so, give rescue breathing through the casualty's nose.

Mouth-to-stoma breathing

Some people have had an operation that removed part of their windpipe. They breathe through an opening called a stoma in the front of the neck (Figure 7–10). Because air passes directly into the windpipe through the stoma instead of through the mouth and nose, you would give rescue breathing through the stoma.

Casualties with dentures

If you know or see that the casualty is wearing dentures, do not automatically remove them. Dentures help rescue breathing by supporting the casualty's mouth and cheeks during mouth-to-mouth breathing. If the dentures are loose, the head-tilt/chin-lift may help keep them in place.

Figure 7–9 If vomiting occurs, turn the casualty on his/her side, and clear the mouth of any matter.

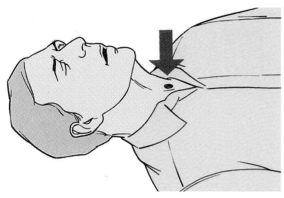

Figure 7–10   You may need to perform rescue breathing on a casualty with a stoma.

Remove the dentures *only* if they become so loose that they block the airway or make it difficult for you to give breaths.

Suspected head, neck, or back injuries

Suspect head, neck, or back injuries in casualties who have experienced a violent force, such as in a motor vehicle crash, a fall, or a diving or sports injury. In such cases minimize movement of the head and neck when opening the airway. Use the jaw thrust method instead of the head-tilt/chin-lift (see Chapter 5).

Summary

- Breathing emergencies include respiratory distress and respiratory arrest.

- Recognizing the signs and symptoms of breathing distress and giving prompt first aid for it is important because this condition can lead to respiratory arrest, which soon leads to death.

- First aid for a penetrating chest wound includes a special dressing to let air escape from the wound but not be sucked into it.

- A casualty in respiratory arrest needs rescue breathing immediately, before a lack of oxygen causes damage to the heart and brain, leading to death.

- After clearing the airway, give rescue breathing to the casualty; if there are no signs of circulation, give CPR.

- Vary the method of rescue breathing appropriately for children and infants.

Cardiovascular Emergencies

Objectives

After reading this chapter, you should be able to:

1. Differentiate between heart attack, angina, and cardiac arrest.
2. List at least four signs and symptoms of a heart attack.
3. Describe first aid for heart attack.
4. Identify cardiovascular disease risk factors that can be controlled.
5. Describe how to give CPR to an adult, child, and infant.
6. Describe two signs and symptoms of life-threatening external bleeding.
7. Describe first aid for external bleeding.
8. List two purposes of bandaging.
9. Describe how to minimize the risk of infectious disease transmission when controlling external bleeding.
10. Describe at least five signs and symptoms of internal bleeding.
11. Describe first aid for internal bleeding.
12. List at least four signs and symptoms of shock.
13. Describe ways to lessen shock.
14. Describe first aid for fainting.
15. Describe first aid for a stroke.
16. Define the key terms for this chapter.
17. Identify the reason for rapid defibrillation.
18. Describe how to use an AED.

Key Terms

angina pectoris A cardiovascular condition in which the heart muscles need more oxygen than they are getting, causing intermittent chest pain or pressure, usually more frequent with exertion or stress.

arteries Large blood vessels that carry oxygen-rich blood from the heart to the body.

atherosclerosis Cardiovascular condition in which cholesterol and other material build up inside the arteries, causing narrowing.

avulsion The complete severing of a body part.

bandage Material used to wrap or cover a part of the body or to hold a dressing or splint in place.

blood volume The total amount of blood circulating in the body.

capillaries Tiny blood vessels linking arteries and veins that transfer oxygen and other nutrients from the blood to body cells and remove waste products.

cardiac arrest Condition in which the heart has stopped or beats too irregularly or too weakly to pump blood effectively.

cardiopulmonary resuscitation (CPR) First aid combining rescue breathing and chest compressions for a casualty whose breathing and heart have stopped.

cardiovascular disease Disease of the heart and blood vessels; also called heart disease.

After reading this chapter and completing the class activities, you should be able to:

1. Demonstrate how to give CPR to an adult, child, and infant.

2. Demonstrate techniques for controlling severe bleeding.

3. Decide what first aid to give in an example of a situation in which someone has persistent chest pain.

4. Decide what first aid to give in an example of a situation in which someone is in cardiac arrest.

5. Decide what first aid to give in an example of a situation in which a person is bleeding.

cholesterol   A fatty substance that can cause fatty deposits on artery walls that may restrict blood flow.

clotting   The process of blood thickening at a wound site to seal a blood vessel and stop bleeding.

coronary arteries   Blood vessels that supply the heart muscle with oxygen-rich blood.

direct pressure   Pressure one puts on a wound to control bleeding.

dressing   A pad placed directly over a wound to absorb blood and other body fluids and to prevent infection.

defibrillation   An electric shock administered to correct a life-threatening heart rhythm.

elevation   Technique to help slow the flow of blood from a wound by raising the injured body part above the level of the heart.

external bleeding   Bleeding outside the body.

fainting   A loss of consciousness caused by a temporary reduction of blood flow to the brain.

heart attack   A sudden illness in which heart muscle tissue is dying from not getting enough oxygen because of a sudden blockage of one of the coronary arteries.

internal bleeding   Bleeding inside the body.

pressure bandage   A bandage applied firmly to put pressure on a wound to help control bleeding.

risk factors   Conditions or behaviours that increase the chance that a person will develop a disease or injury.

shock   The failure of the circulatory system to provide enough oxygen-rich blood to all parts of the body.

stroke   A disruption of blood flow in the brain, causing weakness and/or speech problems; also called a *cerebrovascular accident* (CVA).

veins   Blood vessels that carry oxygen-poor blood from all parts of the body to the heart.

ventricular fibrillation   A life-threatening condition in which the heart muscle quivers rather than pumping blood.

ventricular tachycardia   A life-threatening condition in which the heart muscle contracts too quickly for an adequate pumping of blood to the body.

In the primary survey, you identify and care for immediate threats to a casualty's life. Your first aid priorities are the casualty's airway, breathing, and circulation (the ABCs). In Chapters 6 and 7 you learned how to open a casualty's airway and how to give rescue breathing to a casualty who has signs of circulation but is not breathing.

This chapter describes how to recognize and care for cardiovascular emergencies, which involve the heart and the circulation of blood. You will learn first aid for a casualty having a *heart attack* and *cardiopulmonary resuscitation (CPR)* for a casualty whose heart stops beating, called *cardiac arrest.*

Circulation also involves moving blood to all body tissues. Severe bleeding impairs the circulation of blood and can be a life-threatening emergency. This chapter also describes first aid for bleeding and for casualties of stroke.

Angina Pectoris

Some people with coronary artery disease sometimes feel intermittent chest pain or pressure. This condition is called *angina pectoris.*

Anatomy and Physiology of Angina Pectoris

Angina pectoris develops when the heart needs more oxygen than it gets. When the coronary arteries have become narrow and the heart needs more oxygen, such as during physical activity, emotional stress, or temperature extremes, heart muscle tissues may not get enough oxygen. This situation causes the pain.

Causes of Angina Pectoris

Any condition that limits the blood to the heart may cause angina. These include coronary artery disease, high blood pressure, anemia, and certain heart disorders and other diseases. Because there are many different causes, only a doctor can know what causes someone's angina.

PREVENTION

Angina Pectoris

Preventing angina involves preventing the conditions that cause it. Although some of these disorders cannot be prevented, many can. High blood pressure can be controlled with diet, exercise, weight control, and medication. Coronary artery disease can be prevented with a diet low in fat, cholesterol, and salt; regular exercise; and not smoking. The later section on prevention of heart attack discusses these factors in more detail.

Signs and Symptoms of Angina Pectoris

Chest pain that is often described as being tight, heavy, or a pressure and may spread to the neck, jaw, and arms.

- Pain usually lasts less than 10 minutes.
- Pain usually relieved by rest.
- Sometimes breathing difficulty, sweating, nausea, or dizziness.

FIRST AID

Angina Pectoris

Casualties who know that they have angina usually have with them prescribed medication for the pain, such as nitroglycerin. If the casualty asks you, help him or her with the medication. It comes as a small tablet that is placed under the tongue, as a spray used in the mouth, or in patches placed on the chest. Nitroglycerin enlarges the blood vessels to make it easier for the heart muscle to get blood. Nitroglycerin usually works in just a few seconds and may cause a headache. Have the casualty sit or lie down. You will learn more about nitroglycerin later in this chapter.

Reducing the heart's demand for oxygen, such as by stopping physical activity, often relieves angina symptoms.

If the person has not been diagnosed by a doctor as having angina, do not ignore this pain because it could be a heart attack. Call EMS immediately and help the casualty rest comfortably.

Heart Attack

Anatomy and Physiology of Heart Attack

The heart is a muscular organ that acts like a pump. The ribs and sternum protect it in front and the spine protects it in back (Figure 8–1). Oxygen-poor blood is brought to the right side of the heart and is pumped to the lungs to pick up oxygen. The oxygen-rich blood returns to the left side of the heart and is pumped to all parts of the body. Valves direct the blood through the heart (Figure 8–2). For the circulatory system to be effective, the respiratory system must also be working so that the blood can pick up oxygen in the lungs.

Like all tissues, the heart needs continuous oxygen. The *coronary arteries* bring oxygen to the heart (Figure 8–3, *A*). If heart muscle tissue does not get enough blood, it dies. If too much

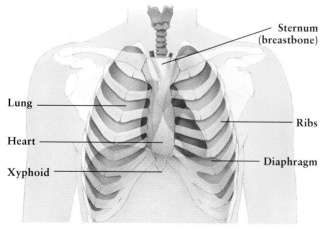

Figure 8–1   The heart is located in the middle of the chest, behind the lower half of the sternum.

tissue dies, the heart cannot pump effectively. The sudden blockage of a coronary artery leading to death of heart muscle is called a *heart attack*. A heart attack can cause an irregular heartbeat and prevent blood from circulating effectively.

Causes of Heart Attack

Heart attack is usually caused by *cardiovascular disease*, which is disease of the heart and blood vessels. This is the leading cause of death for adults in Canada. Every year about 50,000 Canadians die of coronary artery disease. Cardiovascular disease develops as *cholesterol* and other material gradually build up inside the coronary arteries. This condition, called *atherosclerosis*, causes narrowing of the arteries. When coronary arteries narrow, a clot can completely block the artery, causing a heart attack (Figure 8–3, *B*). Atherosclerosis can also occur in other arteries, such as in the brain, causing stroke.

PREVENTION

Heart Attack

Although a heart attack may seem to strike suddenly, cardiovascular disease develops gradually. A diet high in cholesterol and fats, lack of exercise, high blood pressure, and smoking all contribute to cardiovascular disease, which can begin as early as the teenage years. Prevention of cardiovascular disease and heart attack depends on controlling one's risk factors for developing the disease.

Risk factors for heart disease
Various *risk factors* increase the chances of a person having heart disease. Some risk factors cannot be changed. For instance, men have a higher risk for heart disease. Having a family history of heart disease also increases your risk.

However, many risk factors for heart disease can be controlled. Smoking, a diet high in fats, high blood pressure, obesity, and lack of routine exercise

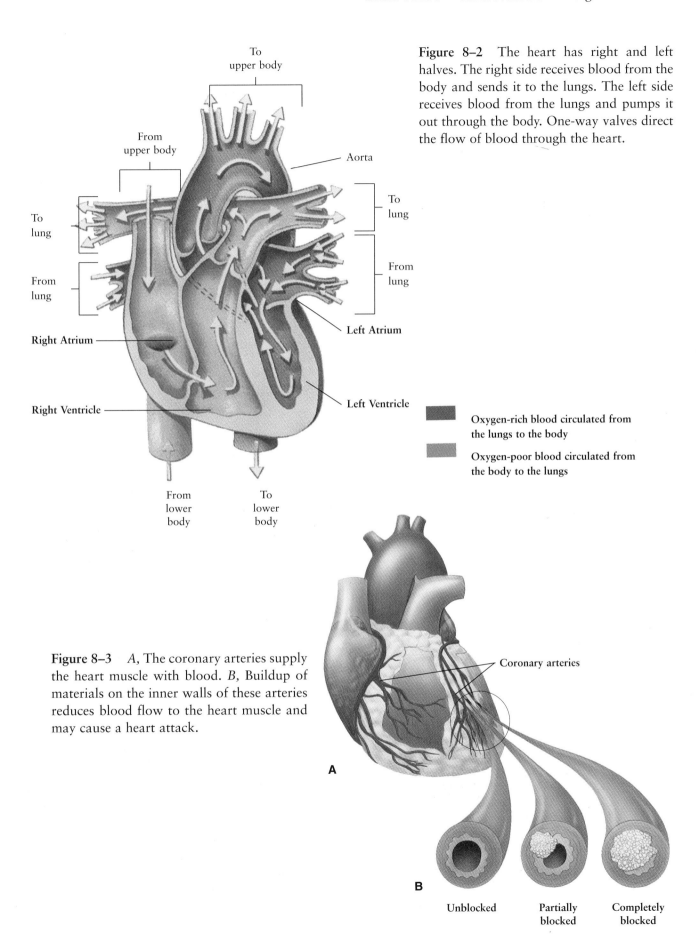

To upper body

From upper body

To lung

From lung

Right Atrium

Right Ventricle

From lower body

To lower body

Aorta

To lung

From lung

Left Atrium

Left Ventricle

Figure 8–2 The heart has right and left halves. The right side receives blood from the body and sends it to the lungs. The left side receives blood from the lungs and pumps it out through the body. One-way valves direct the flow of blood through the heart.

Oxygen-rich blood circulated from the lungs to the body

Oxygen-poor blood circulated from the body to the lungs

Figure 8–3 *A,* The coronary arteries supply the heart muscle with blood. *B,* Buildup of materials on the inner walls of these arteries reduces blood flow to the heart muscle and may cause a heart attack.

Coronary arteries

A

B

Unblocked

Partially blocked

Completely blocked

The Heart as a Pump

Too often we take our hearts for granted. As a mechanical pump, the heart is very reliable. The average heart beats about 70 times each minute, more than 100,000 times a day. During the average lifetime, the heart will beat nearly three billion times. The heart pumps almost 5 litres of blood per minute, over 150 million litres in an average lifetime. The heart pumps blood through over 90,000 kilometers of blood vessels.

are all risk factors. When one risk factor, such as high blood pressure, is combined with other risk factors, such as obesity or cigarette smoking, the risk of heart attack is greatly increased.

Controlling risk factors

Controlling risk factors means a change in lifestyle to reduce the chances of future disease (Figure 8–4). The three major risk factors that can be controlled are cigarette smoking, high blood pressure, and intake of fats.

Cigarette smokers have more than twice the chance of having a heart attack and two to four times the chance of cardiac arrest than nonsmok-

ers. The earlier a person started using tobacco, the greater the risk. Giving up smoking rapidly reduces the risk of heart disease. After a number of years, the risk becomes the same as if the person never smoked. If you do not smoke, do not start. If you do smoke, quit.

High blood pressure can damage blood vessels in the heart and other organs. You can often control high blood pressure by losing weight, changing your diet, and taking medications when prescribed. Everyone should have regular blood pressure checks.

A diet high in fats and cholesterol increases the risk of heart disease. You should eat only small amounts of foods high in cholesterol, such as egg yolks, organ meats, shrimp, and lobster, and those high in fats, such as beef, lamb, veal, pork, ham, whole milk, and whole milk products. Limiting one's intake is easier than you think. Moderation is the key. Make changes whenever you can by substituting low-fat milk or skim milk for whole milk, margarine for butter, trimming visible fat from meats, and broiling or baking rather than frying. Read labels carefully. A "cholesterol free" product may still be high in fat.

Also control your weight, and exercise regularly. Excess calories are stored as fat. Obese middle-aged men have nearly three times the risk of a

PREVENT HEART DISEASE

Smoker
High-cholesterol diet
High blood pressure
Overweight
No exercise

Nonsmoker
Low-cholesterol diet
Normal blood pressure
Normal weight
Exercise regularly

TAKE ACTION!

Figure 8–4   Control risk factors; do not let them control you.

fatal heart attack than normal-weight, middle-aged men. Routine exercise improves muscle tone and helps in weight control. Exercise also improves your chances of surviving a heart attack.

Benefits of controlling risk factors

Controlling your risk factors really works. In the past 20 years, deaths from cardiovascular disease and stroke have decreased dramatically, partly because of people's lifestyle changes. People are becoming more aware of their risk factors for heart disease and are taking action to control them. If you do this, you can improve your chances of living a long and healthy life.

> **If you have a heart attack and have a cardiac arrest, your chances of survival are poor. Ignoring the risk factors and waiting for a cardiac arrest is like putting an ambulance at the bottom of a 100-foot cliff. Once you fall off the cliff, even the best care may not be able to save your life. But preventing cardiovascular disease is like building a barrier at the top of the cliff to keep you from tumbling to your death. Begin today to control your risk factors.**

Signs and Symptoms of a Heart Attack

Heart attack may result from a condition of atherosclerosis that may go undetected for years, producing no signs or symptoms before the heart attack occurs. Some people may have early warning signals (such as angina) when the heart does not receive enough blood. Others may have a heart attack or even cardiac arrest without any warning at all.

The major symptom of a heart attack is chest pain or discomfort that persists. This pain may be similar to pain caused by indigestion, muscle spasms, or other conditions. Brief, stabbing chest pains or pain that gets worse when you bend or breathe deeply is usually not caused by a heart attack.

Heart attack pain can range from discomfort to an unbearable crushing feeling in the chest. The

casualty may describe it as an uncomfortable pressure, squeezing, tightness, aching, or heavy feeling in the chest. The pain is usually felt in the centre of the chest behind the sternum. It may spread to the shoulder, arm, neck, or jaw. It is constant and usually not relieved by resting, changing position, or usual painkillers. Many heart attack casualties try to explain the pain as heartburn or indigestion.

Any person with chest pain that is severe, lasts longer than 10 minutes, or includes other heart attack signs and symptoms should seek emergency medical care immediately.

The following may also signal a heart attack:

- Neck, shoulder, abdominal or back pain
- Breathing difficulty, such as noisy breathing, shortness of breath, or breathing faster than normal
- Pulse may be faster or slower than normal or irregular
- The skin may be pale or bluish in colour
- Nausea and vomiting
- The face may be moist, or the casualty may be sweating profusely

The key signal of a heart attack is persistent chest pain. If the chest pain is severe or chest discomfort does not cease within 10 minutes, call EMS immediately and begin first aid for a heart attack. Please note that some people do not experience any chest pain when having a heart attack, and women may experience abdominal or back pain instead.

Signs and Symptoms of Heart Attack

Persistent chest pain
Abdominal or back pain (women)
Difficulty breathing
Pulse too fast, too slow, or irregular
Pale or bluish skin
Sweating
Nausea and vomiting

A Heart Attack

As in any emergency situation, begin with the emergency action principles:

1. Survey the scene to ensure no danger.
2. Check the casualty for unresponsiveness. If the person does not respond, call EMS.
3. Do a primary survey, and care for life-threatening problems (ABCs). Call EMS for help if necessary.
4. Do a secondary survey, if needed, and care for other problems.
5. Keep monitoring the ABCs until EMS arrives.
6. Help the casualty rest in the most comfortable position and give reassurance.

After the primary survey, the most important step is to recognize any of the heart attack signs and symptoms and take immediate action. A heart attack casualty often denies that the pain or other symptoms are serious. Do not let this change your mind. If you think the person might be having a heart attack, you must act. First, have the casualty stop what he or she is doing and rest comfortably (Figure 8–5).

In the secondary survey, talk to the casualty and others present, if needed, to get more information. Ask these questions if the casualty has persistent chest pain:

- When did the pain start?
- What brought it on?
- Does anything lessen it?
- What does it feel like?
- Where does it hurt?
- Do you have a history of heart disease? If so, do you have medication to take?

If you think the casualty may be having a heart attack or are unsure, ask someone to call EMS for help. If you are alone, make the call yourself. Surviving a heart attack often depends on how soon the casualty receives advanced medical care. Do not try to drive the casualty to the

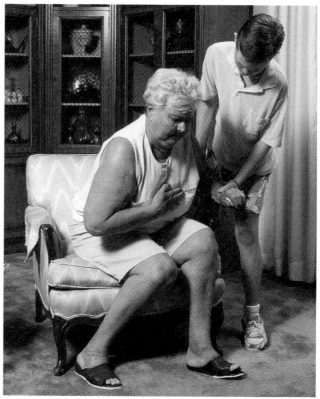

Figure 8–5   The heart attack casualty should rest in a position that helps breathing.

hospital yourself, unless EMS services are not readily available, because cardiac arrest can occur at any time. Call the emergency number right away, before the condition worsens and the heart stops beating.

Keep a calm and reassuring manner when caring for a heart attack casualty. Comfort helps reduce anxiety and eases some of the pain. Watch the casualty closely until EMS arrives. Monitor the vital signs and watch for changes in appearance or behaviour. Since cardiac arrest may occur, be prepared to give CPR.

ASA Administration

Recommendation on ASA and Nitroglycerin for Chest Pain

Current research has shown that early administration of 160–325 mg of ASA (e.g., Aspirin®) during a heart attack can reduce the risk of death by as much as 25%. It is then recommended that all individuals who are experiencing acute onset of chest pain that is cardiac in origin be encouraged to chew 160–325 mg of ASA regardless of whether they take ASA or not. Therefore, an individual who is experiencing chest pain should be assisted with his/her prescribed medications and ASA (whether prescribed or not) in the following way:

- As soon as chest pain is detected, activate the EMS.
- While waiting for medical help, assist the person to the most comfortable position, usually semi-sitting with the head and shoulders raised and supported. Loosen tight clothing at the neck, chest, and waist. Reassure the person. Assist the fully conscious person to take appropriate medications as described below. *If your profession is governed by regulations that preclude this action, you should not proceed.*
- Ask the **fully conscious person** if he/she carries nitroglycerin. If yes, determine if the person has taken Viagra® within the last 24 hours. If yes, explain to the person that they must not take their nitroglycerin because they may develop low blood pressure. Ensure that you have the correct medication before assisting the person. If the person has not taken Viagra®, help them administer nitroglycerin by either tablets or spray. Nitroglycerin tablets are placed under the tongue where they quickly dissolve. Nitroglycerin spray is sprayed under the tongue and is rapidly absorbed. Nitroglycerin starts working within 1 or 2 minutes and works for about 5 to 6 minutes. The nitroglycerin dose may be repeated every 5 minutes until the pain is relieved or until a maximum of three doses have been administered.
- Ask the **fully conscious person** if he/she carries ASA. Ask if he/she is allergic to ASA and/or has asthma. If the **fully conscious person** does not carry nitroglycerin or if the pain is not relieved by the first dose of nitroglycerin, suggest the person chew two children's ASA tablets (80 mg each) or one ASA tablet (regu-

lar strength adult dose = 325 mg). You may offer Aspirin® but you are cautioned to only recommend that the person take Aspirin® and explain why. The individual must make the decision whether or not to take the medication. NOTE: Acetaminophen (e.g., Tylenol®) or Ibuprofen (e.g., Advil®) does not have the same effect as ASA in reducing damage due to heart attacks: do not substitute!

- When the EMS arrives, advise them of any actions or medications that have been taken.
- Monitor respiration and circulation (pulse) and be ready to provide rescue breathing or CPR.

Cardiac Arrest

Anatomy and Physiology of Cardiac Arrest

Cardiac arrest occurs when the heart stops beating or beats too irregularly or too weakly to circulate blood effectively. Breathing soon stops. Cardiac arrest is a life-threatening emergency because vital organs can live only a few minutes without oxygen-rich blood.

Causes of Cardiac Arrest

Cardiovascular disease is the most common cause of cardiac arrest. Drowning, suffocation, and certain drugs can cause breathing to stop, which then causes cardiac arrest. Severe chest injuries or severe blood loss can also cause the heart to beat ineffectively. Electrocution disrupts the heart's own electrical activity and causes the heart to stop.

PREVENTION

Cardiac Arrest

Cardiac arrest can be prevented by preventing its causes. A good diet, exercise, and not smoking help prevent cardiovascular disease (see earlier section). Prevention of drowning, suffocation, and injury involves safety precautions in work, home, and recreational activities. Follow the safety guidelines in later chapters in this book.

Signs and Symptoms of Cardiac Arrest

- Unresponsiveness (unconsciousness)
- Absence of movement by the casualty
- Absence of effective breathing
- Presence of cyanosis or blue colouring of the skin
- Absence of a carotid pulse

Although cardiac arrest can result from a heart attack, cardiac arrest can occur suddenly without any signs and symptoms of a heart attack first. This occurrence is called *sudden death*.

FIRST AID

CPR/AED For Cardiac Arrest

Because the brain and other vital organs live only for a few minutes after the heart stops, the casualty needs CPR, defibrillation, and advanced emergency medical care. CPR combines rescue breathing and chest compressions. Chest compressions make the blood flow when the heart is not beating. Rescue breathing and chest compressions make the lungs and heart function to some extent. CPR increases the casualty's chances of survival by keeping the brain supplied with oxygen until defibrillation can be applied and advanced medical care arrives. Without CPR, the brain cells begin to die within 4 to 6 minutes (Figure 8–6). CPR provides a minimum of the normal blood flow to the brain and heart. Even with CPR, the chance of survival is very slim unless defibrillation can be applied and advanced medical care arrives within 5 minutes.

Anyone with a minimum of training can provide defibrillation with an Automated External Defibrillator. Advanced emergency medical personnel can provide Advanced Cardiac Life Support (ACLS) by administering the appropriate medications in addition to defibrillation.

CPR for adults

Position the casualty flat on the back on a firm surface, with the head on the same level as the heart. Kneel beside the casualty midway between the chest and the head so you can give compressions and breaths (Figure 8–7). Lean over the chest and place your hands in the correct position over the lower half of the sternum. Compress the chest by alternately pressing straight down and releasing in a smooth, uniform pattern.

To achieve the most effective compressions, avoid the lowest point of the sternum. To find the correct hand position for chest compressions for an adult or child:

1. Find the lower edge of the casualty's rib cage. Slide your middle and index fingers up the

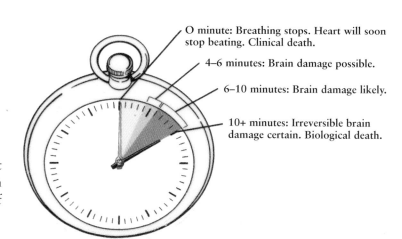

O minute: Breathing stops. Heart will soon stop beating. Clinical death.

4–6 minutes: Brain damage possible.

6–10 minutes: Brain damage likely.

10+ minutes: Irreversible brain damage certain. Biological death.

Figure 8–6 In clinical death the heart and breathing stop. Biological death occurs when there is irreversible death of brain cells.

4. Use the heel of your hand to apply pressure on the sternum. Try to keep your fingers off the chest by interlacing them or holding them upward. Pushing with your fingers can cause inefficient chest compressions or damage to the chest.
5. If you have arthritis or a similar condition, you may use an alternate hand position,

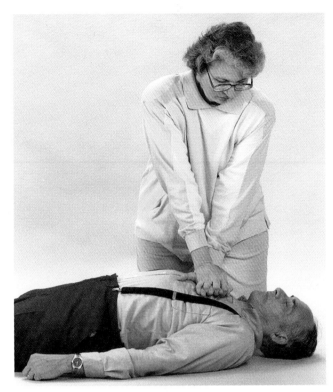

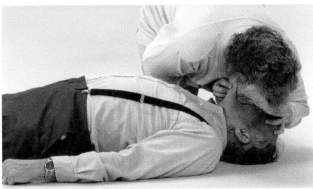

Figure 8–7   Position yourself so that you can give rescue breaths and chest compressions without having to move.

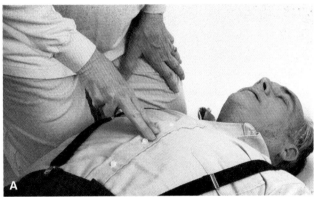

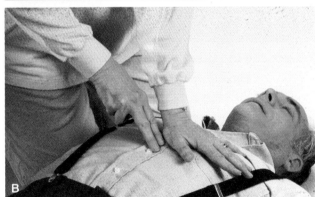

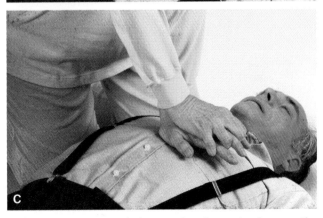

Figure 8–8   *A*, Find the notch where the lower ribs meet the sternum. *B*, Place the heel of your hand on the sternum, next to your index finger. *C*, Place your other hand over the heel of the first. Use the heel of your bottom hand to compress the sternum.

edge of the rib cage to the notch where the ribs meet the sternum (Figure 8–8, *A*). Place your middle finger on this notch. Place your index finger next to your middle finger.
2. Place the heel of your other hand on the sternum next to your index finger (Figure 8–8, *B*). The heel of your hand should rest along the length of the sternum.
3. Once the heel of your hand is in position on the sternum, place your other hand directly on top of it (Figure 8–8, *C*).

grasping the wrist of the hand on the chest with the other hand (Figure 8–9).

The correct hand position provides the most effective compressions.

Clothing usually does not interfere with correct hand position. Sometimes a thin layer of clothing helps keep your hands from slipping when the casualty's chest is moist with sweat. If you cannot find the correct hand position, bare the casualty's chest.

Your own body position is important also. Compressing the chest straight down makes the best blood flow and is less tiring for you. Kneel at the casualty's chest with your hands in the correct position. Straighten your arms and lock your elbows with your shoulders directly over your hands (Figure 8–10). When you press down in this position, you will be pushing straight down onto the sternum. Locking your elbows and keeping your arms straight prevent you from tiring quickly.

Compressing the chest requires little effort in this position. When you press down, the weight of your upper body creates the force needed to compress the chest. Push with the weight of your upper body, not with the muscles of your arms. Push straight down. Do not rock back and forth; rocking results in less effective compressions and unnecessarily uses much needed energy. After each compression, release the pressure on the

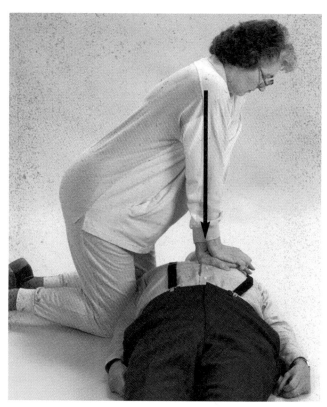

Figure 8–10   With your hands in place, position yourself so that your shoulders are directly over your hands, arms straight and elbows locked.

chest without losing contact with it and let the chest return to its normal position before starting the next compression (Figure 8–11).

Each compression should push the sternum down 3.8 to 5 cm (1½ to 2 inches). The downward and upward movement should be smooth, not jerky. Maintain a steady down-and-up rhythm, and do not pause between compressions. When you come up, release all pressure on the chest but keep your hands on the chest. If your hands slip, start over to reposition them correctly.

Give compressions at the rate of about 100 per minute. As you do compressions, count aloud, "One and two and three and four and five and six and. . ." up to 15. Counting aloud helps you pace yourself. Push down as you say the number and come up as you say "and." You should do the 15 compressions in about 9 seconds. Even though you are compressing the chest at a rate of about 100 times per minute, you will

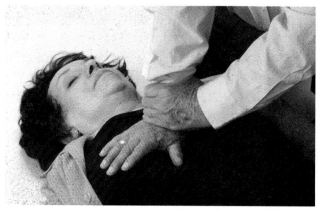

Figure 8–9   Grasping the wrist of the hand positioned on the chest is an alternate hand position for giving chest compressions.

only actually do approximately 70 compressions in a minute because you must also do rescue breathing.

Do 4 cycles of 15 compressions and 2 breaths. For each cycle, give 15 chest compressions, then open the airway and give 2 full breaths (Figure 8–12). This cycle should take about 13 seconds. For each new cycle of compressions and breaths, find the correct hand position first.

After 4 cycles of CPR, check to see if the casualty has signs of circulation. Then continue CPR. Check circulation again every few minutes.

Two-Rescuer CPR for an Adult

If two rescuers trained in CPR arrive at the scene they should first identify themselves to each other. One rescuer should then call EMS if this has not already been done. The second rescuer should begin the primary survey while the first rescuer kneels on the opposite side of the casualty near the chest (if possible) and waits for direction. When directed by the second rescuer, the first rescuer should begin a series of 15 chest compressions at a rate of about 100 per minute. The first rescuer should then pause to allow the second rescuer to give the casualty two breaths, each breath lasting a full 2 seconds. Both rescuers should continue for four cycles of 15 compressions and two breaths before stopping to recheck breathing and circulation. The second rescuer

should recheck breathing and circulation for no more than 10 seconds before directing the first rescuer to resume chest compressions if required. Breathing and circulation should be checked every few minutes thereafter. If it becomes necessary for the rescuers to switch positions for whatever reason, it should be done on completion of the second rescuer giving two breaths. After the rescuers have changed positions the rescuer who is now in position next to the casualty's head will recheck breathing and circulation before directing the first rescuer to resume chest compressions.

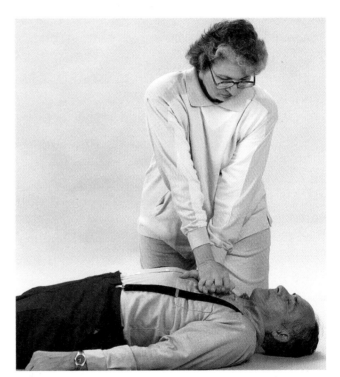

Figure 8–12   For adults, give 15 compressions, then 2 breaths.

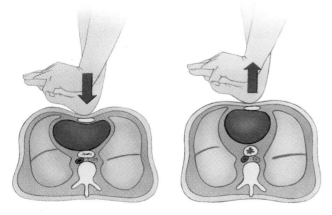

Figure 8–11   Push straight down with the weight of your body then release, allowing the chest to return to its normal position.

Automated External Defibrillation (AED)

Sudden cardiac arrest continues to be the number one cause of death in Canada. In more than 80% of the cases, rapid defibrillation would be beneficial. However, research has shown that maximum benefit occurs when defibrillation is provided in under 5 minutes from the point of collapse. In Canada, casualties wait an average of 9 minutes before this form of help arrives. This response time can be decreased and survival rates increased if more defibrillators are made available and more people are trained to use them.

Public Access Defibrillation (PAD) is a movement to make Automated External Defibrillators (AEDs) readily accessible in locations such as sporting arenas or shopping centres. Public Access Defibrillation also promotes changes in legislation to allow individuals to use AEDs without having to seek prior approval from a physician. This would allow responders such as police officers, lifeguards, and firefighters as well as members of the general public who have access to an AED to use them to save lives.

Automated External Defibrillators employ cutting-edge technology that removes the need for extensive training before being used. Minimal training and following of the voice prompts provided by the AED are all that is required to successfully defibrillate a casualty.

Basically, when properly applied, an AED will detect the presence or absence of a shockable heart rhythm. If the AED detects either ventricular tachycardia (VT) or ventricular fibrillation (VF) it will advise the user by voice prompt to deliver the shock. This is done by depressing a clearly marked button.

Considerations when using an AED

- It is important that absence of circulation has been confirmed before an AED is attached to a casualty. The rescuer should look for signs of absent circulation, which include unre- sponsiveness, no movement, absence of effective breathing or coughing, and absence of a pulse. No more than 10 seconds should be used to check for circulation.

- Use of an AED on someone under 8 years of age (or < 25 kg) is not recommended. While children occasionally do experience VT or VF, it is not common and present AED technology is not suitable for this age group.

- The rescuer or bystander must not touch the casualty during the analyze mode or when a shock is about to be given. Movement prevents the AED from correctly analyzing the heart's rhythm. Also, contact with a casualty when a shock is being delivered could result in injury to the bystander or rescuer.

- If the casualty has a medicine patch such as a nitroglycerin patch or nicotine patch on in the area of where they are going to be shocked, it needs to be removed to prevent burns to the casualty (the rescuer should be wearing gloves to prevent the medicine in the patch from being absorbed through the skin).

- If the casualty's skin is very wet, it should be dried before the AED is attached. This ensures the AED is able to both analyze the rhythm and deliver the shock.

- If the casualty has excessive chest hair, it should be removed before the AED is attached. This ensures the AED is able to both analyze the rhythm and deliver the shock.

- The casualty may have a pacemaker implanted in the area where one of the electrodes is intended to go. If you observe a small scar and a matchbox-size lump on the chest, reposition the electrode approximately 1" (2.5 cm) away.

- No change in the way an AED is used is required if the rescuer encounters
  - A casualty who is pregnant
  - A casualty who has traumatic injuries

Using an AED

While it is true that using an AED is a very simple procedure, familiarization with its operation will reduce delay during an emergency.

The majority of AEDs use an On/Off button, an Analyze button, and a Shock button.

Turning the AED on will result in a voice prompt advising the rescuer to "Connect Electrodes." Most electrodes have a diagram on them to indicate where to place them. Make sure the electrodes are firmly attached to the chest before proceeding.

The next voice prompt will advise the user to "Press Analyze." It is very important that there be no touching or movement of the casualty while the AED is analyzing the casualty's rhythm.

Should the AED determine that a shock be delivered, a voice prompt will advise the user "Shock Advised." A rising whine will occur to indicate that the AED is charging for the shock.

When the AED is ready to deliver the shock, it will prompt the user to "Stand Clear" and "Push to Shock." A hi-low alarm will sound until the shock button is pushed. **It is very important that no one be in contact with the casualty when the shock button is pushed. The rescuer should look around to ensure this prompt is being followed.**

When the rescuer is confident that no one is in contact with the casualty, he or she should press the shock button. It is common for casualties to experience an involuntary contraction of their muscles as the current passes through them.

The AED will automatically reanalyze the casualty and continue to advise the user of the next step.

Should the AED not detect a shockable heart rhythm, it will advise the user to continue CPR for 1 minute before reanalyzing the heart rhythm.

CPR for the Child

CPR for children is similar to the technique for adults (Figure 8–13). However, because children's breath and heart rates are faster, it is necessary to change the ratio of compressions to ventilations from 15:2 to 5:1.

Start by kneeling at the child's side. Place your hand closest to the child's head on the forehead to keep it in the head-tilt position. This helps to maintain an open airway during chest compressions. Place your other hand on the lower half of the child's sternum and lock your arm out straight. Using your body weight compress the child's sternum straight down 2.5 to 3.8 cm (1 to 1 1/2 inches). Compressions should be performed at a rate of about 100 times a minute. After every five chest compressions stop to give one rescue breath. Make sure you use both hands to perform the head-tilt/chin-lift when giving rescue breaths. In order to maintain this pace it is necessary to drop the word "and" when you count out loud.

CPR for the Infant

CPR for infants is similar to the technique for children. However, because of their smaller size you need only use two or three fingers to compress the infant's chest.

Start by kneeling next to the infant. Alternatively, you may place the infant on a table or hold the infant in your arms. If you decide to do so make sure you can control the infant to keep him/her from receiving injuries. Place two or three fingers on the infant's sternum one finger width below an imaginary line drawn between the infant's nipples. Compress the infant's sternum straight down 1.2 to 2.5 cm (1/2 to 1 inch). Compress the sternum at a rate of at least 100 times per minute. After every fifth compression stop to give one breath. Be careful to only open the infant's airway far enough to allow the breath to go in and give small puffs of air rather than full rescue breaths. In order to maintain this pace it is necessary to drop the word "and" when you count out loud.

Circulation check in infants

The signs of circulation in infants are similar to that of adults and children:

- Unresponsiveness (unconsciousness)
- Absence of movement by the casualty
- Absence of effective breathing
- Presence of cyanosis or blue colouring of the skin
- Absence of a brachial pulse

To check for a brachial pulse in an infant begin by raising the infant's arm above its head. Place one or two fingers on the underside of the arm half way between the elbow and the shoulder. Push in against the upper arm bone gently.

Take no more than 10 seconds to perform the circulation check. If you are not absolutely positive that circulation is present begin CPR.

When to stop CPR. Once you begin CPR, stop CPR only if:

- Your personal safety is threatened.
- The casualty's heart starts to beat on its own.
- Another trained rescuer arrives on the scene and takes over.
- You are too exhausted to continue.
- An AED is available and someone there is trained and authorized to use it.

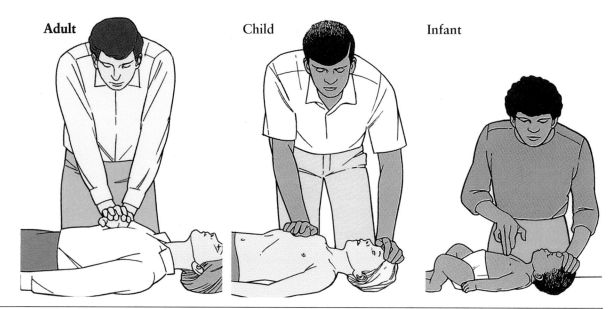

	Adult	**Child**	**Infant**
HAND POSITION:	**Two hands** on lower ½ of sternum	**One hand** on lower ½ of sternum	**Two fingers** on lower ½ of sternum (one finger width below nipple line)
COMPRESS:	3.8 – 5 cm (1½ – 2 in)	2.5 – 3.8 cm (1 – 1½ in)	1.2 – 2.5 cm (½ – 1 in)
BREATHE:	Slowly **until chest rises** (2 seconds per breath)	Slowly **until chest rises** (1 to 1.5 seconds per breath)	Slowly **until chest rises** (1 to 1.5 seconds per breath)
CYCLE:	15 compressions 2 breaths	5 compressions 1 breath	5 compressions 1 breath
RATE:	15 compressions in about 9 seconds	5 compressions in about 3 seconds	5 compressions in about 3 seconds

Figure 8–13 The technique for chest compressions differs for adults, children, and infants.

If the casualty's heart starts but he or she is still not breathing, keep giving rescue breathing. If the casualty is breathing and has a heartbeat, place the person in the recovery position and carefully monitor the ABCs until EMS arrives.

Stroke

Anatomy and Physiology of Stroke

A *stroke,* also called a cerebrovascular accident (CVA), is a disruption of blood flow to a part of the brain that is serious enough to damage brain tissue (Figure 8–14).

Causes of Stroke

Stroke can be caused by a blood clot that lodges in the arteries in the brain. Other causes include an artery in the brain that ruptures, a head injury, or tumour.

PREVENTION

Stroke

The risk factors for stroke are similar to those for heart disease. You can help prevent stroke with the same lifestyle changes discussed in the earlier section on preventing cardiovascular disease.

Signs and Symptoms of Stroke

- Sudden weakness and/or numbness of the face, arm, or leg, usually only on one side of the body
- Difficulty talking or understanding speech
- Sudden, severe headache
- Dizziness or confusion
- Unconsciousness
- Loss of bladder control

A transient ischemic attack (TIA) is a temporary episode that is like a stroke and is sometimes called a "mini-stroke." Like a stroke, TIA causes reduced blood flow to the brain. A TIA is a warning sign that a stroke may occur.

FIRST AID

Stroke

As in any situation, start with the emergency action principles:

1. Survey the scene to ensure no danger.
2. Check the casualty for unresponsiveness. If the person does not respond, call EMS.
3. Do a primary survey, and care for life-threatening problems (ABCs). Call EMS for help if necessary.

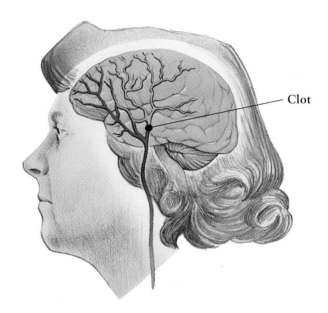

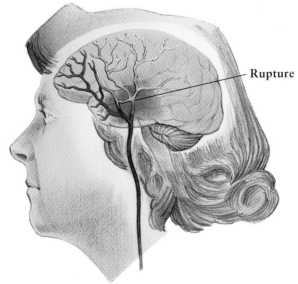

Figure 8–14 A stroke can be caused by a blood clot or bleeding from a ruptured artery in the brain.

4. Do a secondary survey, if needed, and care for other problems.

5. Keep monitoring the ABCs until EMS arrives.

6. Help the casualty rest in the most comfortable position and give reassurance.

Provide this additional care to a casualty of a stroke:

1. If there is fluid or vomitus in the casualty's mouth, place him or her in the recovery position with the affected side up to allow any fluids to drain out of the mouth. You may have to use a finger sweep to remove some of the material from the mouth.

2. Stay with the casualty until EMS arrives, and monitor his or her ABCs. This can be an extremely frightening experience so your reassurance is really important.

Bleeding

Bleeding is the escape of blood from *arteries, veins,* or *capillaries. Internal bleeding* stays inside the body and is often difficult to recognize. *External bleeding* outside the body is usually visible (Figure 8–15). Any uncontrolled bleeding is a life-threatening emergency. Check for severe bleeding during the primary survey, although you may not identify internal bleeding until the secondary survey, if at all.

Anatomy and Physiology of Blood and Vessels

The blood has three major functions:

1. Transporting oxygen, nutrients, and wastes
2. Protecting against disease by producing antibodies and defending against infection
3. Maintaining constant body temperature by circulating throughout the body

Blood is channeled through blood vessels (Figure 8–16). Arteries carry oxygen-rich blood away from the heart. Arteries become smaller the farther they go from the heart. Capillaries are microscopic blood vessels linking arteries and veins. They transfer oxygen and nutrients from the blood to the cells. Capillaries carry waste products, such as carbon dioxide, from the cells to the veins. The veins carry waste products to the heart and lungs and from there to the kidneys and intestines for elimination.

Blood in the arteries travels faster and under greater pressure than blood in the capillaries or veins. Blood flow in the arteries pulses with the heartbeat; blood in the veins flows more slowly and evenly.

Bleeding causes several body reactions. The brain, heart, and kidneys immediately try to compensate for blood loss to maintain the flow of oxy-

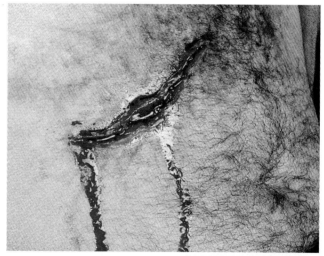

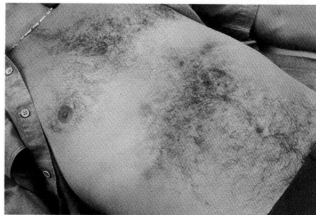

Figure 8–15   External bleeding is more obvious than internal bleeding.

gen-rich blood to the vital organs. The blood at the wound site tries to clot to stop the flow. *Clotting* is the process of the blood thickening to seal an opening and stop bleeding. The body starts to make extra red blood cells to help transport more oxygen to the cells. Excess body fluid normally removed from the body is reabsorbed into the bloodstream to try to keep *blood volume* constant.

Bleeding severe enough to reduce the blood volume to a critical level is life threatening because not enough oxygen reaches the vital organs.

External Bleeding

Causes of external bleeding

External bleeding occurs when a blood vessel is opened to the outside of the body, such as through a tear in the skin. Minor bleeding, such as a scraped knee, usually stops by itself within 10 minutes when the blood clots. However, if the damaged blood vessel is too large or the blood is flowing too fast to clot, bleeding may become life threatening, especially in children and infants whose blood volume is much smaller than an adult's.

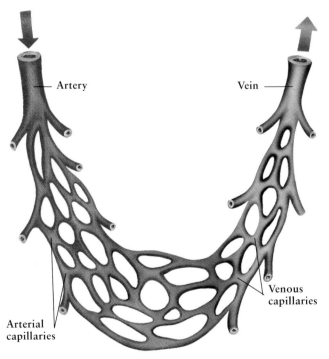

Artery

Vein

Venous capillaries

Arterial capillaries

Figure 8–16   Blood flows through the three major types of blood vessels: arteries, capillaries, and veins.

Signs and symptoms of major external bleeding

Each type of blood vessel bleeds differently. Arterial bleeding is often rapid and profuse and is potentially life threatening. Its high concentration of oxygen gives arterial blood a bright red colour. Because arterial blood is under more pressure, it usually spurts from the wound, making it difficult for clots to form. Arterial bleeding is harder to stop.

Venous bleeding (bleeding from the veins) is more common because veins are closer to the skin's surface. Because it is oxygen poor, venous blood is dark red or maroon. Venous blood flows steadily from the wound without spurting. Only damage to veins deep in the body, such as those in the trunk or thigh, causes profuse venous bleeding that is hard to control.

Capillary bleeding, the most common type, is usually slow because the vessels are small and the blood is under low pressure. The blood is usually less red than arterial blood. It looks like blood oozing from the wound. Clotting occurs easily.

FIRST AID

Major external bleeding

External bleeding is usually easy to control. *Direct pressure* with a bandage or your gloved hand on the wound can stop bleeding. Pressure on the wound restricts the blood flow and allows clotting to occur. If the casualty's injury and pain allow it, *elevation* of the injured area also slows the flow of blood to assist clotting. Pressure can be kept on a wound with a *pressure bandage*. Rest and reassurance also help reduce the flow. A tourniquet, a tight band placed around an arm or leg to help constrict blood flow to a wound, is no longer recommended because too often it does more harm than good.

Always start with the emergency action principles:

1. Survey the scene to ensure no danger.
2. Check the casualty for unresponsiveness. If the person does not respond, call EMS.
3. Do a primary survey, and care for life-threatening problems (ABCs). Call EMS for help if necessary.
4. Do a secondary survey, if needed, and care for other problems.
5. Keep monitoring the ABCs until EMS arrives.
6. Help the casualty rest in the most comfortable position, and give reassurance.

For external bleeding give this first aid:

1. Do not waste time trying to wash the wound first. Place direct pressure on the wound with a **dressing** or any clean cloth, such as a washcloth, towel, or handkerchief. Using a pad or cloth helps keep the wound free from microbes. Place a hand over the pad and apply firm pressure (Figure 8–17, *A*). If you do not have a pad or cloth available, have the injured person apply pressure with his or her hand. As a last resort, use your own gloved hand.
2. Elevate the injured area above the level of the heart if you do not suspect a broken bone (Figure 8–17, *B*).

International Assistance—*Canadian Couple Gives First Aid in the United States*

A few months ago I realized how fortunate I am to be trained to deal with life-threatening emergencies. The valuable knowledge I received during a Red Cross First Aid course proved to be beneficial, not only to two accident casualties, but also to me and my husband.

On an afternoon in May 1992 we were heading home from the United States, travelling along the highway toward the border when two vehicles raced past us at a tremendous speed. Shortly afterward the driver of one car lost control and his vehicle flipped over six times down the road.

Within minutes we approached the accident scene and both driver and passenger had already been removed from the car. Seeing gasoline and sparks coming from the car, we realized that the casualties were still in some danger. Once it was safe to approach I surveyed the scene and had a closer look at the casualties. Fortunately, both were conscious. One had no external bleeding and was very coherent; the other had a serious head injury with a great deal of bleeding. While I was applying pressure on the wound, my husband asked for a first aid kit and asked an onlooker to call for an ambulance.

Then a woman came up and identified herself as a nurse, and with her assistance we bandaged the head wound and continued trying to calm both casualties. They did not want to lie down, but finally agreed to take up a resting position. By the time the rescue vehicle arrived both casualties were at last calm and still conscious.

Once the paramedics started treatment I was allowed to stay and assist. Their procedures included the application of a cervical collar, administration of oxygen, the use of a spinal board for both casualties, a check for vital signs, secondary assessment, transport, and most of all providing reassurance and making the casualties feel as comfortable as possible.

One and a half hours later everything was under control. I was not only thanked by the two casualties but also by the paramedics for my time and assistance. I can truly say that the Red Cross First Aid training I received gave me the ability to act quickly, ease discomfort, prevent further injury, and provide appropriate assistance. Never once did I feel inadequate or in the way.

S.G. Port Coquitlam, B.C.

3. Apply a pressure **bandage** to hold the gauze pads or cloth in place (Figure 8–17, C).

4. If blood soaks through the bandage, add more pads to help absorb the blood. Do not remove any blood-soaked pads.

5. Continue to monitor the airway and breathing. Watch the casualty for any signs and symptoms of the condition worsening. If bleeding seems controlled, provide additional care as needed.

6. Wash your hands as soon as possible.

7. If the casualty has an **amputation** in which a body part has been completely severed, try to retrieve the severed body part. Wrap the part in sterile gauze, if available, or in any clean material such as a washcloth. Place the wrapped part in a plastic bag and put it on ice. Make sure the part is transported to the medical facility with the casualty.

A good way to remember the basics of first aid for external bleeding is the acronym RED:

> R - rest
> E - elevate the injured area above the heart
> D - direct pressure on the bleeding site

Internal Bleeding

Internal bleeding is the escape of blood from arteries, veins, or capillaries into spaces in the body. Capillary bleeding causes mild bruising beneath the skin and is not serious. But deeper bleeding from arteries or veins can result in severe blood loss.

Causes of internal bleeding

Severe internal bleeding usually occurs in injuries caused by a violent blunt force, such as in a car crash when the driver is thrown against the steering wheel or when someone falls from a height. Internal bleeding may also occur when an object like a knife or bullet punctures the skin and damages internal structures. In any serious injury, suspect internal bleeding. Internal bleeding can also occur from a fractured bone that ruptures an organ or blood vessels.

Signs and symptoms of internal bleeding

Internal bleeding is more difficult to recognize than external bleeding because the signs and symptoms are less obvious and may take time to appear:

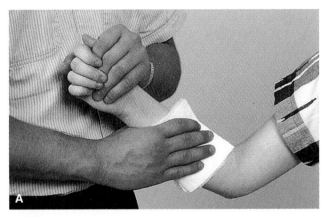

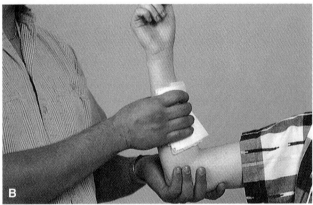

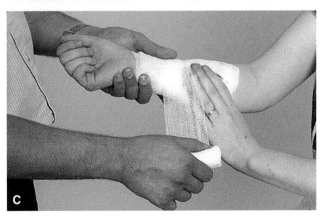

Figure 8–17 *A,* Apply direct pressure to the wound using a sterile gauze pad or clean cloth. *B,* Elevate the injured area above the level of the heart if there is no fracture. *C,* Apply a pressure bandage. The casualty may be able to help you.

- Discolouration of the skin (bruising) in the injured area
- Soft tissues, such as those in the abdomen, that are tender, swollen, or hard
- Anxiety or restlessness
- Rapid, weak pulse
- Rapid breathing
- Skin that feels cool or moist or looks pale or bluish
- Nausea and vomiting
- Excessive thirst
- Declining level of consciousness

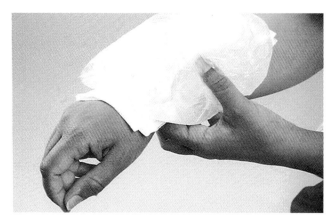

Figure 8–18   For a minor internal injury, apply ice to help control pain and swelling.

FIRST AID

Internal bleeding

As in any situation, start with the emergency action principles:

1. Survey the scene to ensure no danger.
2. Check the casualty for unresponsiveness. If the person does not respond, call EMS.
3. Do a primary survey, and care for life-threatening problems (ABCs). Call EMS for help if necessary.
4. Do a secondary survey, if needed, and care for other problems.
5. Keep monitoring the ABCs until EMS arrives.
6. Help the casualty rest in the most comfortable position and give reassurance.

Controlling internal bleeding depends on the severity and site of the bleeding. Minor closed wounds do not require special medical care. Direct pressure on the area decreases bleeding. Elevating the injured part helps reduce swelling. Cold can help control both pain and swelling. When applying ice or a chemical cold pack, place a gauze pad, towel, or other cloth between the ice and the skin (Figure 8–18). Apply the cold for 15 minutes every hour.

If you suspect internal bleeding caused by serious injury, call EMS immediately. There is little you can do to control serious internal bleeding effectively. Do not dismiss a closed wound as "just a bruise." Evaluate whether there may be more serious injuries to internal organs. If a person complains of severe pain or cannot move a body part without pain, or if you think the force that caused the injury was great enough to cause serious damage, seek medical attention immediately. Care for these injuries is described in later chapters. Severe internal bleeding may cause the casualty to go into shock.

Shock

Causes of Shock

Shock is usually caused by extensive internal or external bleeding, as the loss of blood leads to low blood volume and decreased oxygen supply to the vital organs. Extensive burns and other large fluid losses, such as diarrhea and vomiting in children, can also cause shock.

Signs and Symptoms of Shock

The signs and symptoms of shock are similar to those of severe internal and external bleeding:

- Pale, cold, clammy skin
- Weakness
- Anxiety
- Confusion
- Unconsciousness
- Weak, rapid pulse

Remember, you do not have to see any bleeding or know the cause of shock to give care that may help save the casualty's life.

FIRST AID

Shock

Always follow the emergency action principles:

1. Survey the scene to ensure no danger.
2. Check the casualty for unresponsiveness. If the person does not respond, call EMS.
3. Do a primary survey, and care for life-threatening problems (ABCs). Call EMS for help if necessary.
4. Do a secondary survey, if needed, and care for other problems.
5. Keep monitoring the ABCs until EMS arrives.
6. Help the casualty rest in the most comfortable position, and give reassurance.

In addition, help the casualty maintain normal body temperature (Figure 8–19) and encourage him or her to lie down.

Fainting

Fainting is a form of shock in which the casualty has a partial or complete loss of consciousness. It is caused by a temporary reduction of blood flow to the brain. Fainting can be triggered by an emotional shock such as the sight of blood. It may be caused by pain, medical conditions such as heart disease, standing for long periods of time, or overexertion. Some people, such as pregnant women or the elderly, may faint because of a sudden change in position, such as moving from a sitting or lying down position to one of standing up.

Fainting may occur without any warning at all, or the casualty may first feel lightheaded, dizzy, nauseated, or sweaty.

The first aid for fainting begins with the emergency action principles. Do not assume the person merely fainted, since he or she may have become unconscious because of a life-threatening

problem such as severe shock or cardiac arrest. Always check the ABCs to ensure that no life-threatening problem exists. If there is any doubt about the cause of the fainting, call EMS.

Usually fainting resolves by itself and the casualty regains consciousness within a minute or two.

Shock: The Domino Effect

- An injury causes severe bleeding.
- The heart attempts to compensate for the disruption of blood flow by beating faster. The casualty first has a rapid pulse. More blood is lost. As blood volume drops, the pulse becomes weak or hard to find.
- The increased work load on the heart results in an increased oxygen demand. Therefore, breathing becomes faster.
- To maintain circulation of blood to the vital organs, blood vessels in the arms and legs and in the skin constrict. Therefore, the skin

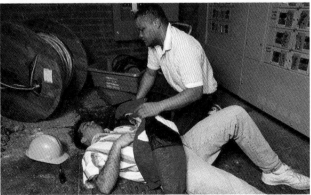

Figure 8–19 *A,* Watch the ABCs of a casualty who is in shock. *B,* Maintain normal body temperature.

appears pale and feels cool. In response to the stress, the body perspires heavily and the skin feels moist.

- Since tissues of the arms and legs are now without oxygen, cells start to die. The brain now sends a signal to return blood to the arms and legs in an attempt to balance blood flow between these body parts and the vital organs.

- Vital organs are now without adequate oxygen. The heart tries to compensate by beating even faster. More blood is lost and the casualty's condition worsens.

- Without oxygen, the vital organs fail to function properly. As the brain is affected, the casualty becomes restless, drowsy, and eventually loses consciousness. As the heart is affected, it beats irregularly, resulting in an irregular pulse. The rhythm then becomes chaotic and the heart fails to pump blood. There is no longer a pulse. When the heart stops, breathing stops.

- The body's continuous attempt to compensate for severe blood loss eventually results in death.

Summary

- It is important to recognize the signs and symptoms of a heart attack and call EMS immediately. Then help the casualty rest until help arrives, assist with any medication, and be prepared to give CPR if cardiac arrest occurs.

- For a casualty in cardiac arrest, starting CPR immediately can help keep the brain and vital organs supplied with oxygen until an AED is available or until EMS arrives to give advanced cardiac life support (ACLS).

- Stay in practice with CPR and remember correct hand position, smooth compressions, cycles of compressions and rescue breaths, and signs of circulation checks.

- Continue CPR until the casualty's heart starts beating, you are relieved by another trained person, you are exhausted, an AED is available or EMS arrives and takes over.

- Cardiovascular disease can often be prevented with a good diet, exercise, and weight control, not smoking, and stress management.

- Severe bleeding is a life-threatening emergency. Control external bleeding with rest, elevation of the area, and direct pressure on the wound (RED). Call EMS for suspected internal bleeding, and help the casualty rest and stay calm.

- Stroke, like cardiovascular disease, can be prevented by minimizing risk factors. First aid includes keeping the airway open and giving reassurance until EMS arrives.

The Secondary Survey

9

Objectives

After reading this chapter, you should be able to:

1. Describe the appropriate time to proceed from the primary survey to the secondary survey.

2. Explain why you should do a secondary survey.

3. Explain how to do each of the steps of the secondary survey: interview the casualty and bystanders, check vital signs, and perform a head-to-toe examination.

4. Explain what you should do if you decide to transport the casualty to the hospital yourself.

5. Define the key terms for this chapter.

After reading this chapter and completing the class activities, you should be able to:

1. Demonstrate a secondary survey.

2. Decide what care to give in an example of an emergency situation in which you do a secondary survey.

3. Demonstrate a hands off and a hands on Head to Toe survey.

Key Terms

secondary survey   A check for other injuries or conditions that require first aid or that could become life-threatening problems if not cared for.

vital signs   Three characteristics that show the casualty's condition: level of consciousness, breathing, and pulse.

In Chapters 2 through 8 you learned how to recognize and give first aid for life-threatening conditions that may result from injuries or illness. You learned how to do the primary survey and check the ABCs to find any problems with the airway, breathing, or circulation. You learned how to give first aid for these life-threatening conditions to help the casualty stay alive until EMS arrives.

You also learned the six emergency action principles to guide your actions in any situation of illness or injury:

1. Survey the scene to ensure no danger.
2. Check the casualty for unresponsiveness. If the person does not respond, call EMS.
3. Do a primary survey and care for life-threatening problems (ABCs). Call EMS for help if necessary.
4. Do a secondary survey, if needed, and care for other problems.
5. Keep monitoring the ABCs until EMS arrives.
6. Help the casualty rest in the most comfortable position and give reassurance.

In this chapter you will learn how to continue with these emergency action principles by doing a secondary survey, the fourth emergency action principle.

Only when you are certain that the casualty has no life-threatening conditions needing immediate attention should you do a *secondary survey*. If you find conditions such as altered level of consciousness, no breathing, no signs of circulation, or severe bleeding during the primary survey, do *not* waste time with the secondary survey. Instead, call EMS and give care only for the immediate life-threatening conditions.

If the casualty is unconscious but has a clear airway, is breathing, has signs of circulation, and has no serious bleeding, it is safe to proceed to the secondary survey after calling EMS because there are no life-threatening conditions to care for first.

Always be sure first that you do not have to give first aid for the casualty's ABCs. Then continue with the secondary survey and place the casualty in the recovery position.

The secondary survey is a way to find other problems that may need first aid. These problems could become serious if not cared for. For example, you might find a broken bone or minor bleeding. The secondary survey has three steps:

1. Interview the casualty and/or bystanders.
2. Check *vital signs*.
3. Perform a head-to-toe examination.

If you can, write down what you find during the secondary survey or have someone else write it down or help you remember. Your findings may be important. Give this information to EMS when they arrive.

Remember that moving a casualty may aggravate the person's condition, so do not move the casualty to do the secondary survey. Most injured people find the most comfortable position for themselves.

Interview the Casualty and/or Bystanders

If the casualty is conscious, start by asking how he or she feels and where it hurts. Ask bystanders what happened. Try to get more information than you did at first when you surveyed the scene quickly to make sure it was safe. Be sure to identify yourself and to get consent (see Chapter 5). Use the casualty's name to make him or her more comfortable. Ask these questions:

1. What happened?
2. Do you feel pain anywhere? Where? What does it feel like?
3. Do you have any allergies?
4. Do you have any medical conditions or are you taking any medication?

With an unconscious casualty, a child, or an adult who has lost consciousness or cannot recall what happened, ask others at the scene. Because a casualty may be frightened, be calm, patient, and reassuring.

Check Vital Signs

The vital signs of the casualty are three characteristics that can provide some idea of the person's condition:

- Level of consciousness
- Breathing
- Pulse

Watch for changes in these and note anything unusual. Check these vital signs about every 5 minutes until EMS arrives.

Level of Consciousness

A healthy person is generally awake and alert. A serious injury or illness can affect consciousness. A change in consciousness may occur some time after you start to give first aid. Watch for these signs and symptoms of altered consciousness, and call EMS if you have not already done so:

- Unresponsiveness to your voice
- Confusion about time and place

Changes in level of consciousness may be caused by many different problems. Keep checking the casualty's ABCs and give first aid for any conditions you find while waiting for EMS.

Breathing

A healthy person breathes regularly, easily, and quietly. Abnormal breathing may result from a problem. Watch for these signs and symptoms:

- Gasping for air
- Noisy breathing, whistling sounds, crowing, gurgling

- Very fast or slow breathing (normal breathing for adults at rest is 10 to 20 breaths per minute; children and infants normally breathe faster)
- Painful breathing
- Very deep or very shallow breathing

Chapter 7 describes what changes in breathing may mean and what first aid to give.

Pulse

In a healthy person the pulse is regular. An abnormal pulse may signal a problem. Check the casualty's pulse for these signs (Figure 9–1):

- Irregular rhythm
- Weak or hard-to-find pulse
- Very fast or slow pulse (normal pulse for an adult is 60 to 100 beats per minute; children and infants normally have a faster pulse)

A faster or weak pulse may signal pain or loss of blood. These changes may be hard for you to feel. Most important, keep checking the pulse to make sure it has not stopped. Chapter 8 describes how to take a pulse, what changes may mean, and what first aid to give.

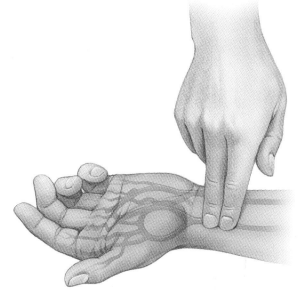

Figure 9–1 Check the pulse in arteries that circulate close to the surface, such as the radial artery in the wrist.

Perform a Head-to-Toe Examination (Hands Off)

The last step of the secondary survey is the head-to-toe examination. Do a careful, systematic examination and be careful not to cause further injury. Start by telling the casualty what you are going to do. Ask the casualty to stay still. *Avoid touching any painful areas or having the casualty move any area in which there is discomfort.* Watch the casualty's facial expressions and listen for any pain in the person's voice. Look for a medical information tag on a Medic Alert necklace or bracelet. This tag may tell you what might be wrong, whom to call for help, and what care to give.

Listed below is an outline of what to do for a physical examination on a conscious casualty:

1. Look over the entire body for bruises or anything that looks unusual. The appearance of the skin and its temperature can signal a problem. For example, a casualty with a breathing problem may have a flushed or pale face. Cool, moist, and pale skin often indicates shock. Check the skin temperature by feeling it with the back of your hand (Figure 9–2).
2. Ask the casualty to move all body parts one at a time to check for pain. Start at the head. If the casualty has neck pain, do not move the neck. If no neck pain is present, ask if the injured person can slowly move his or her head from side to side (Figure 9–3). Check the ears, nose, and mouth for blood or fluids. Check the shoulders by asking the person to shrug them (Figure 9–4). Check the chest and abdomen by asking the person to take a deep breath and then blow the air out (Figure 9–5). Check the arms and hands (Figure 9–6). Check the hips, legs, toes, feet, and ankles (Figure 9–7). Check one arm or leg at a time.
3. If the casualty does not complain of any pain, has no tender areas, and no signs of injury, have the casualty rest for a few minutes in a sitting position (Figure 9–8). Check the vital

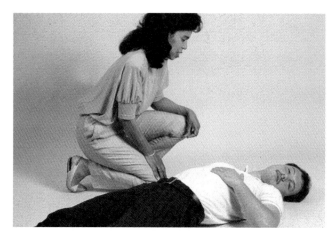

Figure 9–3 If the casualty has no neck pain, ask him to move his head from side to side to check the neck.

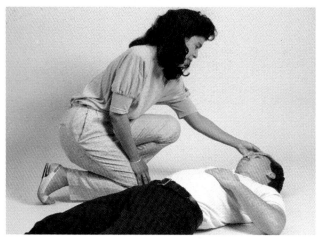

Figure 9–2 Feel the skin with the back of your hand to check the casualty's temperature.

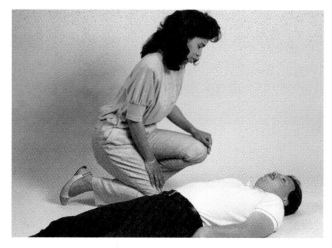

Figure 9–4 Ask the casualty to shrug his shoulders to check the shoulders.

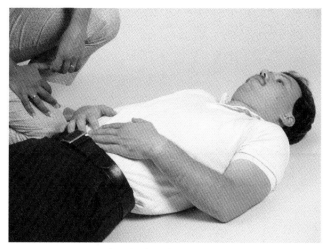

Figure 9–5   To check the chest and abdomen, ask the casualty to breathe deeply and then blow out the air. Ask if any pain was felt.

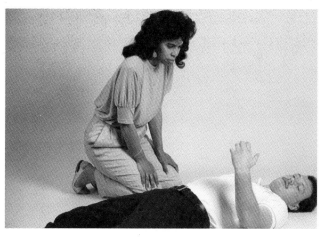

Figure 9–6   Check arms by asking the casualty to bend his arms one at a time.

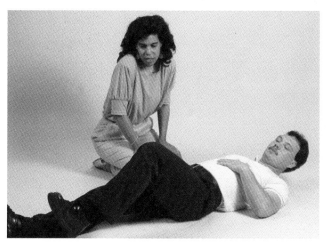

Figure 9–7   Check the legs by asking the casualty to bend his legs one at a time.

signs and monitor the ABCs. If you see no problem, help the casualty to try to stand slowly when ready (Figure 9–9).

4. If the person has pain or dizziness or cannot move a body part, recheck the ABCs. Help the person rest, maintain normal body temperature, and give reassurance. Determine whether first aid is needed and whether to call EMS.

As you do this examination, keep watching the casualty's level of consciousness, breathing, and skin colour. If any problems develop, *stop* whatever you are doing and give first aid *immediately*.

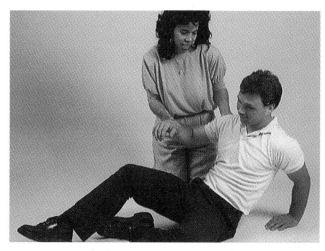

Figure 9–8   If there are no signs of obvious injuries, help the casualty into a sitting position.

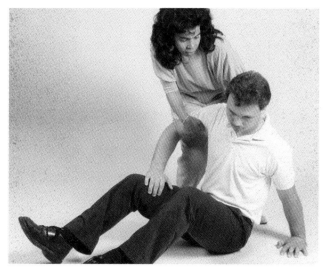

Figure 9–9   Help the casualty slowly stand if you have found no problems.

Perform a Head-to-Toe Examination (Hands On)

A hands-on head-to-toe should only be done once the primary survey has been completed and no interventions are necessary, and the patient is properly positioned. If you suspect a spinal injury and the patient is unresponsive then do not perform a head-to-toe unless there is a second first aider to maintain an open airway.

During the head-to-toe examination, inspect the entire body starting with the head. Look for blood or clear fluids in or around the ears, nose, and mouth. Blood or fluid can indicate a serious head injury. Then proceed with the following steps....

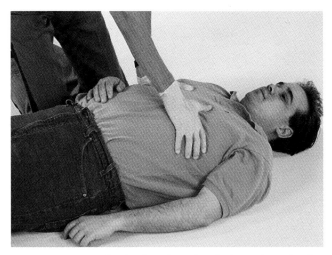

Figure 9–12   Check the chest by feeling the ribs for deformity.

Figure 9–10   To check the neck, look and feel for any abnormalities.

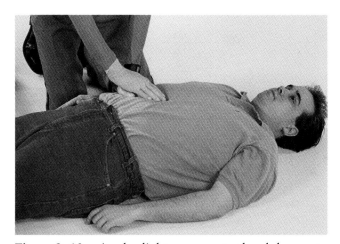

Figure 9–13   Apply slight pressure to the abdomen to see if it is soft or rigid.

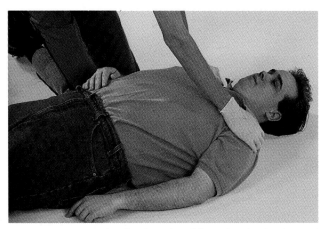

Figure 9–11   Check the shoulders by looking and feeling for deformity.

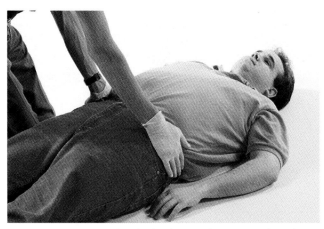

Figure 9–14   To check the hips, place your hands on both sides of the pelvis and push down and in.

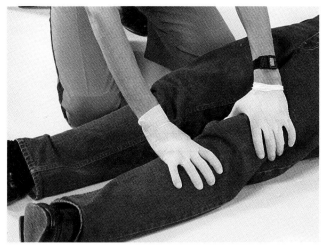

Figure 9–15   Check the legs by feeling for any deformity. If there is no apparent sign of injury.

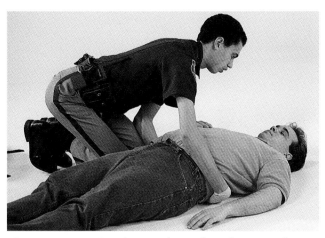

Figure 9–16   Gently reach under the casualty to check the back.

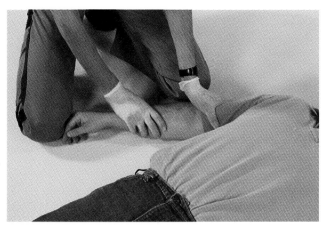

Figure 9–17   Check the arms by feeling for any deformity. If there is no apparent sign of injury.

Give First Aid

After the secondary survey give first aid for any problems you find. Remember the six emergency action principles and continue with steps 5 and 6. If the casualty's condition changes, return to the earlier steps, do another primary survey, or call for EMS if you have not already done so.

Deciding to Transport the Casualty

Never transport a casualty with a life-threatening condition or a chance one may develop. Instead, call EMS and wait for help. A car trip may make the injury worse. Chapter 2 explains in detail when to call EMS. If you are certain the casualty's injuries are minor and it is safe to move the person, you might consider transporting the casualty to the doctor or hospital yourself.

If you do decide to transport the casualty, take someone else with you to help keep the casualty comfortable and watch for any changes in his or her condition. Do not let a casualty drive alone to the hospital because a change in condition can make driving dangerous for the casualty and others.

Summary

- When you respond to an emergency, remember to follow the six emergency action principles (EAPs):

- Survey the scene to ensure no danger.

- Check the casualty for unresponsiveness. If the person does not respond, call EMS.

- Do a primary survey and care for life-threatening problems (ABCs). Call EMS for help if necessary.

- Do a secondary survey, if needed, and care for other problems.

- Keep monitoring the ABCs until EMS arrives.

- Help the casualty rest in the most comfortable position and give reassurance.

- Only do a secondary survey if you are sure the casualty has no life-threatening conditions.

- In the secondary survey interview the casualty and bystanders, check the vital signs, and perform a head-to-toe examination.

- As you give additional first aid for problems you find in the secondary survey, continue to monitor the casualty's ABCs and return to the primary survey or call EMS if needed.

Head and Spine Injuries

10

Objectives

After reading this chapter, you should be able to:

1. Name the most common cause of head and spine injuries.
2. List at least five situations that may cause serious head and spine injuries.
3. List at least six signs and symptoms of head and spine injuries.
4. Describe how to keep the casualty's head and spine still until help arrives.
5. Describe how to care for concussion and injuries to the scalp, eye, and ear.
6. List at least five ways to prevent head and spine injuries.
7. Describe how to care for mouth and jaw injuries, including knocked-out teeth.
8. Define the key terms for this chapter.
9. Decide what first aid to give in an emergency involving probable injuries to the head and spine.

Key Terms

concussion   A temporary impairment of brain function, usually caused by a blow to the head.

in-line stabilization   A way to position and support the head and neck if the casualty must be moved.

spinal column   The column of vertebrae from the skull to the tailbone.

spinal cord   The bundle of nerves from the brain to the lower back, protected inside the spinal column.

vertebrae   The 33 bones of the spinal column.

It's a warm summer day and a group of teenagers are having fun at a backyard pool party. John, the son of the family having the party, told all the guests as they arrived that the pool is too shallow for diving, even in the deep end. After an hour some of the teenagers are chasing each other around the pool and jumping in while they play a wild ball game. When John goes inside for more food and soft drinks, some of the others start making shallow dives into the deep end. Someone throws the ball into the pool and two boys dive in after it; one hits his head on the bottom. Although the others carefully rescue him and immediately call 9-1-1 for help, his injury is serious. He has a broken neck and will be paralyzed for life.

Head and Spine Injuries

Motor vehicle crashes cause about half of all head and spine injuries. Other causes include falls, sports, and violent acts such as assault.

Even those who survive head and spine injuries can have physical and mental difficulties, including paralysis, speech and memory problems, and behavioural disorders. Many casualties are permanently disabled.

First aid correctly given can prevent some head and spine injuries from leading to death or disability. In this chapter you will learn how to recognize when a head or spine injury may be serious. You will also learn how to give the right care for injuries to the head and spine. Head injuries may include concussion and injuries to the scalp, eye, or ear.

Anatomy and Physiology of Head and Spine Injuries

Injuries to the head or spine can damage bones such as the skull or vertebrae and tissues such as the brain and the *spinal cord*. Determining how much damage has taken place in head and spine injuries is not easy. Usually the only way to learn is by an x-ray examination. Because you cannot know for sure, always give care as if the injury were serious.

The Brain

Injuries to the head can affect the brain. Bleeding from a ruptured vessel in the brain can build up pressure within the skull and damage brain tissue (Figure 10–1).

Bleeding within the skull can occur rapidly or slowly. This bleeding will result in changes in consciousness. An altered level of consciousness is often the first and most important sign of a serious head injury.

The Spine

The spine is a strong, flexible column that supports the head and the trunk. It contains and protects the spinal cord, the bundle of nerves from

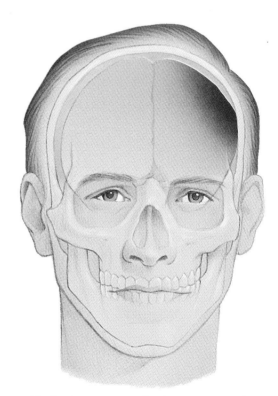

Figure 10–1   Injuries to the head can break blood vessels in the brain. Pressure builds within the skull as blood builds up, causing brain damage.

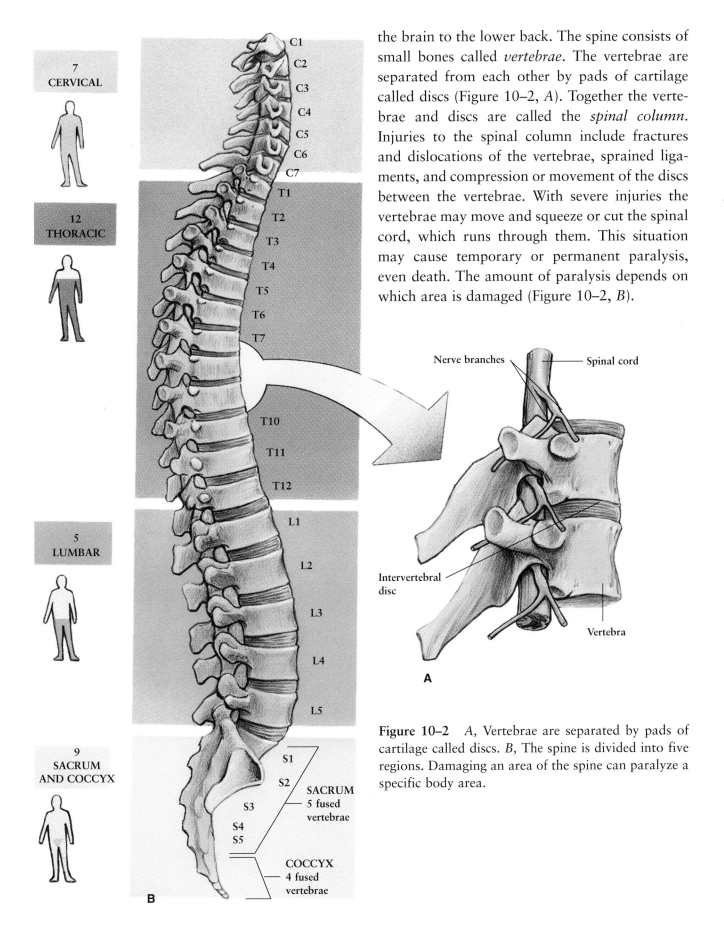

the brain to the lower back. The spine consists of small bones called *vertebrae*. The vertebrae are separated from each other by pads of cartilage called discs (Figure 10–2, *A*). Together the vertebrae and discs are called the *spinal column*. Injuries to the spinal column include fractures and dislocations of the vertebrae, sprained ligaments, and compression or movement of the discs between the vertebrae. With severe injuries the vertebrae may move and squeeze or cut the spinal cord, which runs through them. This situation may cause temporary or permanent paralysis, even death. The amount of paralysis depends on which area is damaged (Figure 10–2, *B*).

Figure 10–2   *A*, Vertebrae are separated by pads of cartilage called discs. *B*, The spine is divided into five regions. Damaging an area of the spine can paralyze a specific body area.

Causes of Head and Spine Injuries

The cause of the injury often is the first clue you may have in judging the seriousness of a head or spine injury. Strong forces (as in a car crash) are likely to cause serious injury. Injuries should be suspected with the following situations:

- A fall from a height
- Any diving injury
- A person found unconscious for unknown reasons
- Any injury with a strong blow to the head or trunk
- Any injury making a wound in the head or trunk
- A crash involving a driver or passengers
- Any person thrown from a motor vehicle
- Any injury in which the person's helmet is broken
- A lightning strike

PREVENTION

Head and Spine Injuries

The following safety practices can help prevent injuries to the head and spine.

- Always wear safety belts and shoulder restraints when driving or riding in a car; small children must be in safety seats approved for the child's age and weight, and the seat must be properly installed (Figure 10–3).
- Wear the right helmet and proper eyewear for activities where protection is needed (Figure 10–4). The helmet should fit comfortably and securely. All bicycle riders should wear a helmet, including adults as well as children and teens. With any work involving flying particles or chemicals, wear protective eyewear.
- Prevent falls around the home and work place

Figure 10–3 Children in cars must ride in properly installed approved safety seats.

with nonslip floors, nonslip tread and handrails on stairs, rugs secured with double-sided adhesive tape, and handrails by the bathtub and toilet when necessary.
- Take safety precautions in all contact sports by wearing proper protection, such as mouthpieces. Never join in a new sport without knowing the rules and risks involved.
- Always be very careful around water:
  - Check water depth and be sure it is deep enough for diving. Pools at homes, motels, or hotels may not be safe for diving.
  - Never dive into an above-ground pool.
  - Always swim with a buddy.
  - Never drink and dive.
  - Before diving, check for objects below the surface, such as logs or pilings.
  - Don't rush into the water or dive head-first into the waves.
  - When bodysurfing, keep your arms out front to protect your head and neck.
  - Inspect mechanical equipment and ladders regularly for worn or loose parts.
  - Use ladders carefully and correctly.
- Do not abuse alcoholic beverages or drugs. Alcohol intoxication is often present in serious vehicular crashes and water injuries. Alcohol slows the reflexes and gives the user

Figure 10–4   Wearing a helmet helps prevent head and spine injuries.

a feeling of false confidence. Since prescription and common drugstore medications can also make driving or operating machinery dangerous, follow the directions.

Signs and Symptoms of Head and Spine Injuries

- Changes in level of consciousness
- Severe pain or pressure in the head, neck, or back
- Tingling or loss of feeling in the fingers and toes
- Loss of movement of any body part
- Unusual lumps on the head or spine
- Blood in the ears or nose
- Heavy bleeding of the head, neck, or back
- Convulsions
- Impaired breathing or vision
- Nausea or vomiting
- Persistent headache
- Loss of balance
- Bruising of the head, especially around the eyes and behind the ears

These signs and symptoms alone do not always mean a serious head or spine injury, but *always* call EMS when you suspect a serious head or spine injury.

FIRST AID

Head and Spine Injuries

Follow the emergency action principles whenever you suspect a head or spine injury:

1. Survey the scene to ensure no danger.
2. Check the casualty for unresponsiveness. If the person does not respond, call EMS.
3. Do a primary survey and care for life-threatening problems (ABCs). Call EMS for help if necessary.
4. Do a secondary survey, if needed, and care for other problems.
5. Keep monitoring the ABCs until EMS arrives.
6. Help the casualty rest in the most comfortable position and give reassurance.

Head and spine injuries can become life threatening. Give the following specific first aid while waiting for EMS help to arrive:

1. Keep the head and spine as still as possible.
2. Maintain an open airway.
3. Monitor consciousness and breathing.
4. Control external bleeding.
5. Maintain normal body temperature.

Keep the Head and Spine as Still as Possible

Steady the injured area and control any bleeding. Because movement of the head and spine can damage the spinal cord, keep the casualty as still as possible while waiting for EMS. Immobilize the head and neck in the position found, and support them in that position until EMS arrives (Figure 10–5).

If the casualty is wearing a helmet, leave it on.

Log Roll

Move a casualty with a suspected neck or back injury only if it is absolutely necessary. You need a spine board (a flat, nonmetal board the same length as the casualty) and at least two other rescuers to assist. One rescuer acts as leader and instructs the others:

1. All rescuers kneel on the same side of the casualty.
2. One rescuer at the head supports the head and neck, while one at the feet supports the feet. Other rescuers pass their hands over the casualty at the chest, hips, and knees (Figure 10–6, A).
3. At the leader's signal, the rescuers roll the casualty toward them onto his or her side. The head and neck are kept aligned with the rest of the body (Figure 10–6, B).
4. The spine board is placed behind the casualty. On the leader's signal, the rescuers roll the casualty back onto the board as one unit (Figure 10–6, C).
5. To secure the casualty immobile on the board, wrap a series of bandages around the casualty and board, including at the forehead, chest, waist, legs, and ankles (Figure 10–6, D).

The rescuers can now carry the casualty on the board away from the danger scene.

Maintain an Open Airway

If the casualty is breathing, give support for the head and neck in the position in which you found the casualty. If the casualty begins to vomit, provide in-line stabilization and roll him or her onto one side to keep the airway clear.

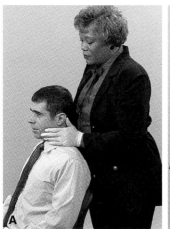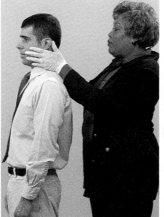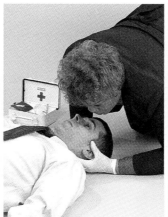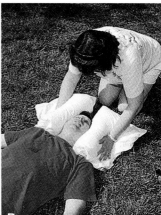

Figure 10–5 Support the casualty's head and neck in the position in which you find the casualty.

Monitor Consciousness and Breathing

While stabilizing the head and neck, watch the casualty's level of consciousness and breathing. A serious injury will affect the person's consciousness. The casualty may say odd things or speak without making sense. The casualty may be drowsy, seem to go to sleep, and then suddenly awaken or pass out. Breathing may become rapid or uneven. Because a head or spine injury can paralyze chest nerves and muscles, breathing can stop. If this happens, give rescue breathing.

Control External Bleeding

Because there are many blood vessels in the head and two major arteries in the neck, the casualty can lose blood quickly. Control any external bleeding with dressings, direct pressure, and bandages (see Chapter 8).

Maintain Normal Body Temperature

A serious injury to the head or spine can disrupt the body's normal heating or cooling system. The person can then go into shock. Minimizing shock by maintaining normal body temperature is important (see Chapter 8).

FIRST AID

Specific Head Injuries

The head is easily injured because it lacks padding of muscle and fat. You can feel bone just below the surface of the skin over most of the head (Figure 10–7).

In addition to the six emergency action principles, give first aid for the following specific head injuries.

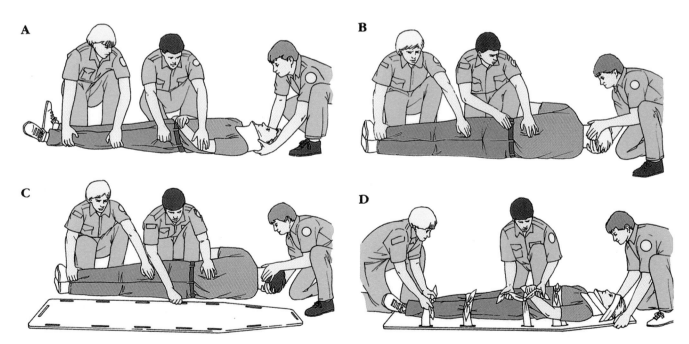

Figure 10–6   The log roll emergency move for the casualty with suspected neck or back injury. *A,* Rescuers in position, with head and neck supported in line with the body. *B,* Roll the casualty as a unit. *C,* Position the spine board and roll the casualty back onto it. *D,* Secure the casualty immobilized on the board before transporting the casualty. *Note:* These illustrations depict an EMS team in action. As a first aider, you may not have items such as cervical collars and spine boards available. In that case, improvise.

Concussion

A *concussion* is usually a temporary injury. In most cases the casualty loses consciousness for only a few minutes and may say that he or she "blacked out" or "saw stars." Unconsciousness sometimes lasts longer, or the casualty may be confused or have memory loss. Anyone suspected of having a concussion should be seen by a physician.

Scalp Injury

Scalp bleeding is usually controlled with direct pressure. Apply dressings and hold them in place with your hand. Set the dressings with a roller-type or a triangular bandage (Figure 10–8, *A* and *B*). Be gentle, because the skull may be fractured. If you feel a depression, a soft area, or pieces of bone, do not put direct pressure on the wound unless bleeding is severe. Call EMS immediately. Try to control bleeding with pressure on the area around the wound (Figure 10–9). Check the area carefully because hair may hide part of the wound. If you are unsure of the seriousness of the injury, call EMS.

Eye Injury

Eye injuries can involve the bone and soft tissue surrounding the eye or the eyeball itself. A blunt object may injure the eye area, or an object may penetrate the eyeball. Care for wounds around the eyeball just as you would for any other soft tissue injury.

Injuries to the eyeball are very serious and require special care. Never put direct pressure on the eyeball. Follow these guidelines for first aid:

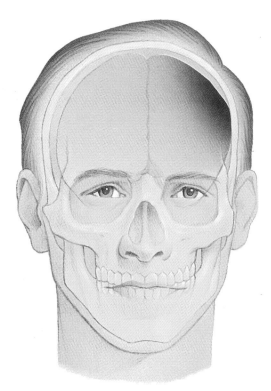

Figure 10–7   The head is easily injured because it lacks the padding of muscle and fat found in other areas of the body.

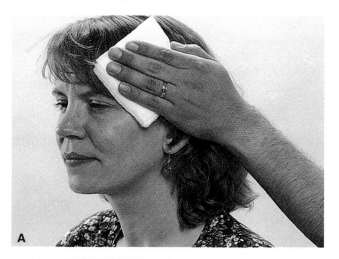

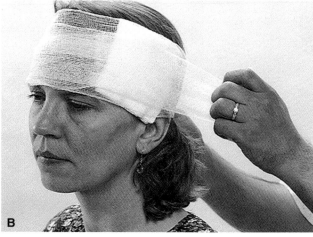

Figure 10–8   *A*, Apply pressure to control bleeding from a scalp wound. *B*, Then secure dressings with a bandage.

Figure 10–9 To keep from putting direct pressure on a deep scalp wound, apply pressure with your hands to the area around the wound.

1. Place the casualty on his or her back.
2. Do not attempt to remove any object impaled in the eye.
3. Place a sterile dressing around the object (Figure 10–10, A).
4. Stabilize any impaled object in place as best you can (Figure 10–10, B and C).

A casualty with a foreign body in the eye, such as dirt, sand, or slivers of wood or metal, may feel severe pain and may have difficulty opening the eye. Give the following first aid for a foreign object or chemical in the eye:

1. Try to remove the foreign body by having the person blink several times. The eye will produce tears that may wash out the object.
2. Gently flush the eye with water.
3. If the object remains, the casualty should see a doctor as soon possible.

Ear Injury

Either the soft tissue of the ear or the eardrum within the ear may be injured. Recreational injuries typically cause ear injuries.

If you are sure the bleeding is just from the soft tissues of the ear, apply direct pressure to the affected area.

However, if the casualty has a serious head or spine injury and blood or other fluid is in the ear canal or draining from the ear, follow these guidelines:

1. *Do not* attempt to stop this drainage with direct pressure.
2. Cover the ear lightly with a sterile dressing.
3. Call EMS immediately.

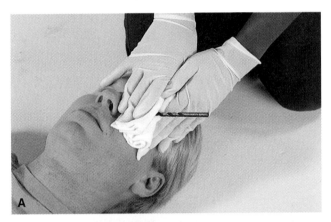

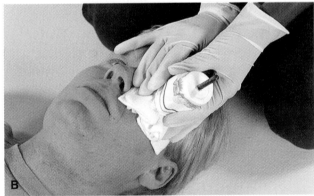

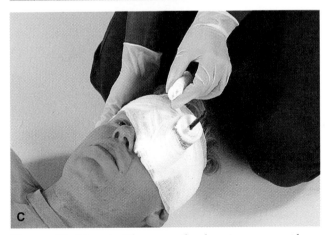

Figure 10–10 *A,* Place sterile dressings around an object impaled in the eye. *B,* Support the object with a paper cup. *C,* Carefully bandage the cup in place.

Internal injury may be caused by a direct blow to the head or sudden pressure changes such as those occurring with an explosion or a deep-water dive. The casualty may lose hearing or balance or feel inner ear pain. Call EMS for such injuries.

For a foreign object, such as dirt, an insect, or cotton lodged in the ear canal, give the following first aid:

1. If you can easily see and grasp the object, remove it.

Now Smile

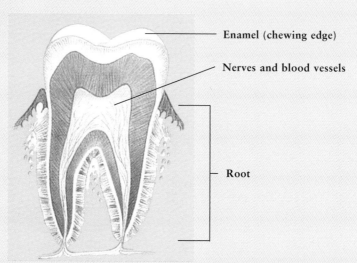

Enamel (chewing edge)

Nerves and blood vessels

Root

Knocked-out teeth no longer spell doom for pearly whites. Most dentists can successfully replant a knocked-out tooth if they can do so quickly and if the tooth is properly cared for.

Replanting a tooth is similar to replanting a tree. On each tooth, tiny root fibres called periodontal fibres attach to the jawbone to hold the tooth in place. Inside the tooth, a canal filled with bundles of blood vessels and nerve ends runs from the tooth into the jawbone and surrounding tissues.

When these fibres and tissues are torn from the socket, it is important that they be replaced within an hour. Generally, the sooner the tooth is replanted, the greater the chance it will survive. The knocked-out tooth must be handled carefully to protect the fragile tissues. Be careful to pick up the tooth by the chewing edge (crown), not the root. Do not rub or handle the root part of the tooth. It is best to preserve the tooth by placing it in a closed container of cool, fresh milk until it reaches the dentist. Milk is not always available at an injury scene; water may be substituted.

A dentist or emergency room doctor will clean the tooth, taking care not to damage the root fibres. The tooth is then placed back into the socket and secured with special splinting devices. The devices keep the tooth stable for 2 to 3 weeks while the fibres reattach to the jawbone. The bundles of blood vessels and nerves grow back within 6 weeks.

References

Bogart, J, DDS, Executive Director, American Academy of Pediatric Dentists: Interview, April 1990.

Medford, H, DDS: Acute care of an avulsed tooth. Ann Emerg Med 11:559, October 1982.

2. Do not try to remove any object by using a pin, toothpick, or a similar sharp item. You could force the object farther back or puncture the eardrum.

3. Try to remove the object by pulling down on the earlobe, tilting the head to the side, and shake or gently strike the head on the affected side.

4. If the steps above do not easily remove the object, the casualty should see a doctor as soon as possible.

Mouth and Jaw Injuries

Your primary concern for any injury to the mouth or jaw is to ensure an open airway. Injuries in these areas may cause breathing problems if blood or loose teeth obstruct the airway.

If the casualty is bleeding from the mouth and you do not suspect a serious head or spinal injury, place the casualty in a seated position with the head tilted slightly forward. This will allow any blood to drain from the mouth. If this position is not possible, place the casualty on his or her side to allow blood to drain from the mouth.

For injuries that penetrate the lip, place a rolled dressing between the lip and the gum. You can place another dressing on the outer surface of the lip. If the tongue is bleeding, apply a dressing and direct pressure. Applying cold to the lips or tongue can help reduce swelling and ease pain. If the bleeding cannot be controlled, summon more advanced medical personnel.

If the injury knocked out one or more of the casualty's teeth, control the bleeding and save any teeth so that they can be reinserted. To control the bleeding, roll a sterile dressing and insert it into the space left by the missing tooth. Have the casualty bite down to maintain pressure (Figure 10–11).

Opinions vary as to how a tooth should be saved. One thought is to place the dislodged tooth or teeth in the casualty's mouth. This, however, is not always the best approach, since a crying child could aspirate the tooth. Also, the tooth

Figure 10–11   If a tooth is knocked out, place a sterile dressing in the space left by the tooth. Tell the casualty to bite down.

could be swallowed with blood or saliva. You also may need to control serious bleeding in the mouth. Because of these concerns, it is best to place the tooth in a cup of milk. If milk is not available, the tooth can be placed in water.

If the injury is severe enough for you to summon more advanced medical personnel, give the tooth to them when they arrive. If the injury is not severe, the casualty should immediately seek a dentist who can replant the tooth. Time is a critical factor if the tooth is to be successfully replanted. Ideally, the tooth should be replanted within an hour after the injury.

Injuries serious enough to fracture or dislocate the jaw can cause other head or spinal injuries. Be sure to maintain an open airway. Check inside the mouth for bleeding. Control bleeding as you would for other head injuries. Minimize the movement of the head and neck. Summon more advanced medical personnel.

Summary

- To judge whether a head or spine injury may be serious, you must consider its cause. If you are unsure, call EMS.

- As with any injury, follow the six emergency action principles.

- Control bleeding as necessary, usually with direct pressure on the wound, but be careful not to apply pressure to a possible skull fracture.

- If you suspect a fracture of the skull or spine, minimize movement of the injured area by immobilizing the head and neck in the position found. Maintain an open airway.

- First aid for an eye injury includes stabilization and bandaging of an impaled object and flushing out any foreign object.

- First aid for an ear injury includes stopping soft tissue bleeding with direct pressure, attempting to remove a foreign object, and calling EMS for internal ear injuries.

- First aid for mouth and jaw injuries includes maintaining an airway, preserving knocked-out teeth in milk and controlling bleeding and swelling.

Musculoskeletal Injuries

Objectives

After reading this chapter, you should be able to:

1. Identify the four main structures of the musculoskeletal system.

2. List at least three signs and symptoms of serious bone, muscle, and joint injuries.

3. Describe the general care for bone, muscle, and joint injuries.

4. List four principles of splinting.

5. Identify three types of splints.

6. Define the key terms for this chapter.

After reading this chapter and completing the class activities, you should be able to:

1. Show how to splint a body part.

2. Decide what first aid to give in an example of an emergency involving a bone, muscle, or joint injury.

Key Terms

bandage   Material used to wrap or cover a part of the body or to hold a dressing or splint in place.

binder   A bandage used to hold an injured arm to the chest.

bone   The dense, hard tissue that forms the skeleton.

dislocation   The displacement of a bone from its normal position at a joint.

extremities   The upper extremities are the arms, forearms, and hands; the lower extremities, the thighs, legs, and feet.

fracture   A break in bone tissue.

immobilize   To use a splint or other method to keep an injured body part from moving.

joint   Where two or more bones are joined.

ligament   A fibrous band that holds bones together at a joint.

muscle   A soft tissue that lengthens and shortens to create movement.

pelvis   The lower part of the trunk containing the intestines, bladder, and reproductive organs.

skeletal muscles   Muscles that attach to bones.

splint A device used to immobilize body parts.

sprain The stretching and tearing of ligaments and other soft tissues at a joint.

strain The stretching and tearing of muscles and tendons.

tendon A fibrous band that attaches muscle to bone.

Bone, muscle, and joint injuries are common. They range from a simple bruise to a severe fracture or dislocation. First aid helps lessen pain and prevent further damage.

Although bone, muscle, and joint injuries are almost always painful, they are rarely life threatening. However, without first aid they can lead to serious problems and even permanent disability. An understanding of the body's framework will help you care for these injuries.

Anatomy and Physiology of Bone, Muscle, and Joint Injuries

The musculoskeletal system is made up of bones that form the skeleton along with muscles, *tendons*,

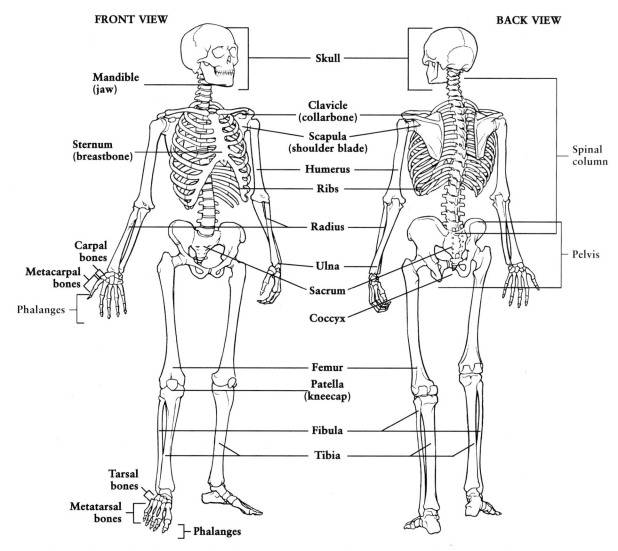

FRONT VIEW

BACK VIEW

Skull

Mandible (jaw)

Clavicle (collarbone)

Scapula (shoulder blade)

Sternum (breastbone)

Humerus

Ribs

Spinal column

Radius

Carpal bones

Metacarpal bones

Ulna

Phalanges

Sacrum

Pelvis

Coccyx

Femur

Patella (kneecap)

Fibula

Tibia

Tarsal bones

Metatarsal bones

Phalanges

Figure 11–1   The bones of the skeleton give the body its shape and protect vital organs.

ligaments, and joints. Together, this system gives the body shape, form, and stability. Bones and muscles work together to make the body parts move.

Skeleton

The skeleton is formed by over 200 bones of various sizes and shapes and makes up the framework on which the body is formed (Figure 11–1). The skeleton protects vital organs and other soft tissues. The skull protects the brain (Figure 11–2, *A*). The ribs protect the heart and lungs (Figure 11–2, *B*). The spinal column protects the spinal cord (Figure 11–2, *C*). Bones that can be seen or felt beneath the skin provide landmarks for locating parts of the body (Figure 11–3).

Bones

Bones are hard, dense, strong tissues. Some bones store and make red blood cells. Bone injuries can bleed and are usually painful. Such bleeding can even become life threatening if not controlled.

Bones have many different sizes and shapes. Bones are weakest at the points where they change shape and therefore usually fracture at these points.

Muscles

Muscles are soft tissues. The body has over 600 muscles (Figure 11–4). Most are *skeletal muscles*, which attach to the bones.

Unlike the other soft tissues, muscles can shorten and lengthen to make body parts move.

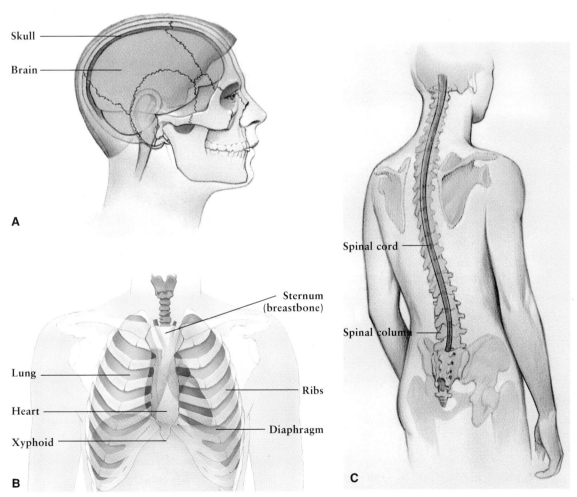

A

Skull
Brain

B

Sternum (breastbone)
Lung
Heart
Xyphoid
Ribs
Diaphragm

C

Spinal cord
Spinal column

Figure 11–2 *A,* The immovable bones of the skull protect the brain. *B,* The rib cage protects the lungs and heart. *C,* The vertebrae protect the spinal cord.

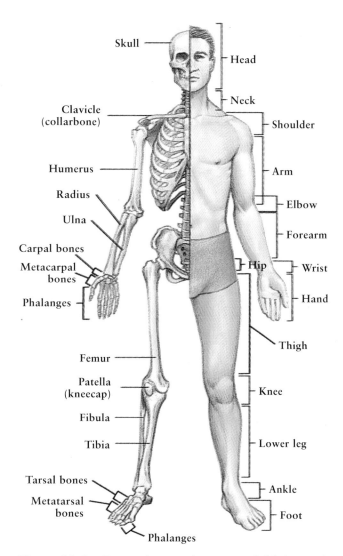

Figure 11–3 Bones that can be seen and felt beneath the skin provide landmarks for locating parts of the body.

Through the nerves, the brain directs muscles to move. Skeletal muscles also protect the bones, nerves, and blood vessels. Most skeletal muscles are attached to bone at each end by tendons. Muscles and their tendons stretch across joints. Injuries to the brain, the spinal cord, or the nerves can affect muscle control.

Joints

A *joint* is formed where two or more bones come together. Most joints allow motion, but some are fused together, such as the bones of the skull, to form solid structures.

Joints are held together by ligaments. All joints have a normal range of movement. When a joint is forced beyond its normal range, ligaments stretch and can tear. Stretched and torn ligaments make the joint unstable and can produce disability. Unstable joints are also reinjured easily and can develop arthritis in later years.

Causes and Types of Bone, Muscle, and Joint Injuries

Musculoskeletal injuries occur in many ways, such as a fall, an awkward or sudden movement, or an automobile collision. There are four basic types of muscle, bone, and joint injuries:

- fracture
- dislocation
- sprain
- strain

Fracture

A *fracture* is a break, chip, or crack in a bone (Figure 11–5). Fractures are usually caused by direct or indirect forces. Strong twisting forces and muscle contractions can also cause a fracture.

An open fracture is one with an open wound. Open fractures often occur when the limb is badly bent, causing bone ends to tear the skin, or when an object pierces the skin and breaks the bone. Closed fractures, which leave the skin unbroken, are more common. Open fractures are more serious because of the risks of infection and blood loss. Although fractures are rarely life threatening, any fracture of a large bone can cause shock because bones and soft tissues are damaged and may bleed heavily.

Fractures are not always obvious, but the amount of force that caused the injury often suggests a possible fracture.

Dislocation

A *dislocation* is a separation of a bone from its normal position at a joint (Figure 11–6). Dislocations are usually caused by strong forces. Some joints, such as the shoulder or fingers, dislocate relatively easily because their bones and ligaments provide less protection.

When bone ends are forced far enough beyond their normal position, ligaments stretch and tear. The strong force causing a dislocation can also cause a fracture and can damage nearby nerves and blood vessels. Dislocations are generally obvious injuries because the joint appears deformed.

Sprain

A *sprain* is the tearing of ligaments at a joint when the bones are forced beyond their normal range of motion (Figure 11–7). The sudden forcing of a joint can completely rupture ligaments and dislocate the bones. The bones may also fracture.

Mild sprains, which only stretch ligaments, generally heal quickly. The casualty may feel pain for a short time and return to activity with little or no soreness. For this reason people often neglect sprains and the joint is often reinjured. Severe sprains usually cause pain when the joint is moved or used. The joints of the ankle, knee, fingers, and wrist are most commonly sprained.

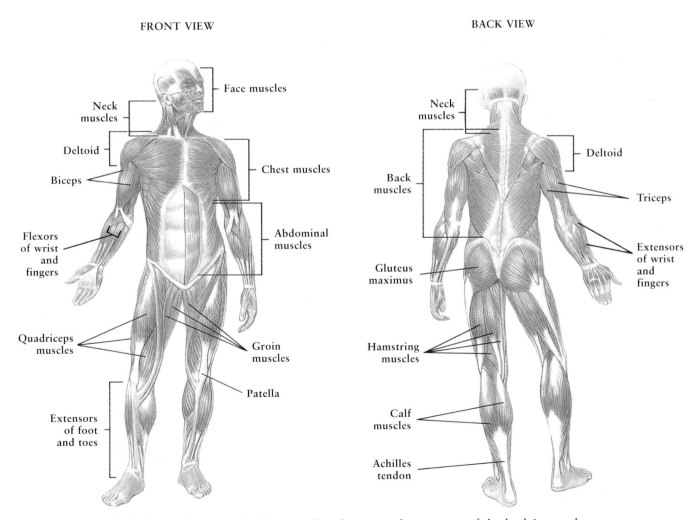

FRONT VIEW   BACK VIEW

Figure 11–4 Skeletal muscles, muscles that attach to bones, make up most of the body's muscles.

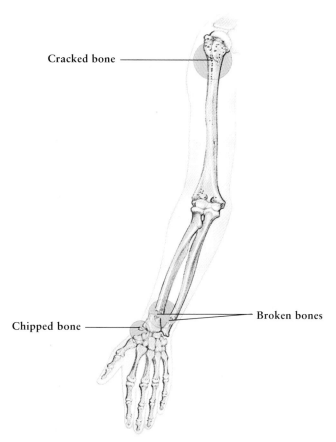

Figure 11–5 Fractures include chipped or cracked bones and bones broken all the way through. Fractures are not always obvious.

A sprain can be more disabling than a fracture. A healed bone stays strong and is no more likely to break again. However, once ligaments are stretched or torn, they can make the joint less stable and more likely to be injured again.

Strain

A *strain* is a stretching and tearing of a muscle or tendon (Figure 11–8). It is sometimes called a "muscle pull" or "tear." Strains often result from lifting something too heavy, working a muscle too hard, or moving suddenly or awkwardly. Strains are common in the neck or back, the front or back of the thigh, or the back of the lower leg. Neck and lower back strains can be very painful.

Like sprains, strains are often neglected, leading to reinjury. Strains can recur chronically, especially in the neck, lower back, and thigh.

Muscle Cramps

Although not an injury, muscle cramps are a type of pain that occurs after heavy exercise or if the

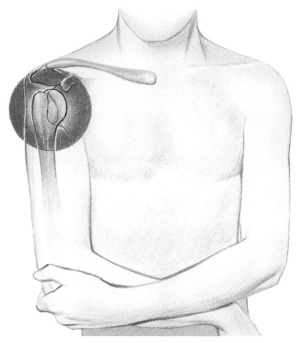

Figure 11–6 A dislocation is a displacement of a bone from its normal position at a joint.

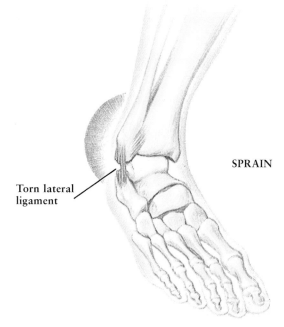

Figure 11–7 A sprain results when bones that form a joint are forced beyond their normal range of motion.

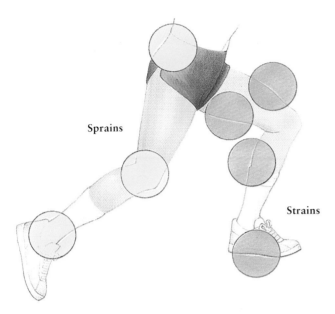

Figure 11–8   Sprains involve the soft tissues at a joint. Strains usually involve the soft tissues stretching between joints.

arm or leg is in the same position for a long time. Stretching and massaging the area, resting, and changing one's position are usually enough for the pain to stop. Heat cramps may feel like muscle cramps but occur when the muscles lose fluids after exercise in the heat (see Chapter 13).

Specific Bone, Muscle, and Joint Injuries

In the upper *extremities*, the wrist, hands, and shoulder are often injured. It is common for a falling person to try to break the fall with an outstretched arm, and the arm receives the force of the body's weight. This can cause a severe sprain, fracture, or dislocation of the hand, wrist, or shoulder, or all three.

Shoulder injuries

The most common shoulder injuries are sprains, but the shoulder may also be fractured or dislocated.

The most frequently injured bone of the shoulder is the collarbone (clavicle). Usually it is

fractured in a fall (Figure 11–9). The casualty usually feels pain in the shoulder area and sometimes down the arm. The person usually tries to ease the pain by holding the arm against the chest (Figure 11–10). Since the collarbone lies over major blood vessels and nerves to the arm, the injured area must be immobilized to prevent further injury.

A shoulder dislocation, often called a shoulder separation, is common. Like fractures, dislocations often result from falls. They happen in sports such as football and rugby when a player attempts to break a fall with an outstretched arm or lands on the point of the shoulder. The impact

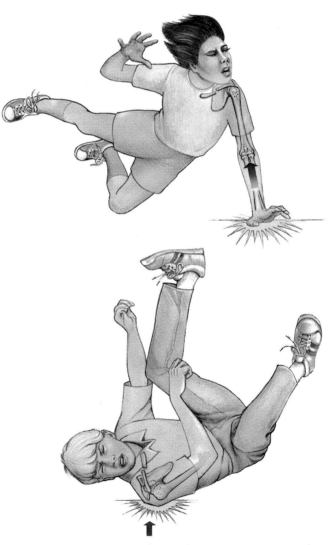

Figure 11–9   A collarbone fracture is commonly caused by a fall.

Figure 11–10   Someone with a fractured collarbone usually supports the arm on the injured side.

can force the arm against the shoulder joint (Figure 11–11), resulting in the tearing of ligaments and the displacement of bones.

Upper arm injuries

The upper arm bone, the humerus, can be fractured at any point. The upper end of the humerus often fractures when elderly persons and young children fall. Breaks in the middle of the bone occur mostly in young adults. The blood vessels and nerves supplying the entire arm may be damaged.

Forearm, wrist, and hand injuries

Fractures of the two forearm bones, the radius and ulna, are more common in children than adults. If a person falls on an outstretched arm, both bones may break, but not always in the same place, making the arm look S-shaped. Such a fracture may cause bleeding or a loss of movement in the wrist and hand.

Wrist sprains and fractures are common, but determining the extent of the injury is often difficult.

Because the hands are used so much, they are very susceptible to injury. Most injuries to the hands and fingers involve only minor damage. However, a serious injury may damage nerves, blood vessels, tendons, ligaments, and bones. Home, recreational, and industrial injuries often cause cuts, burns, and fractures of the hands.

Pelvis injuries

The *pelvis* is the lower part of the trunk and contains the bladder, reproductive organs, and part of the large intestine, including the rectum. It is made up of a group of large bones that form a protective girdle around the organs inside. Major arteries (the femoral arteries) and nerves pass through the pelvis. Injuries to the pelvis may involve bleeding from minor soft tissue injuries or serious injuries to bone and internal structures.

A great force is required to cause serious injury to the pelvis. Pelvic injuries may be caused

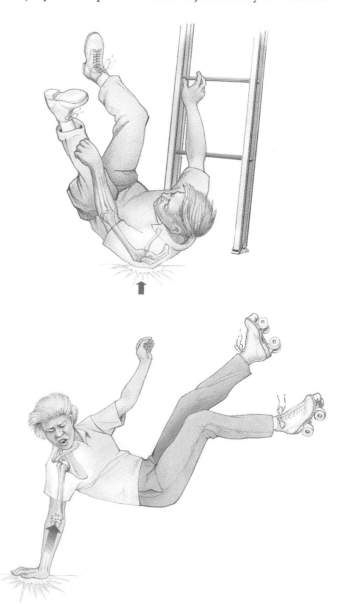

Figure 11–11   Dislocations are often the result of a fall.

by blunt or penetrating forces such as those occurring with falls and automobile crashes. Soft tissue damage, including severe bleeding, may result from punctures or lacerations caused by fractured pelvic bones.

Thigh and lower leg injuries

The femur, or thighbone, is the largest bone in the body and bears most of the weight of the body. Thigh injuries range from bruises and torn muscles to severe injuries such as fractures or dislocations (Figure 11–12). Most femur fractures involve the upper end of the bone at the hip. Even though the hip joint itself is not involved, such injuries are often called hip fractures. Injuries to the leg can be very serious. The femoral artery, the major supplier of blood to the legs, can be damaged by a fracture of the femur, causing a life-threatening blood loss.

Knee injuries

The knee is easily injured. Knee injuries range from cuts and bruises to sprains, fractures, and dislocations. A deep cut in the area of the knee can cause a severe joint infection. Sprains, fractures, and dislocations of the knee are common in sports.

Because the kneecap lies just beneath the skin, it is easily bruised, cut, dislocated, or fractured. Violent forces to the front of the knee, such as those caused by hitting the dashboard of a motor vehicle or by falling and landing on bent knees, can fracture the kneecap.

Ankle and foot injuries

Ankle and foot injuries are commonly caused by twisting forces. Injuries range from minor sprains that heal with rest to fractures and dislocations.

Fractures of the feet and ankles can occur from a twisting and falling injury. Any great

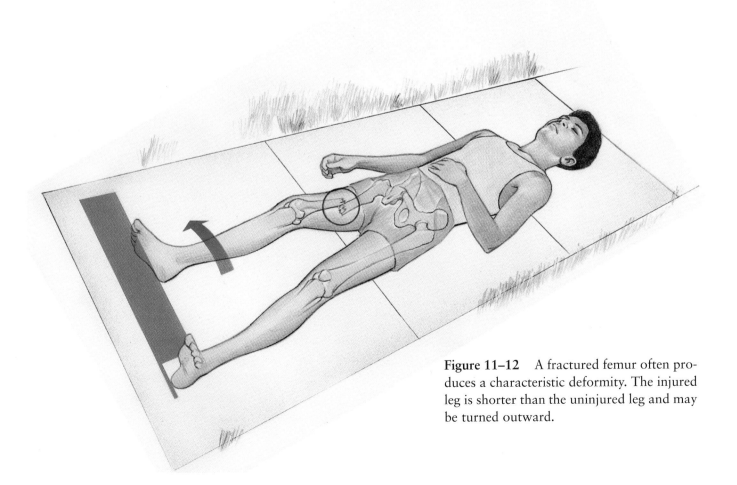

Figure 11–12   A fractured femur often produces a characteristic deformity. The injured leg is shorter than the uninjured leg and may be turned outward.

force, such as something falling and landing on the foot, can cause fractures. The impact of landing hard on the foot may also be sent up the legs and result in an injury elsewhere such as the knee, hip, or spine (Figure 11–13).

PREVENTION

Bone, Muscle, and Joint Injuries

Many of the safety practices listed in Chapters 10 and 15 also apply to the prevention of bone, muscle, and joint injuries. Everyday activities such as driving, playing sports, or working around the house cause most such injuries. Therefore, consider the safety of your everyday activities and environment.

Figure 11–13 In a jump or fall from a height, the impact can be sent up the legs, causing injuries to the knees, hips, or spine.

Exercise is good for the whole musculoskeletal system, in addition to the muscles. An effective exercise program, such as aerobics, jogging, cycling, or walking, strengthens the body and helps prevent injury.

Signs and Symptoms of Bone, Muscle, and Joint Injuries

The following signs and symptoms generally occur in most injuries:

- Pain
- Tenderness
- Swelling
- Inability to use the injured part normally

The following may occur with more severe injuries:

- Discolouration of the skin
- Deformity
- External bleeding
- A feeling of bones grating or a feeling or sound of a snapping at the time of injury

Pain, swelling, and tenderness often occur with any significant injury. Swelling is caused by internal bleeding but by itself is not a sure sign of how severe an injury is. Discolouration is also caused by bleeding in tissues, usually changing from red to a dark red or purple. This usually takes hours to develop.

Deformity includes swelling, abnormal lumps, ridges, depressions, or unusual angles in body parts. Marked deformity is often a sign of fracture or dislocation (Figure 11–14). Comparing the injured part to an uninjured part may help you detect deformity.

The casualty may tell you he or she cannot move or that it is too painful to move. Often the muscles contract to try to hold the injured part in place.

Signs and Symptoms of Sprains and Strains

Sprains or strains are fairly easy to tell apart. With a sprain the pain, swelling, and deformity are generally confined to the joint area. In most strains, pain, swelling, and any deformity are generally in the areas between the joints.

Bone, Muscle, and Joint Injuries

Follow the emergency action principles whenever you suspect a significant bone, muscle, or joint injury:

1. Survey the scene to ensure no danger.
2. Check the casualty for unresponsiveness. If the person does not respond, call EMS.

Figure 11–14   Marked deformity is often a sign of fracture or dislocation.

3. Do a primary survey and care for life-threatening problems (ABCs). Call EMS for help if necessary.
4. Do a secondary survey, if needed, and care for other problems.
5. Keep monitoring the ABCs until EMS arrives.
6. Help the casualty rest in the most comfortable position and give reassurance.

Some bone, muscle, and joint injuries produce protruding bones, bleeding, or great pain. Do not be distracted. Such injuries are rarely life threatening. But be sure to call EMS if:

- The injury involves the head, neck, or back.
- The injury makes walking or breathing difficult.
- You suspect multiple injuries.

General Care

The general care for all bone, muscle, and joint injuries is similar. You do not have to know the specific type of injury. Avoid causing any more pain. Keep the casualty as comfortable as possible. Just remember the acronym RICE:

R - rest
I - immobilize
C - cold
E - elevate

Rest

Avoid any movements that cause pain. Help the casualty find the most comfortable position. If you suspect head, neck, or back injuries, leave the casualty lying flat.

Immobilization

If you suspect a serious injury, you must *immobilize* the injured part before giving additional care such as applying ice or elevating the injured part. If EMS is expected within minutes, keep the person from moving but do not splint the part.

The purposes of immobilizing an injury are to:

- Lessen pain.
- Prevent further damage.
- Reduce the risk of further bleeding.
- Reduce the possibility of loss of circulation to the injured part.
- Prevent closed fractures from becoming open fractures.

You can immobilize an injured part with a *splint,* sling, or *bandages* to keep it from moving. A splint is a device that keeps an injured part in place. An effective splint must extend above and below the injury (Figure 11–15, *A* and *B)*. For instance, to immobilize a fractured bone, the splint must include the joints above and below the fracture. To immobilize a sprain or dislocation, the splint must include the bones above and below the injured joint.

When using a splint, follow these four basic principles:

- Splint only if you can do it without causing more pain to the casualty.
- Splint an injury in the position you find it.
- Splint the injured area and the joints above and below the injury site.
- Check for proper circulation before and after splinting by asking the person if the fingers or toes feel numb and by checking whether the fingers or toes feel warm and are pink in the nailbeds.

Types of Splints. There are three types of splints: soft, rigid, and anatomic. Soft splints include folded blankets, towels, pillows, and slings or bandages (Figure 11–16). A sling is a triangular bandage tied to support an arm, wrist, or hand. A folded triangular bandage can be used to hold dressings or splints in place. A wad of cloth or bandages can serve as effective splints for small body parts such as the hand or fingers (Figure 11–17). Rigid splints include boards, metal strips, and folded magazines or newspapers (Figure 11–18). Anatomic splints use the body itself as a splint. For example, an arm can be splinted to the chest. An injured leg can be splinted to the uninjured leg.

You are unlikely to have commercial splints at hand. If they are available, however, be familiar with them before you use them. Commercial splints include padded board splints, air splints, and specially designed flexible splints (Figure 11–19). Follow these general rules:

1. Support the injured part. If possible, have the casualty or a bystander help you keep movement of the injured part to an absolute minimum (Figure 11–20, *A*).
2. Cover any open wounds with a dressing and bandage to help control bleeding and prevent infection.
3. If using a rigid splint, pad the splint so that it is shaped to the injured part (Figure 11–20, *B*).

Figure 11–15   *A,* To immobilize a bone, splint the joints above and below the fracture. *B,* To immobilize a joint, splint the bones above and below the injured joint.

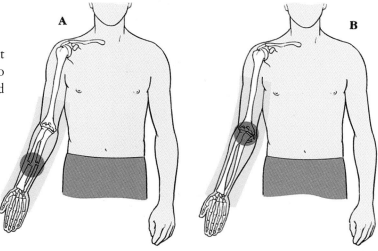

Figure 11–16 Soft splints include a folded blanket, a towel, a pillow, and a sling or bandage.

Figure 11–18 Rigid splints include boards, metal strips, and folded magazines or newspapers.

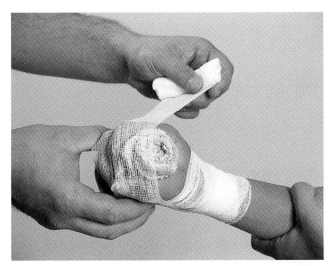

Figure 11–17 A wad of cloth and bandages can effectively splint small body parts.

4. Hold the splint in place with bandages (Figure 11–20, C).
5. Every 15 minutes check to make sure that the splint is not too tight. Loosen the splint if the casualty complains of numbness.

Cold

With all injuries except open fractures, apply ice or a cold pack. Cold helps ease pain and reduce swelling by constricting blood vessels. A general rule for cold application is 15 minutes every hour for the first 24 to 48 hours after the injury.

Figure 11–19 Commercial splints.

Place gauze or cloth between the cold pack and the skin to prevent damage to the skin. You can make an ice pack with ice in a plastic bag wrapped with a cloth. Do not put a cold pack on an open fracture because pressure to the site could cause discomfort. With sprains or strains,

Figure 11–20   *A,* Support the arm above and below the injury site. The casualty can help you. *B,* Pad a rigid splint to conform to the injured body part. *C,* Then secure the splint in place.

once the swelling has gone down (usually 2 or 3 days after the injury) heat may be applied to increase the blood flow and speed healing.

Elevation
Elevating the injured area helps slow the flow of blood, reducing swelling. If possible, raise the injured area above the level of the heart. Do not try to elevate a part you suspect is fractured until it is splinted or if raising the area causes additional pain or discomfort.

Summary of general care
After the injury has been immobilized, recheck the ABCs. Help the casualty rest in the most comfortable position, apply ice or a cold pack, maintain normal body temperature, and provide reassurance. Determine what additional care is needed and whether to call EMS for an ambulance. Continue to note the casualty's level of consciousness, breathing, and skin colour. Watch for signs and symptoms, such as shock, that may indicate the casualty's condition is worsening.

FIRST AID

Specific Injuries

Always first follow the general principles of first aid for all musculoskeletal injuries. The following are additional kinds of first aid for some specific injuries.

Hand injuries
The hand structures are delicate. With deep cuts the hand should be immobilized to prevent further injury. With a suspected finger or thumb dislocation, *do not* attempt to put the bones back into place.

Pelvic injuries
Do not move the casualty unless necessary. If possible, try to keep the casualty lying flat or in a com-

fortable position. Control any external bleeding and cover any protruding organs. If you suspect a spinal injury, do not move the casualty. Always call EMS. Take steps to minimize shock, and help the casualty maintain normal body temperature. Continue to monitor the ABCs until EMS arrives.

A pelvic injury may involve the genitals, the external reproductive organs. Any injury to the genitals is extremely painful. Care for the wound as you would for any other. Injuries to the genital area can be embarrassing for both the casualty and the rescuer. Explain briefly what you are going to do, and do it. Acting in a timid or hesitant manner will only make the situation more difficult.

Thigh and lower leg injuries

A fracture in the lower leg may involve one or both bones. Because they lie just beneath the skin, open fractures are common (Figure 11–21). Lower leg fractures may cause a severe deformity in which the lower leg is bent at an unusual angle, as well as pain and inability to move the leg. In such cases, if the casualty's leg is supported by the ground, do not move it. Help the casualty rest in the most comfortable position. A fractured thighbone can injure the femoral artery, and serious bleeding can result. Therefore, be sure EMS is called, carefully monitor vital signs, and watch for shock developing.

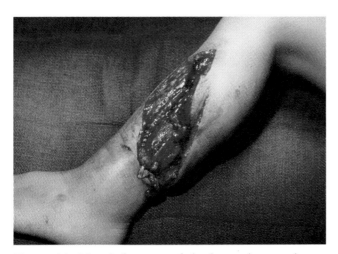

Figure 11–21 A fracture of the lower leg can be an open fracture.

Knee injuries

As with all bone injuries, help the casualty rest in the most comfortable position. If the knee is bent and cannot be straightened without pain, support it in the bent position (Figure 11–22). If the knee is straight or can be straightened without pain, secure it to the uninjured leg as you might do for an injury of the thigh or lower leg. Apply ice or a cold pack. Call EMS to have the casualty transported to a medical facility.

Ankle and foot injuries

You should care for all ankle and foot injuries as if they are serious. Use a bulky rolled blanket or pillow to hold the injured part steady. As with other lower extremity injuries, if the ankle or foot is painful to move, if it cannot bear weight, or if the foot or ankle is swollen, a doctor should see the injury.

Considerations for Transporting a Casualty

If you think the emergency is life threatening, do not transport the casualty yourself: call EMS immediately. Some injuries are not serious enough for EMS but may still require a doctor's care. If you transport the casualty yourself, splint the injury before moving the casualty. See Chapters 2 and 8 for more detailed information on moving a casualty.

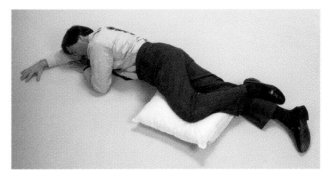

Figure 11–22 Support a knee injury in the bent position if the casualty cannot straighten the knee.

Summary

- Since it is hard to tell the type and severity of a bone, muscle, or joint injury, always care for it as if it is serious.

- If EMS is on the way, do not move the casualty.

- Always follow the emergency action principles. Control any bleeding, minimize pain and shock, and monitor the ABCs.

- Remember **RICE**: help the casualty Rest, Immobilize the injured part, apply Cold or ice to the injured area, and Elevate the injured area.

Soft Tissue Injuries

12

Objectives

After reading this chapter, you should be able to:

1. List two signs of closed wounds.
2. Describe how to prevent infection of an open wound.
3. List at least four signs and symptoms of an infected wound.
4. Describe how to care for an infected wound.
5. List two purposes of bandaging.
6. Describe how to care for open and closed wounds and wounds with an impaled object.
7. Describe first aid for bleeding in the abdomen.
8. List the four causes of burn injury.
9. List situations when to call EMS for a burn injury.
10. Describe the care of the three types of burns caused by heat.
11. Describe how to care for burns caused by chemicals or electricity.
12. Describe first aid for frostbite.
13. Define the key terms for this chapter.

Key Terms

abdomen   The middle part of the trunk containing the stomach, intestines, liver, spleen, and other organs.

bandage   Material used to wrap or cover a wound or to hold a dressing or splint in place.

burn   An injury caused by heat, chemicals, electricity, or radiation.

closed wound   A wound with damaged soft tissues beneath the skin but the skin is not broken.

dressing   A pad placed directly over a wound to absorb blood and other body fluids and to prevent infection.

first degree burn   A superficial burn of only the top layer of skin; the skin will look red and dry.

frostbite   A serious condition in which body tissues such as the fingers, toes, ears, and nose freeze.

open wound   A wound with a break in the skin.

second degree burn   A partial-thickness burn through both layers of skin; the skin may blister and look red and wet.

After reading this chapter and completing the class activities, you should be able to:

1. Demonstrate how to care for a major open wound.

2. Decide what care to give in an example of an emergency situation involving soft tissue injuries.

soft tissue The layers of skin, fat, muscles, and other body soft structures.

third degree burn A full-thickness burn through both layers of skin and the tissues below them; skin may be charred.

wound An injury to soft tissues.

Bruises, cuts, and burns are all soft tissue injuries that occur daily. Most soft tissue injuries are minor, needing only an adhesive bandage or ice and rest. However, some are more severe and need prompt medical attention. This chapter describes how to recognize and care for the most common injuries—soft tissue injuries.

Anatomy and Physiology of Soft Tissues

The *soft tissues* include the layers of skin, fat, and muscles that protect the underlying body structures (Figure 12–1). The skin is the body's largest single organ. It protects the body, helps control body temperature, and senses the environment through nerve endings.

The skin has two layers. The outer layer, the epidermis, blocks germs that can cause infection. The deeper layer, the dermis, contains nerves, sweat and oil glands, and many blood vessels. Most soft tissue injuries are painful and are likely to bleed. Under the skin is a layer of fat. This layer helps maintain body temperature. The muscles are under the fat layer.

Most soft tissue injuries involve the outer layers. However, powerful forces can damage all the soft tissue layers.

Causes and Types of Soft Tissue Injuries

A soft tissue injury is called a *wound*. A wound is a *closed wound* when the soft tissue damage occurs under the skin, leaving the outer layer unbroken. A wound is an *open wound* if there is a break in the skin's outer layer.

Burns are a special kind of soft tissue injury. A burn occurs when intense heat, certain chemicals, electricity, or radiation touches the skin.

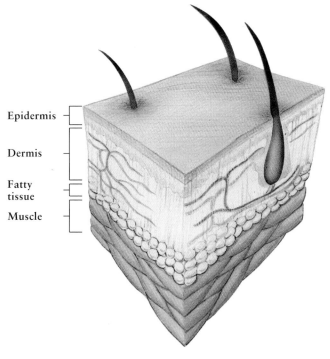

Epidermis

Dermis

Fatty tissue

Muscle

Figure 12–1 The soft tissues include the layers of skin, fat, and muscle.

First degree burns damage only the outer layer of skin. *Second degree burns* damage both layers of skin. *Third degree burns* go through the layers of skin and damage other soft tissues and even bone.

Closed Wounds

Closed wounds are more common than open wounds. The simplest closed wound is a bruise, also called a *contusion* (Figure 12–2). Bruises result when some force impacts the body, such as when you bump your leg on a table. This impact can damage soft tissue layers and vessels beneath the skin, causing internal bleeding. When blood and other fluids seep into nearby tissues, the area discolours and swells. At first, the area may only look red. As more fluid leaks into the area, it turns dark red or purple. Violent forces can cause more severe soft tissue injuries involving larger blood vessels and the deeper layers of muscle. These injuries can result in heavy bleeding beneath the skin.

Open Wounds

Open wounds are injuries that break the skin. They can be as minor as a scrape or as severe as a deep penetrating wound. Any break in the skin can let in microbes.

There are four main types of open wounds:

- Abrasions
- Lacerations
- Avulsions
- Punctures

With an abrasion, the most common open wound, the skin is rubbed or scraped away (Figure 12–3). This type often occurs when a child falls and scrapes his or her hands or knees. The scraping exposes nerve endings and usually causes pain. Bleeding is light and easily controlled. Dirt and other matter can be rubbed into the skin, making it important to clean the wound and to remove all visible dirt.

A laceration is a cut with jagged or smooth edges (Figure 12–4). This type is commonly caused by sharp-edged objects, such as knives or broken glass, or blunt forces that split the skin. Deep lacerations can damage layers of fat and muscle. Lacerations usually bleed freely.

With an avulsion a piece of skin and sometimes other soft tissue is torn away (Figure 12–5). A partly avulsed piece of skin may remain attached like a flap. Bleeding is usually heavy if deeper soft tissue layers are involved. Sometimes

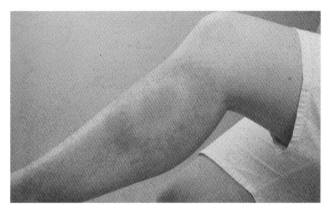

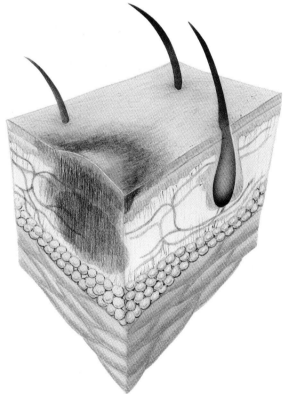

Figure 12–2   The simplest closed wound is a bruise (also called a contusion).

a force is so great that a body part, such as a finger, may be cut off. In such cases bleeding is usually not as bad as you might expect because the blood vessels contract to slow bleeding. Surgeons can sometimes reattach the severed body part.

A puncture wound occurs when the skin is pierced with a pointed object such as a nail, piece of glass, splinter, or bullet (Figure 12–6). Because the skin usually closes, external bleeding is not heavy, but internal bleeding can be very serious. An object that remains stuck in the open wound is called an impaled object (Figure 12–7). An object may also pass clear through a body part, making wounds at both the entry and the exit points. Puncture wounds can be dangerous because they easily become infected. Objects cutting into the soft tissues carry germs, such as tetanus. Tetanus produces a powerful poison that affects the nervous system and muscles. For example, jaw muscles will tighten, causing "lockjaw." Though not common, tetanus can cause disability and even death.

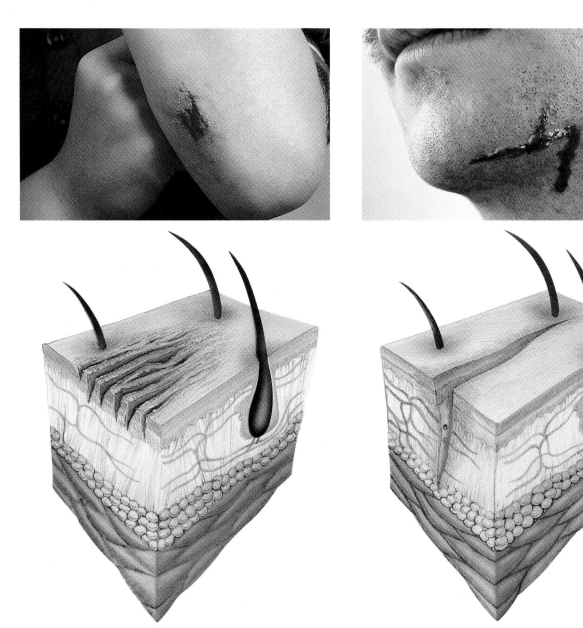

Figure 12–3   Abrasions can be painful, but bleeding is easily controlled.

Figure 12–4   A laceration may have jagged or smooth edges.

PREVENTION

Soft Tissue Injuries

Many soft tissue injuries can be prevented. There are three general ways to prevent injuries:

- People can think about safety and change their behaviour. They can avoid dangerous conditions or activities. They can wear appropriate protective gear—helmets, padding, and eyewear—and buckle up when driving or riding in motor vehicles (see also Chapter 15).
- Laws such as those requiring the use of seat belts and occupational safety regulations can change dangerous conditions and behaviour.
- Product and environmental safeguards, such as airbags in cars, can prevent injuries without people having to change their habits.

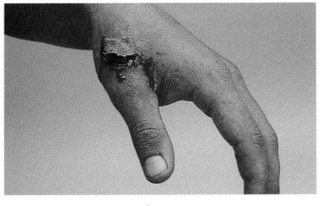

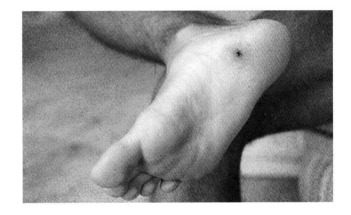

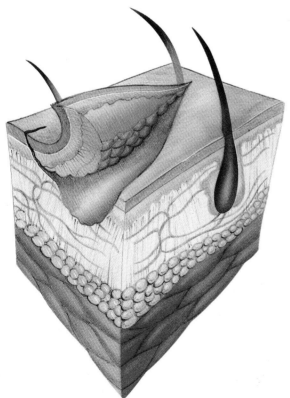

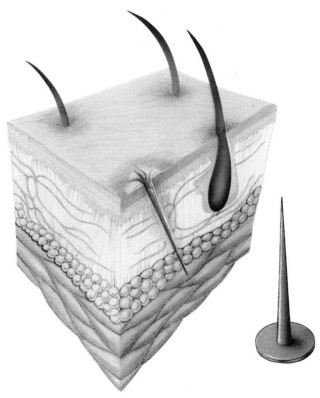

Figure 12–5 In an avulsion, part of the skin and other soft tissue are torn away.

Figure 12–6 A puncture wound results when skin is pierced by a pointed object.

Preventing Infection

When an injury breaks the skin, you must try to prevent infection. The best first defence is to clean the area. For wounds not bleeding heavily, wash the area with soap and water. Most soaps remove harmful bacteria. You do not need to wash wounds that require medical attention because you may cause greater tissue damage or bleeding and because medical professionals will do the cleansing when they treat the casualty. If you expect a long delay before obtaining medical aid, you should clean the wound.

Always be sure to wash your hands after giving first aid, and wear gloves whenever possible when coming in contact with a casualty's body fluids. For additional information, see also Chapter 2 on prevention of infections.

Infections can be prevented with current immunizations. Immunizations help the immune system defend against infections, such as tetanus. Getting a tetanus booster shot is recommended every 5 to 10 years.

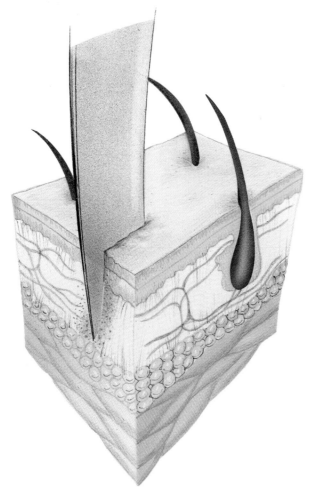

Figure 12–7   An impaled object remains stuck in a wound.

Signs and Symptoms of Soft Tissue Injuries

The signs and symptoms of serious soft tissue injuries include:

- Heavy bleeding
- Damage to deep layers of body tissue
- Severe swelling or discolouration
- Severe pain or the casualty's inability to move a body part

You can easily recognize the first signs and symptoms of infection that may develop one or two days after the injury:

- The area around the wound becomes swollen, red, and warm.
- The area may throb with pain.
- Some wounds have a pus discharge (Figure 12–8).

Serious infections may cause a person to develop a fever and feel ill. You may see red streaks in the skin progressing from the wound.

Soft Tissue Injuries

First Aid for Closed Wounds

Most minor closed wounds do not require special medical care. Direct pressure on the area decreases bleeding. Elevating the injured part helps

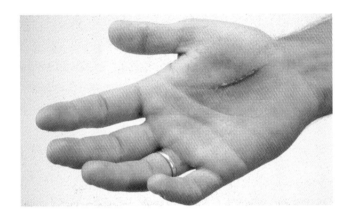

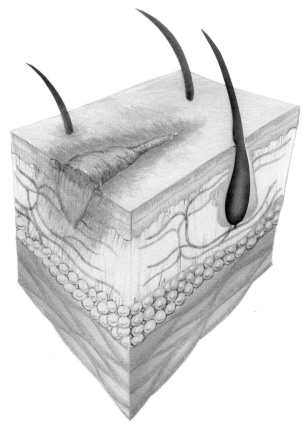

Figure 12–8 An infected wound may become swollen and may have a pus discharge.

reduce swelling. Cold can help control both pain and swelling. When using ice or a chemical cold pack, place a gauze pad, towel, or other cloth between the ice and the skin. Apply the cold for 15 minutes every hour as long as the pain persists.

Remember that a closed wound might be more than "just a bruise." Consider possible serious injuries to internal organs or muscles. Take the time to see whether more serious injuries could be present. If a person feels severe pain or cannot move a body part without pain or if you think the force that caused the injury was great enough to cause serious damage, seek medical attention immediately. Care for these injuries is described in previous chapters.

First Aid for Major Open Wounds

A major open wound is one with severe bleeding, with deep tissue damage, or with an impaled object. Severe bleeding can be life threatening and should be controlled in the primary survey (see Chapter 8).

Follow the emergency action principles whenever you suspect a significant open wound.

1. Survey the scene to ensure no danger.
2. Check the casualty for unresponsiveness. If the person does not respond, call EMS.
3. Do a primary survey and care for life-threatening problems (ABCs). Call EMS for help if necessary.
4. Do a secondary survey, if needed, and care for other problems.
5. Keep monitoring the ABCs until EMS arrives.
6. Help the casualty rest in the most comfortable position and give reassurance.

Give the following additional first aid for a major open wound:

1. Do not waste time trying to wash the wound but attempt to control the bleeding. Remember the acronym RED for **R**est, **E**levation, and **D**irect pressure.

2. Use a sterile dressing or any clean covering such as a towel or handkerchief to put pressure on the wound to stop the bleeding. If no pad or cloth is available, have the injured person use his or her hand. As a last resort, use your own gloved hand.

3. If a body part has been completely cut off, try to find the body part. Wrap the part in sterile gauze or any clean material such as a washcloth. Place the wrapped part in a plastic bag. If possible, keep the part cool by placing the bag on ice. Make sure the part is taken to the medical facility with the casualty.

If the casualty has an impaled object in the wound that is bleeding, follow these additional guidelines:

1. *Do not* remove the object.
2. Use bulky dressings to stabilize it. Any movement of the object can result in further tissue damage (Figure 12–9, *A*).
3. Control bleeding by bandaging the dressings in place around the object (Figure 12–9, *B*).

Dressings and Bandages

All open wounds need a covering to help control bleeding and prevent infection. These coverings are called *dressings* and *bandages*.

Dressings

Dressings are pads put on the wound to absorb blood and other fluids and prevent infection. Commercial sterile dressings are best. Most let air reach the wound to promote healing. Standard dressings include cotton gauze in various sizes. Dressings with nonstick surfaces are useful for moist wounds.

Bandages

A bandage is any material you can use to wrap or cover a body part. Bandages are used to hold dressings in place, to control bleeding, to protect a wound from dirt and infection, to support an injured limb or body part, and to apply pressure to a wound. Many types, shapes, and sizes of bandages are available.

In emergencies when sterile commercial dressings and bandages are not available, you can improvise with clean towels or other material such as clothing.

To use bandages to control bleeding, follow these general guidelines (see Chapter 8 for more detailed information):

1. If you can, elevate the injured body part above the level of the heart.
2. When bandaging an arm or leg, do not cover

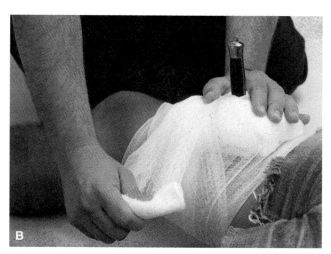

Figure 12–9   *A*, Use a bulky dressing to support an impaled object. *B*, Use bandages over the dressing to control bleeding.

fingers or toes unless you must. By checking these parts, you can see if the bandage is too tight. If fingers or toes become cold or numb or begin to turn pale or blue, loosen the bandage slightly. Note that elastic bandages can block blood flow if not used properly.

3. If blood soaks through the bandage, use more dressings and another bandage. *Do not* remove the blood-soaked ones.

First Aid for Minor Open Wounds

A minor wound is one, such as an abrasion, in which damage is only on the surface and bleeding is light. To care for a minor wound, follow these general guidelines:

- Wash the wound with soap and water.
- Place a sterile dressing or bandage over the wound and bandage it.

Stitches needed?

A major wound should always be seen by a doctor, but you may have to decide when a minor wound should be seen by a doctor for stitches. Stitches are usually needed for face and hand lacerations when the edges of skin do not fall together or for any wound longer than 1 to 2 cm (1/2 to 1 inch). Stitches speed healing, decrease chances of infection, and help prevent scarring. The doctor should place them as soon as possible after the injury.

First Aid for Infection

If you see signs of infection developing in a wound, care for it by keeping the area clean, applying warm, wet compresses and an antibiotic ointment, and seek medical care immediately.

First Aid for Bleeding in the Abdomen

Most injuries to the *abdomen* involve only soft tissues. Often these injuries are only minor cuts, scrapes, and bruises that can be cared for with the usual first aid for minor external bleeding. Severe injuries can cause severe bleeding or impair breathing.

Because the abdomen contains many organs important to life, injury to this area can be fatal. These internal organs are not as protected as some other body areas (Figure 12–10). Most important are the organs that are easily injured or tend to bleed profusely when injured, such as the liver and spleen.

The liver is very rich in blood. It is delicate and can be torn by blows from blunt objects or penetrated by a fractured rib. The resulting bleeding can be severe and can be fatal. The spleen may rupture when the abdomen is struck forcefully by a blunt object. Since the spleen stores blood, an injury can cause a severe loss of blood in a short time and can be life threatening.

Abdominal injuries often occur in motor vehicle collisions to occupants not wearing seat belts. Falls, sports mishaps, and other forms of trauma may also cause such injuries.

The following are the signs and symptoms of abdominal injuries:

- Severe pain
- Bruising
- External bleeding
- Nausea
- Vomiting (sometimes vomit containing blood)
- Weakness
- Pain, tenderness, or a tight feeling in the abdomen

Bleeding in the abdomen can be external or internal. Even if you see no bleeding, the rupture of an organ can cause serious internal bleeding that results in shock. Injuries to the abdomen can be very painful. Serious reactions can occur if organs leak blood or other contents into the abdomen.

For any abdominal injury, follow the emergency action principles. Call EMS immediately and try to minimize shock. Maintain normal body temperature. Give the following additional first aid for external bleeding:

1. Carefully position the casualty on the back.
2. *Do not* apply direct pressure.
3. *Do not* push back into the abdomen any organs that may be protruding from the wound.
4. Remove clothing from around wound.

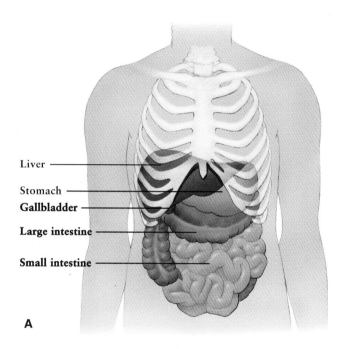

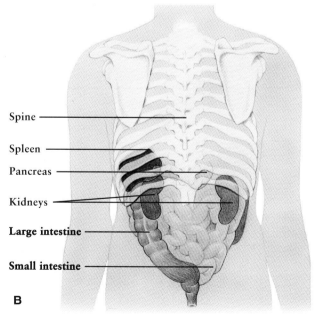

Figure 12–10 Unlike the organs of the chest or pelvis, organs in the abdominal cavity are relatively unprotected by bones.

5. Apply moist, sterile dressings loosely over an open wound. (Warm tap water can be used.)

FIRST AID

Nosebleeds

The nose has many blood vessels that can be easily damaged. Some may bleed extensively. Usually the blood comes out the nostrils, but it may drain to the back of the throat and cause choking or vomiting.

Nose injuries are usually caused by a blow from a blunt object. The result is often a nosebleed. High blood pressure or changes in altitude can also cause nosebleeds.

Give the following first aid for a nosebleed:

1. Have the casualty sit with the head slightly forward while pinching the nostrils together for 10–15 minutes (Figure 12–11).
2. Once you have controlled the bleeding, tell the casualty to avoid rubbing, blowing, or picking the nose, since this could restart the bleeding.
3. Later, you may apply a little petroleum jelly inside the nostril to help keep it from drying out.

Figure 12–11 To control a nosebleed, have the casualty lean forward and pinch the nostrils together until bleeding stops.

4. Seek medical care if the bleeding still continues after using this technique, if bleeding recurs, or if the casualty says the bleeding is the result of high blood pressure.

5. If the casualty loses consciousness, place the casualty in the recovery position to allow blood to drain from the nose. Call EMS immediately.

6. If you think an object is in the nostril, look into the nostril. If you can easily grasp an object, then do so. However, do not probe the nostril with your finger. Doing so may push the object farther into the nose and cause bleeding or make it more difficult to remove later. If you cannot remove the object easily, the casualty should get medical care.

Burns

Anatomy and Physiology of Burns

Burns are a soft tissue injury usually caused by heat but also by chemicals, electricity, or radiation such as with sunburn.

Burns first destroy the top layer of skin, the epidermis. If the burn progresses, the dermis layer is also injured. Burns break the skin and thus can cause infection, fluid loss, and loss of temperature control. Deep burns can damage underlying tissues. Burns can also damage the respiratory system and the eyes.

The severity of a burn depends on
- The temperature involved.
- The cause of the burn: heat, chemicals, electricity, or radiation.
- The length of exposure to the source.
- The location of the burn.
- The extent of the burn.
- The casualty's age and medical condition. In general, people over 60, children under 5, and people with chronic medical problems do not tolerate burns as well as other people.

Causes and Types of Burns

Burns are classified by their causes and their deepness: first degree (superficial), second degree (partial thickness), and third degree (full thickness). The deeper the burn, the more severe it is.

First degree burns
A first degree burn damages only the top layer of skin (Figure 12–12). The skin is red and dry, and

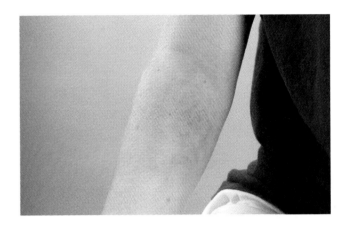

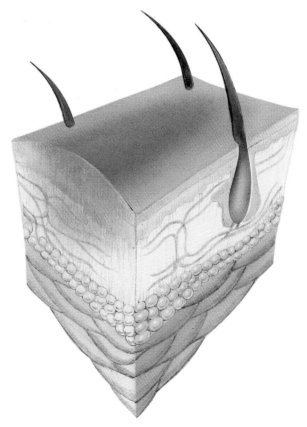

Figure 12–12   A first degree burn.

the burn is usually painful. The area may swell. Most sunburns are first degree burns. First degree burns generally heal in 5 to 6 days without permanent scarring.

Second degree burns

A second degree burn damages both layers of skin—the epidermis and the dermis (Figure 12–13). Heat or very severe sunburn or chemical burns can cause second degree burns. The skin is red and has blisters that may open and leak clear fluid, making the skin appear wet. The burned skin may look patchy. These burns are usually painful, and the area often swells. The burn usually heals in 3 or 4 weeks. Scarring may occur.

Third degree burns

A third degree burn destroys both layers of skin, as well as any or all of the underlying structures—nerves, blood vessels, fat, muscles, and bones (Figure 12–14). Severe heat or fire and electrical burns or lightning can cause third degree burns. These burns can look either charred

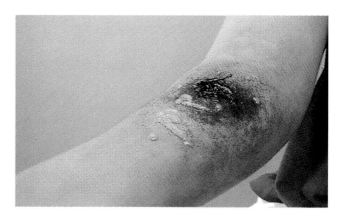

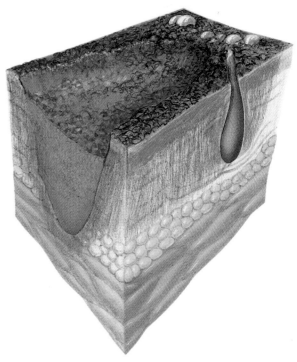

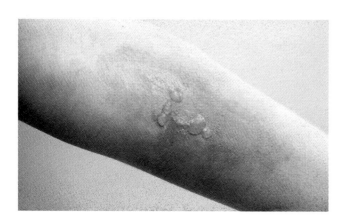

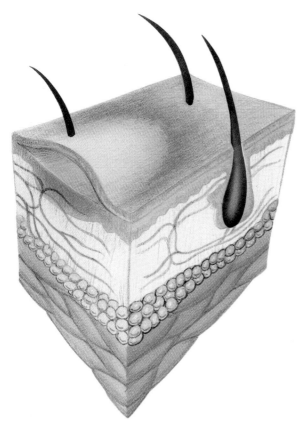

Figure 12–13   A second degree burn.

Figure 12–14   A third degree burn.

(black) or waxy white. They are usually painless because the burn destroys the nerve endings in the skin. Third degree burns can be life threatening if extensive because of the fluid loss that leads to shock. Infection also is likely. Scarring occurs and may be severe. Many third degree burns require skin grafts.

PREVENTION

Burns

Preventing burns starts with preventing fires. Follow these guidelines and see Chapter 15 for more on fire safety:

- Keep matches away from children. Never leave children alone without proper adult care and attention.
- Keep storage areas clear of materials that could catch fire.
- Never store gasoline or other highly flammable liquids indoors.
- Cook on the stove with pot handles turned in and use only the back burners when possible.
- Keep the hot water tank temperature turned down to 49° Celsius (120° F).
- Do not put water on a grease fire.
- Do not spray aerosol cans near an open flame.
- Be sure your fireplace has a sturdy metal screen. Never leave paper, fabrics, or any other material that could catch fire near the fireplace.

Follow these guidelines to prevent electrical burns:

- Never use electrical appliances near water.
- Repair or discard frayed cords.
- If you have young children, cover electrical outlets with safety caps.

The sun can damage the skin as well as cause burns. Too much sun over long periods can also cause skin cancer and early aging. Follow these guidelines to prevent sunburn:

- Avoid exposure to the sun between 10:00 AM and 3:00 PM.
- Wear proper clothing to prevent over-exposure.
- Use sun screen with a sun protection factor (SPF) of 25.

Finally, prevent lightning strike burns with these guidelines when a thunderstorm threatens:

- Go inside a building or home.
- Get inside a car and roll up the windows.
- Stop swimming or boating and get away from the water as soon as you see or hear a storm. Water conducts electricity.
- Stay away from the telephone, except in an emergency.
- Stay away from telephone poles and tall trees if you are caught outside.
- Stay off hilltops; try to crouch down in a ravine or valley.
- Stay away from farm equipment and small metal vehicles such as motorcycles, bicycles, and golf carts.
- Stay away from wire fences, clotheslines, metal pipes and rails, and other conductors.
- Stay several yards apart if you are in a group.

FIRST AID

Burns

Even after the heat is removed, soft tissue will continue to burn for a few minutes afterwards, causing more damage. Therefore, you need to cool any burned area right away with large amounts of cool water. Do not use ice or ice water. Immerse the body part in cool water or let water flow over the area. You can apply soaked towels, sheets, or other wet cloths to an area that cannot be immersed. Cooling minor burns can prevent blisters from developing, and cooling can help minimize the damage with more serious burns.

Do not try to judge how bad the burn is by how much pain the casualty feels because nerve endings may be destroyed. Most burns should be evaluated by a doctor. Call EMS immediately in these situations:

- Burns that make it hard for the casualty to breathe
- Burns covering more than one body part
- Burns resulting from chemicals, explosions, or electricity

First aid for first degree burns

For minor burns that do not require medical attention, care for the burned area as an open wound. Wash it with soap and water and keep it clean. Keep the area cool with water. Once the burning has stopped, you can apply an antibiotic ointment and watch for signs and symptoms of infection. Your pharmacist or doctor can suggest products for superficial burns such as sunburn.

First aid for second and third degree burns

Follow the emergency action principles whenever you suspect a serious burn.

1. Survey the scene to ensure no danger.
2. Check the casualty for unresponsiveness. If the person does not respond, call EMS.
3. Do a primary survey and care for life-threatening problems (ABCs). Call EMS for help if necessary.
4. Do a secondary survey, if needed, and care for other problems.
5. Keep monitoring the ABCs until EMS arrives.
6. Help the casualty rest in the most comfortable position and give reassurance.

Follow these guidelines for additional first aid for serious burns:

1. Pay close attention to the airway. Burns around the mouth or nose may indicate that the air passages or lungs have been burned (Figure 12–15). If you suspect a burned airway or burned lungs, keep checking breath-ing. Air passages may swell, making it difficult for the casualty to breath.

2. As you do a secondary survey, look for more indications of burn injuries. Look also for other injuries, especially if an explosion or electric shock occurred.
3. Cool the burned area with water but do not try to clean it. Continue to cool the area until the burning or pain stops. Never apply ice directly to second or third degree burns. If the burn involves a large part of the body, do not try to cool it because this may lower the casualty's body temperature. Do not put any kind of grease or ointment on serious burns because these seal in heat and do not relieve pain well. Some home cures like butter or oil can cause infection.
4. Cover the burned area to keep out air, help reduce pain, and prevent infection. Use dry, non-stick, sterile dressings and loosely bandage them in place.
5. Do not break blisters. Intact skin helps prevent infection.
6. Third degree burns can cause shock. Have the casualty lie down unless he or she is having difficulty breathing. Elevate burned areas above the level of the heart, if possible. Burn casualties often feel chilled. Help maintain body temperature by protecting against drafts.

Table 12–1 summarizes the care for burns.

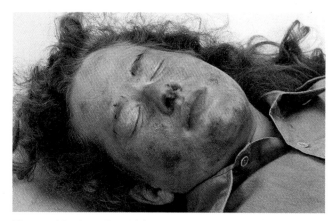

Figure 12–15 Facial burns may suggest that air passages or lungs have been burned.

Table 12–1	Dos and Don'ts of Burn Care

Dos
- Do cool burns by flushing with cool water, or cool cloths in the absence of running water.
- Do cover the burn with a dry, sterile dressing.

Don'ts
- Don't apply ice directly to second or third degree burns.
- Don't touch burns with anything except sterile or clean dressings; do not use absorbent cotton or pull clothes over any burned area.
- Don't remove pieces of cloth that stick to a burned area.
- Don't try to clean a third degree burn.
- Don't break blisters.
- Don't use any kind of grease or ointment on severe burns.

First aid for chemical burns

Chemical burns can occur in both industrial settings and the home. A chemical burn may be caused by household bleach, drain cleaners, toilet bowl cleaners, paint stripper, and lawn or garden chemicals. The chemical keeps burning as long as it is on the skin. Therefore, wash it from the body as quickly as possible. Call the poison centre for further instructions, and they will help you decide if you need to call EMS.

1. Flush the burn with large amounts of cool, running water. Continue flushing until EMS arrives. Do not use a forceful flow of water from a hose because this may further damage burned skin.
2. Have the casualty remove clothes that were in contact with the chemical.
3. Do not forget the eyes. If an eye is burned by a chemical, flush the eye for 15 minutes or until EMS arrives (Figure 12–16). Make sure the water flows from the bridge of the nose outward.

First aid for electrical burns

An electrical current running through the body produces heat that can cause a burn (Figure

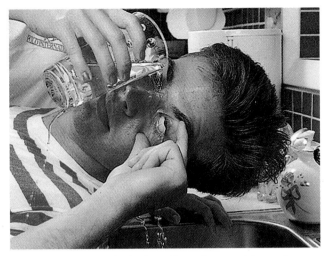

Figure 12–16   Flush the affected eye with cool water in the case of a chemical burn to the eye.

12–17). These burns may appear minor but in fact are very severe, because the tissues below the skin may be severely damaged. Electrical burns are often deep. The casualty will have both an entrance and an exit wound where the electricity entered and left the body.

Electrical incidents cause problems in addition to burns. Electricity can make the heart beat unevenly or even stop. The casualty may stop breathing.

The signs and symptoms of electrical injury include:

- The sound of a sudden loud pop or an unexpected flash of light

Figure 12–17   An electrical burn may severely damage underlying tissues.

- Evidence of exposed power sources nearby
- Unconsciousness
- Dazed, confused behaviour
- Obvious burns on the skin surface
- Breathing difficulty
- Weak, irregular, or absent signs of circulation
- Burns both where the current entered and where it exited, often on the hand or foot

To care for an electrical or lightning burn, always follow the emergency action principles. Also give this specific care:

1. Never approach a casualty of an electrical injury until you are sure the power is turned off. If there is a downed power line, *wait for the fire department and the power company*. If people are in a car with a downed wire across it, tell them to stay in the vehicle.
2. In the primary survey, watch carefully for breathing difficulties or sudden cardiac arrest.
3. In the secondary survey, don't forget the exit wound: look for two burn sites. Cover burned areas with a moist, sterile dressing.
4. A casualty of lightning may also have fractures, including spinal fracture, so do not move him or her. Any burns are a lesser problem.

First aid for radiation burns

Solar radiation and other types of radiation can cause burns. Solar burns are similar to heat burns. Usually they are mild but can be painful (Figure 12–18). They may blister and involve both layers of skin. Care for sunburns like other burns. Cool the area and protect it from further damage from the sun. People are rarely exposed to other types of radiation unless working in special settings such as certain medical, industrial, or research settings.

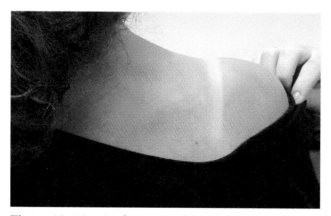

Figure 12–18   Sunburns can be painful.

Frostbite

Frostbite is a type of cold emergency occurring in specific body parts exposed to the cold. It is the freezing of body tissues. In superficial frostbite the skin is frozen but not the tissues below. In deep frostbite both the skin and underlying tissues are frozen. Both types of frostbite are serious. The water in and between the body's cells freezes and swells. The ice crystals and swelling damage or destroy the cells. Frostbite can lead to the loss of fingers, hands, toes, and feet.

Causes of Frostbite

Frostbite is caused by exposure to the cold to the point that the body cannot keep itself or all parts warm. Air temperature, the humidity, and wind all affect how the body maintains its temperature and how much exposure is needed before a body part suffers frostbite.

PREVENTION

Frostbite

Frostbite can usually be prevented with common sense and the following guidelines:

- Avoid exposing any part of the body to the cold in the coldest part of the day.
- Wear a hat and layers of clothing made of tightly woven fibers, such as wool, that trap warm air against your body. Keep vulnerable areas such as the fingers, toes, ears, and nose protected and covered.

- Drink plenty of warm fluids to help the body maintain its temperature. If hot drinks are not available, drink plenty of plain water. Avoid caffeine and alcohol, which hinder the body's heat-producing mechanisms.
- Take frequent breaks from the cold to let your body warm up to better withstand brief periods of exposure to extreme cold.

Signs and Symptoms of Frostbite

Depending on the circumstances and how long the casualty is exposed to the cold, frostbite may occur by itself or along with hypothermia, which is the cooling of the whole body rather than the freezing of a specific part (see Chapter 13). The following are the signs and symptoms of frostbite:

- Lack of feeling in the affected area
- Skin that appears waxy
- Skin that is cold to the touch
- Skin that is discoloured (flushed, white, yellow, blue)

FIRST AID

Frostbite

If the casualty shows signs of both frostbite and hypothermia, give first aid first for the hypothermia (Chapter 13) because it can lead to death if the person is not warmed immediately. Even in this case do not ignore frostbite, which, if serious, can require the amputation of the affected part. Follow the emergency action principles first, and then give the following specific care for frostbite (Table 12–2):

1. Cover the affected area.
2. Handle the area gently and never rub it because this causes further damage.
3. Warm the area gently by immersing the affected part in water warmed to 40.5°C (105°F). If possible, use a thermometer to check the water; if not possible, consider the water too warm if it is uncomfortable to your touch.

Table 12–2   First Aid for Frostbite
Cover affected area
Handle gently, never rub
Soak affected part in water warmed to 40.5°C (105°F)
Do not let affected part touch bottom or sides of container
Keep in water until red and warm
Bandage with dry, sterile dressing

4. Keep the frostbitten part in the water until it looks red and feels warm.
5. Bandage the area with a dry, sterile dressing. If fingers or toes are frostbitten, place cotton or gauze between them. Avoid breaking any blisters.
6. Get the casualty to a doctor as soon as possible.

Summary

- To care for soft tissue injuries, follow the basic guidelines to control bleeding and minimize the risk of infection.

- With minor wounds, cleanse the wound to prevent infection.

- With major wounds, control bleeding and seek medical attention. Use dressings and bandages to help control bleeding, reduce pain, and prevent infection.

- Bleeding in the abdomen can be life threatening and requires special care for the casualty while waiting for EMS.

- With burn injuries, follow the emergency action principles and cool the burned area with water unless a large part of the body is affected. Cover it with moist sterile dressings. Take measures to prevent infection. Check the airway and monitor breathing. Be prepared to give first aid for shock.

● With electrical burns, check carefully for additional problems such as cardiovascular problems and fractures.

● For frostbite, warm the area gently in tepid water, cover the area with dry sterile bandages, and seek medical attention.

Sudden Medical Conditions

Objectives

After reading this chapter, you should be able to:

1. Identify at least four general signs and symptoms of sudden illness.

2. Describe first aid for a person having a diabetic emergency.

3. Describe first aid for a person having a convulsion and when to call EMS.

4. List at least four signs and symptoms of a heat-related illness and describe when to call EMS.

5. Describe first aid for a person suffering from a heat emergency.

6. List at least three signs and symptoms of hypothermia.

7. Describe first aid for hypothermia.

8. Describe at least three things you can do to prevent heat and cold emergencies.

9. Describe the care of a mother before, during, and after emergency childbirth.

10. Describe how to care for a newborn baby.

11. Define the key terms for this chapter.

Key Terms

contraction   Muscular contraction of the uterus during labour in preparation for childbirth.

convulsion   A temporary brain disorder usually marked by loss of consciousness and often uncontrollable muscle movement; also called a *seizure*.

diabetic   A person with diabetes, whose body does not produce enough insulin, leading to high blood sugar levels.

diabetic emergency   Condition when a diabetic becomes ill because of a blood sugar level that is too high or too low.

epilepsy   A condition that causes convulsions but that can usually be controlled by drugs.

heat cramps   Muscle pains following work in warm temperatures, usually involving the calf and abdominal muscles.

heat exhaustion   A condition that occurs when the body temperature is elevated, usually caused by hard work or exercise in a hot, humid environment.

heat stroke   A life-threatening condition that develops when the body temperature is extremely elevated and the body cannot cool itself.

hyperglycemia   A diabetic condition in which too much sugar is in the bloodstream.

After reading this chapter and completing the class activities, you should be able to:

1. Decide what first aid to give in an example of someone becoming ill suddenly.

2. Decide what first aid to give in an example of a situation of a heat or cold emergency.

hypoglycemia   A diabetic condition in which too little sugar is in the bloodstream.

hypothermia   A life-threatening condition that develops when the body temperature drops too low, usually from prolonged cold exposure.

insulin   A hormone the body needs to use sugar for energy; frequently used to treat diabetes.

labour   The period of contractions of the uterus preceding childbirth.

Some medical conditions can cause a casualty to become extremely ill and require immediate first aid and emergency medical care. There may be no warning signals. In some cases the person may feel ill or feel that something is wrong.

Many different conditions, such as diabetes, epilepsy, emergencies caused by being too hot or too cold, poisoning, or stroke, can cause a change in a person's level of consciousness. A person may feel lightheaded, dizzy, or weak. He or she may feel sick to the stomach or may vomit. Breathing, pulse, and skin colour may change. The fact that a person looks and feels ill signifies a problem.

In an emergency you may not know the cause, but you can still give first aid. This chapter discusses basic principles of first aid for a casualty of a serious illness. Any time you are unsure about the casualty's condition, call EMS for help.

This chapter discusses sudden medical conditions including diabetic emergency, convulsion, hypothermia, heat stroke, and emergency childbirth.

Diabetic Emergencies

A diabetic emergency can happen only to someone who has diabetes. You may or may not know this information about the person who needs first aid. First aid is based on the general principles of care if you do not know it is a diabetic emergency.

Anatomy and Physiology of Diabetic Emergencies

To function, the body uses sugar as a source of energy. To use sugar, the body needs *insulin*, which the body normally makes itself. If the body does not make enough insulin or does not use it properly, the person has diabetes. This person is called a *diabetic*.

In one type of diabetes, the body produces little or no insulin. This type often begins in childhood and is called *juvenile diabetes*. Most insulin-dependent diabetics have to inject insulin into their bodies every day. In the other type, non-insulin-dependent diabetes, the body makes some insulin but not enough for the body's needs. This condition usually begins later in life.

Causes of Diabetic Emergencies

Diabetic emergencies are caused by an imbalance in the person's sugar and insulin levels. To maintain good blood sugar levels, diabetics must carefully watch their diet and exercise. Insulin-dependent diabetics must also regulate their use of insulin. If these factors are not controlled, either of two types of *diabetic emergency* can occur— too much or too little sugar in the body. This imbalance can become an emergency.

When the insulin level in the body is too low, the sugar level in the blood will become too high.

This condition is called *hyperglycemia* (Figure 13–1, *A*). The body tries to get energy from stored food and energy sources such as fats, but this makes the blood more acid and causes the casualty to become extremely ill. Hyperglycemia can then lead to diabetic coma.

On the other hand, if the insulin is too high, the person will develop a low sugar level. This condition is known as *hypoglycemia* (Figure 13–1, *B*). It is caused by the diabetic

- Taking too much insulin
- Failing to eat enough
- Overexercising and burning off sugar faster than normal

In hypoglycemia the small amount of sugar is used up rapidly, and there is not enough for the brain to work. This will cause the person to become unconscious.

Diabetic Emergencies

Although diabetes itself cannot be prevented, diabetic emergencies often can. It is crucial that someone with diabetes get the right amount of exercise and stay on the diet prescribed by the doctor. Diabetics who need insulin must also be careful in taking the right doses at the right time and monitoring blood sugar levels. A diabetic who controls these factors carefully may never have problems.

Signs and Symptoms of Diabetic Emergencies

The signs and symptoms of hyperglycemia and hypoglycemia differ somewhat, but the major signs and symptoms are similar:

- Changes in the level of consciousness, including dizziness, drowsiness, and confusion, sometimes leading to coma
- Rapid breathing
- Rapid pulse
- Feeling and looking ill

You do not need to be able to tell the difference between hypoglycemia and hyperglycemia because the first aid for both is the same.

Diabetic Emergencies

As always, start with the emergency action principles.

If the person tells you that he or she is a diabetic (or wears a medical alert tag indicating he or she is a

Diabetic Emergencies

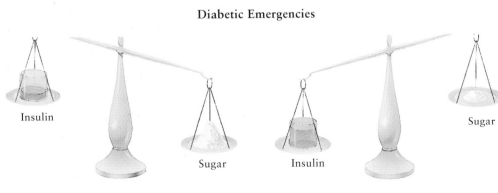

Insulin	Sugar
Sugar	Insulin
Diabetic Coma (hyperglycemia)	**Insulin Shock (hypoglycemia)**
A	**B**

Figure 13–1 *A*, Hyperglycemia occurs when there is not enough insulin in the body, causing a high level of sugar. *B*, Hypoglycemia occurs when the insulin level in the body is high, causing a low level of sugar.

diabetic) and shows the signs and symptoms, then suspect a diabetic emergency. If the casualty can take food or fluids, give him or her something with sugar in it (Figure 13–2). Most candy, fruit juices, and nondiet soft drinks have enough sugar to be effective. Common table sugar, dry or dissolved in a glass of water, also works well. If the person's problem is low sugar (hypoglycemia), the sugar you give will help quickly. If the person already has too much sugar (hyperglycemia), the extra sugar will not cause further harm over a short period of time. Often diabetics know what is wrong and will ask for something with sugar in it. They may carry a source of sugar for such occasions.

If the person is unconscious, do not try to give anything to drink or eat. Instead, watch the ABCs and maintain normal body temperature. If the casualty is unconscious or is conscious but does not feel better within 5 minutes after taking sugar, call EMS.

Convulsions

Anatomy and Physiology of Convulsions

Sometimes when the brain is affected by injury, disease, fever, infection, or unknown reasons, its electrical activity becomes irregular. This condition can cause a loss of body control known as a *convulsion*.

Causes of Convulsions

Fever and certain illnesses and injuries may cause convulsions. A common cause is *epilepsy*. The reason convulsions occur in epilepsy is often unknown. Epilepsy cannot be completely cured, but medications offer very good control. Some people with epilepsy have convulsions from time to time even when taking medication. Someone who stops taking the prescribed medication may then have a convulsion.

Convulsions in infants and young children may be caused by high fever. These are called *febrile convulsions*.

Convulsions

Convulsions resulting from unknown causes cannot be prevented, but the injuries that sometimes lead to convulsions may be prevented. Follow the guidelines throughout this book for preventing injury and for safe work, play, and home life. Taking prescribed medication regularly prevents convulsions for many epileptics. Convulsions in children caused by high fever can sometimes be prevented by controlling the fever before it rises too high. Seek care from a doctor whenever a child's fever rises beyond that considered usual for a cold or flu.

Signs and Symptoms of Convulsion

Before a convulsion occurs the person may hallucinate and see, hear, taste, or smell something not

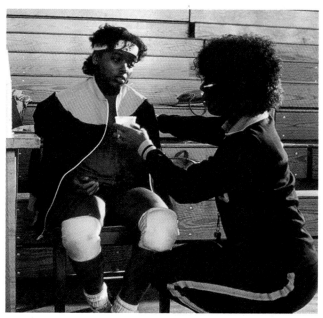

Figure 13–2 If the casualty of a diabetic emergency is conscious, give him or her food or fluids containing sugar.

there or may feel an urgent need to get to safety. If the person recognizes this feeling, he or she may have time to tell bystanders and sit down before the convulsion takes place.

Convulsions range from mild blackouts, which to others seem like daydreaming, to sudden and uncontrolled shaking with unconsciousness lasting several minutes.

FIRST AID

Convulsions

Although a convulsion may look frightening, you can easily help the person. Remember that he or she cannot control the body's movements. Do not try to stop the convulsion or restrain the person.

As always, start with the emergency action principles.

The goal of first aid for convulsions is to protect the casualty from injury and manage the airway, following these steps:

1. Move away nearby objects and furniture that might cause injury. Try to keep the person away from dangerous situations such as fire, heights, or water.
2. Protect the person's head by placing a cushion, such as folded clothing, beneath it.
3. If there is saliva, blood, or vomit in the person's mouth, move him or her into the recovery position so that it drains from the mouth.
4. Do not try to place anything between the person's teeth; biting the tongue or cheek hard enough to cause much bleeding is rare.

After the convulsion the person will be drowsy and confused. Do a secondary survey, checking to see if he or she was injured during the convulsion. Be reassuring and comforting. If the convulsion occurred in public, the casualty may be embarrassed. Ask people not to crowd around the casualty, who will be tired and want to rest. Stay with the casualty until he or she is fully aware of the surroundings.

If you know the casualty has epilepsy, you do not need to call EMS when you see a convulsion starting. The casualty usually recovers quickly. However, call EMS in any of these cases:

- The convulsion lasts more than a few minutes.
- The casualty has repeated convulsions.
- The casualty appears to be injured.
- You are uncertain about the cause of the convulsion.
- The casualty is pregnant.
- The casualty is a known diabetic.
- The casualty is an infant or child.
- The convulsion takes place in water.
- The casualty fails to regain consciousness after the convulsion.

First aid for an infant or child with high fever

An infant or young child with a fever over 39°C (102°F) is at risk for convulsions. Febrile convulsions are usually caused by a rapid rise in body temperature, which is not easily detected. A higher fever can become a medical emergency, and you need to lower the temperature by cooling the body and using medication for fever control, such as acetaminophen. Give a sponge bath with water at room temperature (not icy cold). Because this only temporarily lowers the temperature, the infant or child should see a doctor right away. Most febrile convulsions are not life threatening and do not last long.

Heat Emergencies

The human body generally regulates its temperature very well. However, when the body cannot manage extreme heat, problems result.

Extreme heat can occur both indoors and outdoors, but problems can occur even if the heat is not extreme. The way a person responds to heat is affected by humidity, wind, clothing, the living and working environment, physical activity, age, and personal health.

Heat cramps, heat exhaustion, and *heat stroke* are all caused by exposure to heat. Heat cramps are the least serious but may lead to heat exhaustion and heat stroke. Heat exhaustion is more serious and can lead to heat stroke. Heat stroke is an emergency and can lead to coma and death if the body is not cooled.

Heat emergencies can worsen rapidly once they appear. If the casualty shows any of the signs and symptoms of sudden illness and has been in hot conditions, give immediate first aid to prevent the illness from becoming life threatening.

Anatomy and Physiology of Heat Emergencies

Body temperature must remain constant for the body to work well. Normal body temperature is 37°C (98.6°F). The body produces heat by converting food to energy and by muscle contractions, as in exercise or shivering.

Heat always flows from warm to cooler areas. Since the body is usually warmer than the air around it, it usually gives off heat to the air. The body maintains its temperature by constantly balancing this heat loss with heat production (Figure 13–3). The heat produced in routine activities is usually enough to balance normal heat loss.

When body heat increases, the body removes heat through the skin. Blood vessels near the skin open up in order to bring more warm blood to the surface. Heat then escapes and the body cools (Figure 13–4, *A*). When the air temperature is high, the main source of cooling is the evaporation of sweat. Sweating increases when the body is very warm. However, when the humidity is high, sweat does not evaporate as quickly and has little or no cooling effect.

Causes of Heat Emergencies

Too much body heat is the cause of heat emergencies. Air temperature, humidity, and wind all affect body heat. Exercise or activity in the hot environment increases the risk. Personal factors put some people at greater risk for heat-related conditions:

- Those who work or exercise outdoors
- Elderly people
- Young children
- Those with health problems
- Those who have had a heat-related illness in the past
- Those who have heart disease or other conditions that cause poor circulation
- Those who take medications to eliminate water from the body (diuretics)

Heat cramps, painful spasms of muscles usually in the calf or abdomen, are caused by fluid and salt loss resulting from heavy exercise

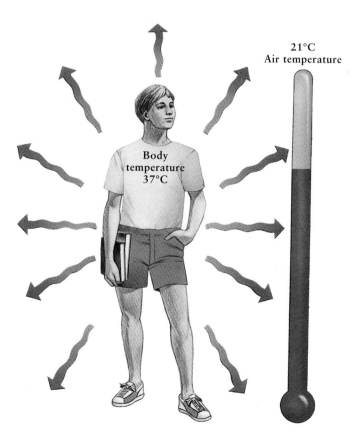

Figure 13–3 Because the body is usually warmer than the surrounding air, it tends to lose heat to the air.

or work outdoors in warm or even moderate temperatures.

Heat exhaustion, the most common heat illness leading to fluid depletion, is caused by exercise or work in a hot environment. Heat exhaustion affects athletes, firefighters, construction workers, factory workers, and others who wear heavy clothing in a hot, humid environment. Fluid loss from excess sweating is not adequately replaced. This loss leads to low blood volume. Blood flow is reduced to vital organs as the body tries to give off heat by increasing blood flow to the skin.

Heat stroke, the least common and most severe heat emergency, occurs when the signs and symptoms of heat exhaustion are ignored. Heat stroke develops when the body cannot cool itself and gradually stops working. Sweating stops because the body tissues have a lower fluid content. The body then cannot cool itself, and body temperature rapidly rises. It soon reaches a level at which the brain and other vital organs, such as the heart and kidneys, cannot function properly.

PREVENTION

Heat Emergencies

Most heat emergencies can be prevented with common sense and these guidelines:

- Avoid being outdoors in the hottest part of the day. If you must work out-of-doors in hot weather, plan your activity for the early morning and evening hours when the sun is not as strong.
- Slow down your activities as it gets hotter, and work or exercise in brief periods.
- Take frequent breaks in a cool or shaded area to let your body cool off so it can withstand brief periods of heat exposure (Figure 13–5).
- Dress for the heat and your activity level. Wear a hat when in the sun and light-coloured cotton clothing to absorb sweat and let air circulate and heat escape.

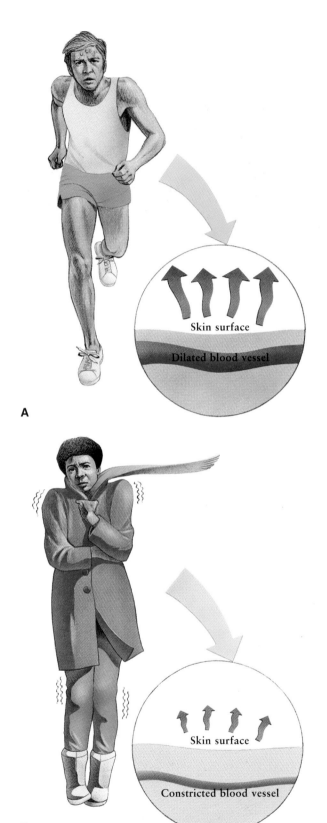

Figure 13–4 *A,* Your body removes heat by dilating the blood vessels near the skin's surface. *B,* The body conserves heat by contracting the blood vessels near the skin.

Figure 13–5   Taking frequent breaks when exercising in extreme temperatures allows your body to readjust to its normal body temperature.

- Drink plenty of fluids—this is the most important action you can take to prevent heat emergencies. Drink cool fluids and avoid caffeine and alcohol, which make the body's temperature-regulating mechanisms less efficient.

Signs and Symptoms of Heat Emergencies

Heat cramps, heat exhaustion, and heat stroke are not necessarily related problems, but a person may progress from one to the next. The signs and symptoms may indicate the particular stage of the casualty in a progressing heat emergency.

Signs and symptoms of heat cramps
- Severe muscle contractions, usually in the legs and the abdomen
- Usually normal body temperature
- Moist skin

Signs and symptoms of heat exhaustion
- Normal or slightly elevated body temperature
- Cool, moist, pale, or red skin
- Headache
- Nausea
- Dizziness and weakness
- Exhaustion

Signs and symptoms of heat stroke
- High body temperature, often as high as 41°C (106°F)
- Red, hot, dry skin, especially in the elderly
- Irritable, bizarre, or combative behaviour
- Progressive loss of consciousness
- Rapid, weak pulse becoming irregular
- Rapid, shallow breathing

The casualty of heat stroke may at first have a strong, rapid pulse, as the heart works hard to rid the body of heat by sending more blood to the skin. Then the circulatory system begins to fail, and the pulse becomes weak and irregular. Without prompt care, the casualty will die.

FIRST AID

Heat Emergencies

As in all emergencies, start with the emergency action principles.

If you suspect the casualty's condition is caused by overexposure to heat, follow these additional first aid steps immediately:

- Cool the body
- Give fluids if the person is conscious

First aid for heat cramps can include lightly stretching the muscle and gently massaging the area (Figure 13–6). The casualty should drink cool liquids or a sports drink. When the cramps stop and if no other signs and symptoms of illness are present, the person can usually become active again. However, he or she should watch carefully for signs and symptoms of developing heat exhaustion and continue to drink plenty of fluids.

When you recognize possible heat exhaustion in an early stage, you can usually reverse it. Move the casualty to a cool or shady place away from the heat and give cool water to drink. These measures let the body's own temperature-regulating mechanisms recover to cool the body.

Figure 13–6 Resting, lightly stretching the affected muscle, and drinking fluids are usually sufficient care to allow the body to recover from heat cramps.

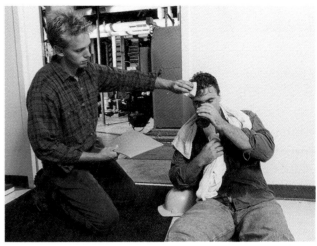

Figure 13–7 For heat exhaustion or the early stages of heat stroke, apply cool water to the entire body and fan the casualty to increase evaporation. Apply ice packs. Give cool water to drink if the casualty is conscious.

Loosen any tight clothing and remove clothing soaked with perspiration. Put cool water on the skin and fan the casualty to increase evaporation.

If the casualty is conscious, drinking cool water slowly helps replace the fluids lost through sweating. The casualty likely is nauseated, and water is less likely to cause vomiting than other fluids and is quickly absorbed into the body. Do not let the casualty drink too quickly. Let the casualty rest, and watch carefully for changes in his or her condition. The person should not return to activities in the heat on this day.

If heat exhaustion progresses, the casualty's condition worsens. Body temperature climbs. The casualty may vomit and show changes in level of consciousness, signaling the beginning of heat stroke.

If you see changes in the casualty's level of consciousness, call EMS and cool the body any way you can. Sponge the entire body with tepid or cool water and fan the casualty to increase evaporation. If you have ice packs or cold packs, put them on the groin, in each armpit, and on the neck to cool the large blood vessels (Figure 13–7). *Do not* apply rubbing (isopropyl) alcohol because it closes the skin's pores and blocks heat loss. Keep the airway open and monitor the ABCs. Putting the casualty in a tub of cool water may not be a good idea because this may make it hard

to maintain an open airway. A person in heat stroke may stop breathing or have a heart attack. Be prepared to do rescue breathing or CPR.

Table 13–1	First Aid for Heat Emergencies
Heat cramps	
Have casualty rest in cool place	
Give cool water or sports drink	
Stretch muscle and massage area	
Heat-related illness	
Have casualty rest in cool place	
Give cool water	
Monitor casualty's condition for signals of worsening	
Loosen tight clothing	
Remove perspiration-soaked clothing	
Apply cool, wet cloths to skin and fan casualty	
Monitor condition carefully	
Call EMS immediately	
Cool the body by any means available	
• Wet towels or sheets	
• Ice packs	
Monitor ABCs	
Be prepared to do rescue breathing or CPR	

When to call EMS

Refusing water, vomiting, and an altered level of consciousness signal that the casualty's condition is worsening. Call EMS immediately. If the person vomits, stop giving fluids and move the casualty into the recovery position to keep the airway clear. Monitor the ABCs and check vital signs. Keep the casualty lying down and continue to cool the body.

Hypothermia

Hypothermia is a general body cooling when the body cannot produce enough heat to stay warm.

Anatomy and Physiology of Hypothermia

The body reacts to cold by contracting blood vessels near the skin to move warm blood to the center of the body. Thus less heat escapes through the skin, and the body stays warm (see Figure 13–4, *B*). If this mechanism is not enough to keep the body warm, shivering starts and produces heat through muscle action. Hypothermia results as the entire body cools when its warming system fails. It can lead to death. In hypothermia body temperature drops below 35°C (95°F). Most medical thermometers do not measure below this point. As the body temperature cools, the heart begins to beat unevenly and eventually stops. Death then occurs.

Causes of Hypothermia

Hypothermia is caused by exposure to the cold to the point that the body cannot keep itself warm. Air temperature, the humidity, whether the skin is wet or dry, and wind all affect how the body maintains its temperature and how much exposure is needed before hypothermia begins.

Some people are more at risk for hypothermia:

- Those who spend much time outdoors in a cold environment
- Elderly people
- Young children
- Those with health problems
- Those who have had hypothermia in the past
- Those who have heart disease or other conditions that cause poor circulation

The air temperature does not have to be below freezing for hypothermia to occur. Elderly people in poorly heated homes, particularly people with poor nutrition and who get little exercise, can develop hypothermia at temperatures even above freezing. The homeless and the ill are also at risk. Substances such as alcohol and barbiturates can also affect the body's normal response to cold, causing hypothermia to occur more easily. Medical conditions such as infection, hypoglycemia, stroke, and brain tumour can also cause it to occur more easily. Anyone remaining in cold water or wet clothing for a long time may develop hypothermia easily.

PREVENTION

Hypothermia

Hypothermia can usually be prevented with common sense and the following guidelines:

- Avoid being outdoors in the coldest part of the day.
- Wear a hat and layers of clothing made of tightly woven fibers, such as wool, which trap warm air against your body. Keep vulnerable areas such as the fingers, toes, ears, and nose protected and covered.
- Drink plenty of warm fluids to help the body maintain its temperature. If hot drinks are not available, drink plenty of plain water. Avoid caffeine and alcohol, which hinder the body's heat-producing mechanisms.
- As soon as shivering starts, get out of the cold and let your body warm up to withstand better brief periods of exposure to extreme cold.
- When near cold water, take extra precaution to avoid falling in.

- If your clothes become wet when you are in the cold, change to dry clothing immediately.

Signs and Symptoms of Hypothermia
- Shivering (may be absent in later stages)
- Numbness
- Lack of coordination
- Confused or unusual behavior
- Body temperature below 35°C (95°F)

FIRST AID

Hypothermia

If the casualty shows signs of both frostbite and hypothermia, give first aid first for the hypothermia because it can lead to death if the person is not warmed immediately (Table 13–2). However, even in this case do not ignore frostbite, which, if serious, can require the amputation of the affected part (see Chapter 12).

Hypothermia is a medical emergency.

As in any emergency, begin with the emergency action principles.

Then give this additional first aid for hypothermia:

1. Remove any wet clothing and dry the casualty.
2. Warm the casualty by wrapping him or her in blankets or putting on dry clothing and moving him or her to a warm place. *Do not* warm the casualty too quickly by immersing him or her in warm water. Rapid rewarming can cause heart problems. Be very gentle in handling the casualty.
3. If available, put hot water bottles, heating pads (if the casualty is dry), or other heat sources on the body, keeping a blanket, towel, or clothing between the heat source and the skin to avoid burns.
4. If the casualty is alert, give warm liquids to drink.

In cases of severe hypothermia, the casualty may be unconscious. Breathing may have slowed or stopped. The pulse may be slow and irregular. Take up to 45 seconds to check the signs of circulation. The body may feel stiff. Monitor the ABCs until EMS arrives, and give rescue breathing if necessary. Be prepared to start CPR.

Emergency Childbirth

It sometimes happens that a pregnant woman in labour is unable to reach a medical facility in time before childbirth begins. In such a case, call EMS immediately. First aid then involves helping the woman before, during, and after the childbirth, as well as caring for the newborn infant.

Anatomy and Physiology of Childbirth

The developing baby is usually positioned head down in the uterus (womb) prior to birth (Figure 13–8). The baby is surrounded by the sac of amniotic fluid, often called the bag of waters, and is connected by the umbilical cord to the placenta in the uterus.

When the body is ready for childbirth, the uterus begins regular *contractions;* this period is called *labour.* The bag of waters may break during labour. The contractions gradually intensify and occur more quickly, and the cervix, the open-

Table 13–2	First Aid for Hypothermia

Call EMS personnel

Warm body gradually by wrapping in blankets or putting on dry clothing

Apply heat sources (hot water bottle, heating pad if victim is dry), if available

Give warm liquids to an alert casualty

Do not rewarm too quickly

Handle gently

ing from the uterus to the birth canal (vagina), expands in preparation for the fetus to move through the birth canal.

Labour may last as long as 16 hours or more for a woman's first child but can be considerably shorter if the woman has had children. A woman who already has one or more children is thus more likely to experience emergency childbirth because labour progresses more rapidly.

During the actual childbirth, contractions, usually coming less than 2 minutes apart, begin to push the baby down the birth canal and out. Complications are rare, with most births being a normal, natural process.

Signs and Symptoms of Impending Childbirth

- Contractions are 2 minutes or less apart.
- The woman says the baby is trying to be born now.
- The woman seems to be straining or pushing as if having a bowel movement.
- The baby's head is showing.

If these signs and symptoms are present, do not try to transport the woman or move her. Call EMS and prepare to assist with the birth.

Emergency Childbirth

First aid for the woman in emergency childbirth is continuous from the last stage of labour to the birth and caring for the mother and baby after the birth. Throughout this process do not leave the woman alone unless absolutely necessary. Follow these general principles:

- If possible have her husband or partner stay with her. Having another woman present usually also provides comfort.
- Arrange as much privacy as possible for the situation.
- Maintain cleanliness of your own hands and the childbirth area.

Care during labour

1. Call EMS immediately.
2. Help the woman be as comfortable as possible, typically by lying on her back with knees raised or on her side. Put a pillow or folded clothing under her head.
3. Keep calm and reassure her that the ambulance is on its way.
4. Time contractions to give this information to arriving EMS personnel.

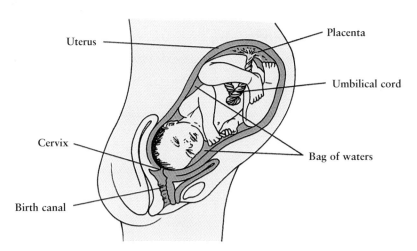

Figure 13–8   Typical position of the fetus in the uterus shortly before birth.

5. Wash your hands.

6. Place clean towels, a blanket, or any available material under her buttocks. Remove her underwear and any clothing in the way, but keep the woman covered with towels or a blanket.

7. Have someone stay at the woman's head. In case she vomits, be ready to turn the head and keep the airway clear.

8. Continue to offer encouragement and reassurance.

9. Do not try anything to delay the delivery.

Care during birth

1. As the baby's head comes out, support it with one hand. Be prepared for the rest of the infant to come out quite rapidly. Do not pull on the baby.

2. If the bag of waters has not broken but still covers the baby's head, gently tear it open with your fingers and remove the membrane from the baby's nose and mouth.

3. If the umbilical cord is around the baby's neck, gently loosen and unwrap it.

4. As the birth progresses, try to keep the baby's mouth and nose wiped clean of mucus and fluids.

5. When the baby's feet are out, hold it carefully facedown with feet slightly elevated. Newborns are slippery; hold firmly but do not squeeze.

6. If a bulb syringe is available, suction the baby's mouth and nose to ease breathing. If not, use a cloth and gently wipe away from the mouth and nose.

7. If the baby is not breathing within 30 seconds of delivery, gently massage the baby's back. Then, if still not breathing, snap your finger against the soles of the baby's feet. If breathing is still not stimulated, start rescue breathing (Chapter 7).

Care for the mother after birth

1. Keep the mother warm.

2. Leave the cord in place and do not pull on it. Clamp or tie the cord while waiting for the placenta to be delivered. Use strips of sterile cloth tied tightly at two different locations 10 and 15 cm (4 and 6 inches) away from the infant. Do not cut the cord.

3. The mother has now entered the third stage of labour. Help the mother rest in the same position in preparation of delivering her placenta. It is normal for women to pass blood vaginally after delivery and to continue to pass blood until after delivering her placenta. Remember that the placenta is a big, round, bloody sac attached to the inner wall of the uterus.

4. Let the placenta and cord drop onto a clean towel, and keep this near the baby. The doctor will want to examine it later.

5. Maintain cleanliness of the childbirth area. If bleeding persists it may be necessary to apply gentle pressure to any bleeding tears. Once bleeding is controlled, place a sanitary pad over the mother's vaginal opening, lower her legs, and ready for transport when the ambulance arrives.

Care for the newborn baby

1. Confirm the baby is breathing, and keep the nostrils clear (newborns breathe through the nose).

2. Keep the baby warm by drying it (but do not try to wash it), wrapping it in clean cloth, holding it or putting it on the mother's abdomen. In a cold environment keep the baby close to your own or the mother's body for warmth.

3. Do not cut the umbilical cord. Arriving EMS personnel will take care of this.

Summary

- You do not need to know the cause of a sudden illness to give first aid care for it. Follow the emergency action principles and the basics of care for any emergency.

- Look for the general signs and symptoms of diabetic emergencies or convulsions (such as changes in consciousness, sweating, confusion, weakness, and the appearance of illness) and give the necessary general care.

- For heat exhaustion or heat stroke, it is important to stop physical activity, cool the casualty, and call EMS.

- Hypothermia is serious and can be life threatening, requiring professional medical care. First aid involves warming the casualty.

- First aid in cases of emergency childbirth involves preparations for delivery, supporting the infant during birth, ensuring the newborn is breathing, and supportive care for mother and child after the birth.

Poisons

Objectives

After reading this chapter, you should be able to:

1. List the four ways poisons enter the body.

2. Describe ways to prevent poisoning.

3. List at least six signs and symptoms of poisoning.

4. Describe the role of a poison centre.

5. Describe the general principles of first aid for any poisoning emergency.

6. Describe the specific first aid for a casualty of ingested, inhaled, and absorbed poison.

7. Describe the specific first aid for an insect bite or sting, marine life sting, tick bite, and animal or human bite.

8. Define the key terms for this chapter.

After reading this chapter and completing the class activities, you should be able to:

1. Decide what first aid to give in an example of an emergency situation involving poisoning.

Key Terms

absorbed poison   A poison that enters the body through the skin.

allergic reaction   The response of the body to a substance to which the person has a hypersensitivity. It can be mild or very severe.

ingested poison   A poison that is swallowed.

inhaled poison   A poison that is breathed into the lungs.

injected poison   A poison that enters the body through a bite, sting, or hypodermic needle.

Lyme disease   An illness transmitted by an infected tick.

poison   Any substance that causes injury, illness, or death when it enters the body.

poison centre   A special health centre that provides information in cases of poisoning.

rabies   A disease caused by a virus transmitted through the saliva of infected animals.

Poisoning results when an external substance enters the body. The substance may be a drug or any chemical substance, taken intentionally or unintentionally, or a poison or microbe that enters the body through a bite, sting, or puncture wound. Poisoning is the third most common cause of accidental death in Canada, with over 500 deaths by poisoning each year.

Most poisonings happen in the home, and most are unintentional. Poisonings occur with both children and adults.

Someone who is hypersensitive to a substance may have an *allergic reaction* when that substance contacts or enters the body. The reaction may be mild or very severe and life threatening, called *anaphylactic reaction* or *anaphylactic shock*. As with other poisonings, this casualty needs immediate first aid (see Chapter 7).

Although you may not think of drugs, medications, and other substances people take on purpose as poisons, they can have a toxic effect on the body if misused or abused. These casualties, too, need first aid.

Poisoning

Causes of Poisonings

A *poison* is any substance that causes injury, illness, or death if it enters the body. A poison can enter the body in four ways: ingestion, inhalation, absorption through the skin (dermal), and injection (Figure 14–1).

Ingested poisons are swallowed or come in contact with the mouth and lips. They include many items found in the home such as medications, cleaning products, pesticides, and plants (Figure 14–2). Many substances not poisonous in small amounts are poisonous in larger amounts.

Figure 14–1 A poison can enter the body in four ways: ingestion, inhalation, absorption, and injection.

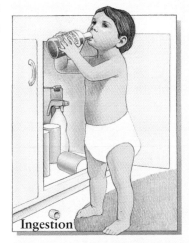
Ingestion

Inhalation

Absorption

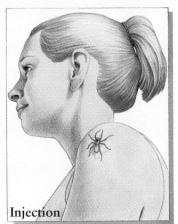
Injection

Figure 14–2 Many common household plants are poisonous.

Any prescription or over-the-counter medication can be toxic if not used according to directions. Overuse of aspirin, for example, not only can cause salicylate poisoning by accumulation, but also increases the risk of side effects such as ulcers and bleeding caused by impaired clotting. Overuse of nasal sprays can lead to dependency and nosebleeds. Laxatives used too often can cause uncontrolled diarrhea and dehydration as well as chemical changes to the blood.

Inhaled poisons are breathed into the lungs. These include gases and fumes such as carbon monoxide from a car exhaust or faulty furnace or heater; nitrous oxide; chlorine gas found in commercial swimming facilities; and fumes from household and industrial products, such as glues, paints, and cleaning solvents.

Absorbed (dermal) poisons enter the body through the skin. They include plants such as poison ivy, poison oak, and poison sumac and fat-soluble chemicals such as solvents, paint strippers, and insecticides.

Injected poisons enter the body through bites or stings of bees, wasps, insects, spiders, ticks, animals, and snakes, or as drugs injected with a needle.

PREVENTION

Poisoning

The best idea is to prevent poisonings in the first place. This sounds simple, but often people do not take enough precautions. For example, most child poisonings happen while the child is being supervised by an adult. Children are curious and can get into things in just a few seconds.

Many substances found in or around the house are poisonous. Children are at great risk because they often put things in their mouths. Many household items and plants are potentially dangerous poisons.

Follow these general guidelines to prevent poisonings:

- Keep all medications, household products, poisonous plants, and other substances well out of the reach of children. Use locked cupboards or special child-resistant latches. Consider all household or drugstore products potentially harmful.
- Use child-resistant safety caps on medications and other products.
- Never call medicine "candy" to entice a child to take it.
- Keep products in their original containers with labels. *Never* store a household product in a food or drink container.
- Use poison symbols to identify dangerous substances, and teach children what the symbols mean.
- Carefully dispose of outdated products.
- Use potentially dangerous chemicals only in well-ventilated areas, and use only as directed.
- Wear proper clothing for any work or recreation that may put you in contact with a poisonous substance (Figure 14–3).
- Keep the poison centre number by your telephone.

You can also prevent the poisoning of insect and spider bites and stings. When in wooded or grassy areas, follow these general guidelines:

- Wear a long-sleeved shirt and long pants.
- Tuck your pant legs into your socks or boots. Tuck your shirt into your pants.
- Wear light-coloured but not bright clothing to make it easier to see tiny insects or ticks. Avoid perfumes.

Figure 14–3 Wear proper clothing for any activity that may put you in contact with a poisonous substance. Follow manufacturer's guidelines and precautions for application of substance.

- In tick-infested areas use a rubber band or tape the area where pants and socks meet so that nothing can get under clothing.
- When hiking in woods and fields, stay in the middle of trails. Avoid underbrush and tall grass.
- Inspect yourself carefully for insects or ticks after being outdoors. If you are outdoors a long time, check yourself often. Check especially in hairy areas of the body (back of the neck and the scalp line).
- If you have pets that go outdoors, spray them with repellent made for your type of pet. Apply the repellent according to the label, and check your pet for ticks often.

If you use an insect repellent, be especially careful. Keep repellents out of the reach of children, and do not put them on children's hands. Be careful around the lips, eyes, and any wounds. Wash the skin later with soap and water to remove the repellent. Check the label; never spray permethrin on the skin but only on clothing. With children do not use any insect repellents with diethyl toluamide (DEET) in concentrations greater than 25%.

Prevention of poisoning in the work place

About one fourth of all workers are exposed to chemical hazards in the work place. To help protect employees, the federal, provincial, and territorial governments have legislated the Workplace Hazardous Materials Information System (WHMIS). WHMIS regulations require employers to clearly label hazardous materials, including all toxic substances, and inform employees about risks and precautions.

To prevent poisonings, workers should observe all warning labels, tags, and placards in the work place and follow the required precautions. The labels state the risk, precautionary measures, and first aid to be given in case of exposure or poisoning. In addition, the employer must have available, for any hazardous substance, a Material Safety Data Sheet (MSDS), which gives additional detailed information. Finally, WHMIS requires that workers who may be exposed to hazardous materials undergo education and training in safety measures and procedures for emergencies. When both employer and employees follow these government guidelines, poisoning can be prevented in the work place.

Signs and Symptoms of Poisoning

The most important factor is to recognize *that a poisoning may have occurred*. Watch for any sign or symptom of poisoning:

- Anything unusual at the scene such as odours, flames, smoke, open or spilled containers, open medicine cabinet, overturned or damaged plant
- General appearance of being ill and signs and symptoms of other sudden illnesses: nausea, vomiting, diarrhea, chest or abdominal pain, breathing difficulty, sweating, salivation, loss of consciousness, and muscle twitching or convulsions
- Burn injuries around the lips or tongue or on the skin
- Drug paraphernalia or empty containers
- Unusual behaviour

If you suspect a poisoning, ask the casualty or others at the scene:

- What type of poison was taken?
- How much was taken?
- When was it taken?

FIRST AID

Poisoning

Even if you do not know the specific substance causing a poisoning, the general care you give is the same. Special *poison centres* in all provinces

can tell you what to do. You should have your poison centre telephone number posted by your phone (Figure 14–4). This number can be found on the first inside page of your telephone directory.

Follow the emergency action principles for any poisoning emergency:

1. Survey the scene to ensure no danger.
2. Check the casualty for unresponsiveness. If the person does not respond, call EMS.
3. Do a primary survey and care for life-threatening problems (ABCs). Call EMS for help if necessary.
4. Do a secondary survey, if needed, and care for other problems.
5. Keep monitoring the ABCs until EMS arrives.
6. Help the casualty rest in the most comfortable position and give reassurance.

In addition, do not give the casualty anything to drink or eat unless directed by the poison centre. With an unknown poison, if the casualty vomits, save some of the vomitus for later medical analysis.

First aid for ingested poisons
Call the poison centre and follow their directions.

Figure 14–4   The local poison centre phone number can be found on the inside page of your telephone directory and should be posted by your phone.

Vomiting *should not* be induced if the casualty:

- Is unconscious
- Is having a convulsion
- Is pregnant
- Ingested a corrosive substance (an acid or alkali) or a petroleum product (such as kerosene or gasoline)
- Has heart disease

Vomiting removes only about half of the poison. The poison centre may tell you to neutralize the poison left with activated charcoal. Follow the directions given by the poison centre.

With some poisons the poison centre may tell you to give the casualty water to drink to dilute the poison in the stomach. Only do this when the poison centre so instructs.

First aid for inhaled poisons

All casualties of inhaled poison need to breathe oxygen as soon as possible. But remember to start with the emergency action principles. Be sure the scene is safe for you to help. Remove the person from the gas or fumes only if it is safe for you to do so. Just moving a casualty into fresh air and calling EMS is a major help. Give first aid for the ABCs as needed.

First aid for dermal (absorbed) poisons

Poisonous substances can be absorbed into the body through contact with poisonous plants such as poison ivy, poison oak, and poison sumac (Figure 14–5) and chemicals such as those used in yard and garden care.

For first aid for poison plant contact, immediately wash the affected area thoroughly with soap and water (Figure 14–6, *A*). Remove any contaminated clothing and avoid contact with it until it has been laundered.

Later care may include the following:

1. If a rash or weeping lesion develops, apply a paste of baking soda and water to the area several times a day for comfort. Lotions such as Calamine® or Caladryl® may be soothing.

Poison sumac

Photo by John Shaw/TOM STACK & ASSOCIATES

Photo by Walt Anderson/TOM STACK & ASSOCIATES

Poison oak

Poison ivy

Photo by Walt Anderson/TOM STACK & ASSOCIATES

Figure 14–5 Many people suffer from contact with poisonous plants whose poisons are absorbed into the body.

2. Antihistamines such as Benadryl® may help dry up the lesions.
3. If the condition worsens or a large area is affected, see a doctor, who may give other medications.

The first aid for dry or wet chemicals on the skin begins by calling the poison centre and following their instructions. The centre may instruct you to do the following:

1. Flush the affected area continuously with large amounts of water (Figure 14–6, B). Even though dry chemicals are activated by water, continuous running water will flush the chemical from the skin quickly. Make sure you are safe by wearing protective gloves.
2. If running water is not available, brush off dry chemicals. Take care not to damage underlying skin. Avoid getting any substance in your eyes or on your skin.

First aid for injected poisons

Insect and animal stings and bites are common injected poisons. The following sections describe first aid for the most common stings and bites of insects, marine life, animals, and ticks.

Insects. Bees and wasps sting the skin, and bees may leave a stinger in the wound. Ants and some other insects bite and do not leave a stinger. Either can be painful but is rarely fatal. However, some people can have a severe allergic reaction to an insect bite or sting, which can result in anaphylactic shock.

First aid for a sting or insect bite:

1. If the stinger is still in the skin, remove it by scraping it away from the skin with your fingernail or a plastic card such as a credit card. Do not use tweezers because pressure can squeeze more poison into the skin.
2. Wash the area with soap and water, and cover it to keep it clean.
3. Put ice or a cold pack over the area to reduce pain and swelling.

4. Watch the casualty for any signs and symptoms of an allergic reaction.

Marine life. Sting rays, certain fish, jellyfish, and other marine animals have painful stings. These may also cause serious problems such as anaphylactic reaction, paralysis, and cardiac and respiratory problems.

For jellyfish and sting ray stings, first bathe the area liberally with sea water, but do not rub the area. Do not use fresh or hot water. Protect yourself by wearing gloves. Remove any tentacles or pieces of the animal. Make a solution of 10 parts water and one part household ammonia, vinegar, baking soda, or meat tenderizer; then apply it to the area. Scrape or shave the area with

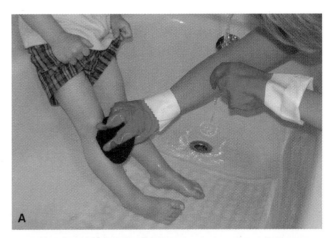

Figure 14–6 *A,* To care for skin contact with a poisonous plant, wear protective gloves and immediately wash the affected area with soap and water. *B,* If chemicals contact the skin or eyes, flush the affected area continuously with large amounts of water.

a razor or knife edge. For a jellyfish sting, applying a cold pack to the area for the first hour will reduce the pain. After the area dries apply a topical corticosteroid, antihistamine, local anesthetic cream every 4 hours for several days.

Call EMS if the casualty
- Does not know what caused the sting
- Is allergic to marine life stings
- Is stung on the face or neck
- Develops any severe problems such as difficult breathing

Animals. The bite of a domestic or wild animal can cause infection. The most serious danger is *rabies*. Rabies is transmitted through the saliva of diseased animals such as skunks, foxes, bats, raccoons, cats, dogs, and cattle. Animals with rabies may act in unusual ways. Rabid animals may salivate, seem partly paralyzed, or act irritable, aggressive, or strangely quiet. If not treated, rabies is fatal. Anyone bitten by an animal suspected to be rabid must get immediate medical attention. Vaccine injections given to the casualty can prevent the disease from occurring. The vaccines used now require fewer injections and have less severe side effects than in the past. If someone is bitten by an animal, try to get him or her safely away from the animal. Do not try to capture it. If the wound is minor, wash it with soap and water. Then control any bleeding and apply a dressing. Watch later for signs and symptoms of infection. If the wound is bleeding seriously, control the bleeding first. Do not clean the wound. The wound will be properly cleaned at a medical facility. Seek medical attention. Call your local emergency number to report the animal bite. The dispatcher will get the proper authorities, such as animal control, to the scene. Most bites come from animals, but people can be bitten by other people, too. Many different microorganisms that live harmlessly in the human mouth can cause infection if the skin is broken. Even a young child's playful bite can lead to serious infection. Give the same first aid as for any animal bite.

Ticks. *Lyme disease* is an illness that people contract from the bite of an infected tick, usually the tiny deer tick, which is difficult to see (Figure 14–7). In areas where Lyme disease is common, it is important to watch for its signs and symptoms because most people who do get it never knew they were bitten. If not treated, Lyme disease can become serious. Lyme disease starts with a rash in a small red area and spreads up to 5 to 7 inches across (Figure 14–8). The person has fever, headache, weakness, and joint and muscle pain that may feel like flu. Later on, the person may develop arthritis, numbness, and a stiff neck; memory loss; seeing or hearing problems; a high fever; and irregular or rapid heartbeat. If you find a tick, remove it with tweezers, grasping it as close to the skin as possible and pulling *slowly* (Figure 14–9). If you do not have tweezers, use a glove, plastic wrap, or a piece of paper to protect your fingers. Wash your hands immediately. Do not try to burn a tick off, do not coat it with petroleum jelly or nail polish, and do not prick it with a pin. If you cannot remove the tick or if its mouth parts stay in your skin, see a doctor. When the tick is out, wash the area with soap and water. Use an antiseptic or antibiotic ointment to prevent infection. If a rash or flu-like symptoms occur later, seek medical help.

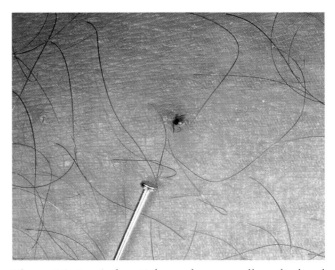

Figure 14–7   A deer tick can be as small as the head of a pin.

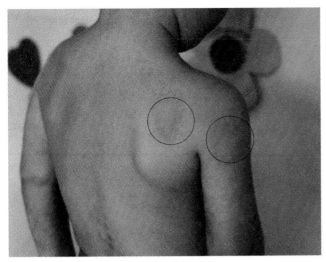

Figure 14–8 A person with Lyme disease may develop a rash.

Figure 14–9 Remove a tick by pulling steadily and firmly with tweezers.

Substance Misuse and Abuse

Substance misuse and abuse refers to a broad range of improperly used medical and nonmedical substances. They are actually methods of poisoning the body. While some substances do not fit well into any category, there are generally three categories: stimulants, depressants, or hallucinogens. Some substances depress the nervous systems, and others speed up its activity. The signs and symptoms can vary greatly and can be similar to those of other medical emergencies. Your initial care for substance misuse or abuse does not require that you know the specific substance taken. This is a form of poisoning, and care follows the same general principles as for poisoning.

Summary

- Allergic reactions to any substance can lead to life-threatening anaphylactic shock requiring immediate first aid.

- Poisonings can occur by ingestion, inhalation, dermal absorption, and injection.

- For suspected poisonings, call the poison centre or your local emergency number; follow their instructions for first aid.

- Follow the emergency action principles to care for life-threatening problems that may result from poisoning.

Healthy Lifestyles

15

Objectives

After reading this chapter, you should be able to:

1. Describe at least two ways your diet can help you to have better health.

2. List at least three ways in which cardiovascular fitness helps you become and stay healthier.

3. Identify two health problems that one can prevent by stopping smoking or never starting.

4. List at least four parts of a home safety plan.

5. Describe how to make a fire escape plan.

6. List at least four things you can do to stay safe at work.

7. Identify the best way to avoid injury in a motor vehicle crash.

8. List at least four ways you can avoid injury in sports.

9. Identify ways that you can personally prepare for disasters that may occur in your area.

Knowing first aid for injuries or medical emergencies is important, but a healthy lifestyle and an awareness of safety issues can prevent many such problems. A healthy lifestyle includes good nutrition, exercise, and safety habits. Such habits may require an attitude change that is hard to make. This chapter helps you understand why you should and how you can build and maintain a healthier lifestyle at home, work, and play.

The key to staying healthy and safe is prevention. Think safety, think prevention, and try to take care of yourself and your family. A healthy lifestyle can prevent illness and injury.

We all have heard various ideas about how to stay healthy. Good diet and exercise, for example, are not new concepts. What we need to do, sometimes, is to try to apply our knowledge about preventing illness and injury. This chapter reviews those principles to help you use them in your own life.

Caring for Your Body

If you care for your body now, you will benefit in the future. Ordinary daily activities—eating, exercising, relaxing, working, and sleeping—are the building blocks of a healthy lifestyle. It's up to you to make the best use of them yourself, because only you can do it.

Nutrition

A healthy lifestyle starts with a healthy diet. A balanced diet includes portions every day from the four basic food groups: carbohydrates, dairy products, protein, and fruit and vegetables (Figure 15–1). Try to eat the following daily:

- At least four servings of enriched, whole-grain breads or cereals. (One serving is one slice of bread or one-half cup of starches such as rice, potatoes, or cereals.)
- Two 8-ounce servings of low-fat dairy foods such as low-fat yogurt and low-fat or skim milk.

- Two to three servings of lean protein foods. (One serving is 2 ounces of chicken, fish, or turkey.)
- Four to five servings of fruits and vegetables with at least one of fruit high in vitamin C and one of a dark green, yellow, or orange vegetable every other day for vitamin A.

Fluids are also important. Drink at least eight glasses of water each day. Try drinking water sometimes instead of a soft drink. Fibre in the diet is also important. Good sources of fibre include whole-grain breads and cereals, fruits, and leafy vegetables.

A healthy diet also involves avoiding foods that are high in salt, fat, and cholesterol. Watch out for all of these, because a product low in one may be high in another. For better eating habits, apply these principles:

- Know the food you buy; read the labels.
- Take the salt shaker off your table.
- Avoid dairy foods except those marked low fat.
- Use unsaturated oils and fats for cooking.

Dairy products

Protein

Carbohydrates

Fruit and vegetables

Figure 15–1 A well-balanced meal plan includes daily servings from the four basic food groups.

Weight Control

You can help prevent many health problems by maintaining an appropriate weight level. Overweight problems contribute to heart disease, high blood pressure, diabetes, and gallbladder disease. Body fat, rather than just weight, leads to these diseases. See your doctor if you are not certain whether you have too much or too little body fat.

Losing weight, especially fat, is not easy. Weight depends on the balance of how much you eat and how much you exercise. If you take in more calories than you use, you gain weight. If you use more calories than you take in, you lose weight.

To lose weight, follow these principles:

- Day-to-day differences in weight may only be changes in fluid; therefore, pick one day and time a week as weigh-in time.
- Consume fewer calories than you use, but try to lose weight only gradually. Too rapid or too much weight loss can also be harmful to your health.
- Regular exercise is a key part of weight control. Any activity—walking to the bus, climbing the stairs, cleaning house—uses calories. The more active you are, the more calories you use.

Exercise

Exercise is good for the heart, lungs, blood vessels, and muscles and helps prevent cardiovascular illness. Even if you have limited time for exercise, strive for cardiovascular fitness, which helps you to:

- Cope with everyday stress
- Control weight
- Fight infections
- Improve self-esteem
- Sleep better

For cardiovascular fitness, you must exercise your heart. Try to exercise at least three times a week for 20 to 30 minutes at your target heart rate. This rate is 65 to 80 percent of your maximum heart rate, which goes down as you get older. The following table shows the target rate ranges for different ages:

Age	Target Heart Rate Range
20	130–160
30	123–152
40	117–144
50	110–136
60	104–128
70	98–120
80	91–112

As you exercise, take your pulse often to stay in this range. Your exercise must be continuous and vigorous to maintain this rate. The "no pain, no gain" theory is not a good way to exercise. In fact, pain usually means you are doing something wrong. Be sure to warm up before strenuous exercise and cool down afterwards.

Turn your daily activities into exercise (Figure 15–2). Walk briskly instead of driving when you can. Take the stairs instead of the elevator. Pedal an exercise bike while watching TV or listening to music. Look for ways to make exercise fun to make it easier to maintain as a regular habit.

If you have not been active or have health problems, see your doctor before starting an exercise program.

Stress Control

Stress is a normal part of life. Coping with stress, however, is an important way to prevent illness and stay healthy. The following activities can help you reduce the amount of stress you feel:

- Develop hobbies that reward your efforts.
- Exercise regularly.
- Avoid coffee, tea, chocolate, soft drinks, or pain relievers that contain caffeine, which decrease your ability to handle stress. Cut back gradually to avoid possible headaches.

- Set goals you can reach. Unrealistic goals will only add to your stress.
- Practice relaxation exercises. Sit or lie quietly in a comfortable position with eyes closed.

Figure 15–2   Build exercise into your daily activities.

Breathe in deeply through your nose and out through your mouth. Focus on your breathing for 10 minutes.

Breaking Unhealthy Habits

Smoking

In the past few decades the dangers of smoking have become well known. Smoking is banned or restricted in many work sites, as well as on many airlines and in other public places (Figure 15–3). Cigarette smoking is the most preventable cause of heart and lung disease. Cigarette smoking causes most cases of lung cancer. Fortunately, the risk of lung cancer starts diminishing as soon as you stop smoking. Never starting to smoke or stopping helps you prevent many kinds of illness.

Cancer is not the only danger of smoking. Smoking also causes heart disease and heart attacks. A pregnant woman who smokes also can cause harm to her unborn baby.

Smokeless tobacco is also dangerous. Chewing tobacco and snuff cause cancer of the mouth, tongue, and nasal passages.

To stop smoking and stop using tobacco is difficult, but most ex-smokers and former users say they feel better physically and emotionally. Numerous programs are available to help smokers break the habit.

Figure 15–3   Because of the dangers of smoking, the government and many private groups discourage or ban smoking.

Alcohol

Alcohol is the most widely used drug in our society. Although millions of people drink beer, wine, or liquor, alcohol in large amounts has many unhealthy effects on the body. Alcohol ingested by pregnant women may also have harmful effects on the unborn child.

Alcohol impairs judgment and reflexes and makes driving unsafe. An average 160-pound person can reach an unsafe blood alcohol level after just two drinks in an hour or less.

Only time can make you sober after having too much to drink. Black coffee and a cold shower may make you feel more alert, but the body still needs time for the effects of alcohol to wear off. Any group driving to a party should always have a designated, nondrinking driver for the return trip.

At any party help keep drinking under control with these principles:

- Have nonalcoholic beverages available.
- Never drink and drive—this applies to boats and recreational vehicles as well as cars.
- Take no more than one drink per hour.
- Do not drink before a party.
- Avoid drinking when angry or depressed.
- Eat plenty of food before and while drinking.
- Avoid salty foods that may make you thirsty and cause you to drink more.
- Do not play drinking games.

Medical and Dental Care

Everyone should have regular medical, dental, and eye checkups. Preventing disease is far better than treating disease after it develops. People need different types of medical examinations, depending on age, medical history, and other factors. Ask your doctor what tests you may need and how often.

See your dentist twice a year for a teeth cleaning and checkup (Figure 15–4). Change your toothbrush often. Brush and floss each day to

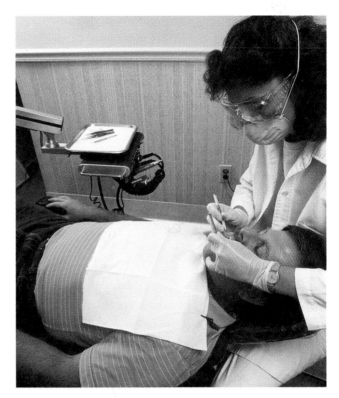

Figure 15–4   Visit your dentist twice a year for a cleaning and checkup.

prevent gum and tooth disease. Gum disease increases as one gets older.

If you wear glasses, see your eye doctor for regular checkups. If you do not wear glasses, you still need checkups because your vision can change anytime. Glaucoma, which can lead to blindness, can cause major damage even before any symptoms develop. If you wear contact lenses, always follow the instructions for use and cleaning. Discard contact lens solutions after the expiration date.

Protect your hearing. Loud noise and music can lead to hearing loss. Avoid loud music in a headset.

Safety Practices

Injuries are a major cause of death and disability. Prevent injuries with good safety habits in your home, motor vehicle, work, and recreation.

Safety at Home

Millions of injuries occur in homes each year. Good safety habits will make your home safer (Figure 15–5). Safety at home is fairly simple and relies mostly on common sense. Look around your home and think "safety"—what can you do to prevent any possible injury? The following steps will help make your home a safer place:

- Post emergency numbers and other important numbers near all phones.
- Make sure that stairways and hallways are well lighted.
- Equip stairways with handrails. If elderly people live in your home, put grab rails by the toilet and in the bathtub or showers. If small children live in your home, put gates at the head and foot of the stairways.
- Keep medicines and poisonous substances separate from each other and out of reach of children in secured cabinets. (See Chapter 14 for more poisoning prevention ideas.)
- Keep your heating and cooling systems and all appliances in good working order. Check heating and cooling systems annually before use.
- Follow instructions for electrical tools, appliances, and toys.
- Turn off the oven and other appliances after use. Unplug heat-producing appliances such as an iron, curling iron, or portable heater.
- Make sure your home has a working fire extinguisher that is easy to reach.

PREVENT INJURIES AT HOME

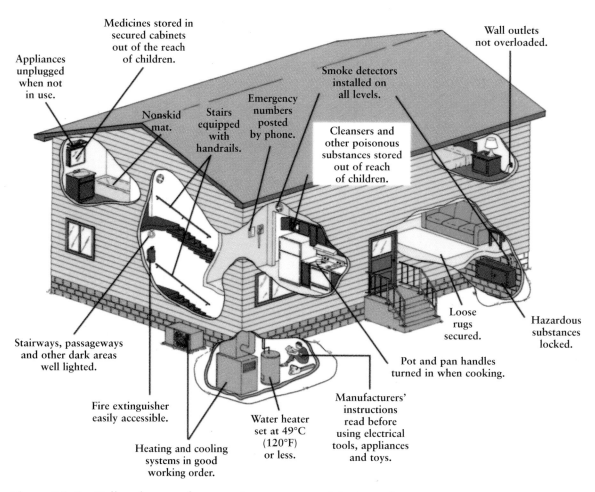

Figure 15–5 Follow home safety practices to prevent injuries at home.

- Keep firearms in a locked place, out of the reach of children, and separate from ammunition.

This list does not include all the safety measures you need to take in your home. If young children or elderly individuals live with you, take additional steps. See the Canadian Red Cross Society book *ChildSafe* for more information on making your home safe for infants and small children.

Fire safety

Fires are caused by heating equipment, appliances, electrical wiring, cooking, and in other unexpected ways.

Plan and practice a fire escape route with your family (Figure 15–6):

- Gather all family members and housemates. Sketch a floor plan of all rooms with doors, windows, and hallways. Include each floor of the home.
- Draw the escape plan with arrows showing two ways, if possible, to get out of each room. Sleeping areas are most important, since most fires happen at night. Plan to use stairs only.
- Plan where everyone will meet after leaving the building.
- Assign someone to call the fire department after leaving the burning building. Many locations use 9-1-1 for the emergency number. When you travel, take a moment to find out the local emergency number and keep it on hand.

Practice these guidelines for escape from fire:

- If there is smoke, crawl low to escape. As smoke rises, breathable air is often close to the floor.
- Make sure children can open windows, go down a ladder, or lower themselves to the ground. Practice with them. Always lower children to the ground first before you go out.
- Get out quickly and never return to a burning building.
- If you cannot get out, stay in the room and stuff door cracks and vents with towels,

rags, or clothing. If there is a phone, call the fire department, even if rescuers are already outside, and tell the dispatcher your exact location.

Ask your local fire department for other safety guidelines.

It is best to try to prevent burns and fires in the first place with these guidelines:

- Install smoke detectors on every floor of your home and maintain them. Many homes have smoke detectors that do not work because of old or missing batteries. A handy way to remember the batteries is to change them twice a year when you reset your clocks for daylight savings time.
- Keep a fire extinguisher in the kitchen and know how to use it.

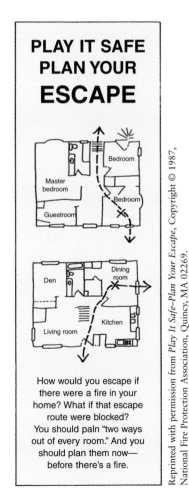

Reprinted with permission from *Play It Safe–Plan Your Escape*, Copyright © 1987, National Fire Protection Association, Quincy, MA 02269.

Figure 15–6   Plan a fire escape route for your home.

- Turn pots on the stove so that their handles do not stick out.
- Lift the far edge of lids on hot pans first to prevent burns from steam.
- Keep flammables and matches out of the reach of children.
- Always take special care when smoking.
- Don't leave children alone while you cook.
- Keep all electrical cords clear of counter edges where toddlers may pull on them and cause appliances to fall on them.
- Double check before leaving the kitchen to make sure that burners are turned off.
- Keep curtains and clothing away from fireplaces and stoves.

Fire safety away from home is also important. Knowing how to exit from a hotel in a fire could save your life.

- Find the fire exits and extinguishers on your floor.
- If you hear an alarm while in your room, feel the door first and do not open it if it is hot (Figure 15–7).
- Do not use the elevator.
- If the hall is not smoky, use the stairs to leave. If the hall is filled with smoke, crawl to the exit.
- If you cannot get to the exit, go back to your room. Turn off the ventilation system, stuff door cracks and vents with wet towels, and telephone the front desk or the fire department to report the fire and your location.

Safety at Work

Most people spend a third of their day at work. To be safe at work, follow these guidelines:

- Know fire evacuation procedures.
- Know the location of the nearest fire extinguisher and first aid kit.
- Keep flammable substances away from heat, sparks, and flame. Never pour a flammable liquid down the drain.

- Wear appropriate safety gear for the job, including protective eye wear. Wear appropriate clothing. When around machinery, avoid loose clothing and jewelry that may become caught in it.
- Follow safety rules when operating or using any equipment or hand tools.
- Take care around compressed air and compressed gas cylinders. Use, move, and store gas cylinders correctly.
- Be sure the work place is clean and orderly, with noncluttered and nonslippery floors and aisles and unobstructed stairways and exits.
- Follow safe practices when using ladders and stepladders.
- Handle work materials carefully, and use correct methods for lifting and carrying heavy loads.

Figure 15–7 In a fire do not open a door if it feels hot.

- When working with hazardous materials, pay attention to warning labels and safety data sheets from Workplace Hazardous Materials Information Systems (WHMIS).
- Make sure the employer and other workers support safety practices and comply with appropriate regulations of the Occupational Health and Safety Act.
- Be aware of other recommended safety equipment and procedures (Figure 15–8).

Motor Vehicle Safety

For safety in motor vehicles, follow these guidelines:

- **Buckle up—always.** Wearing a seat belt is the easiest and best way to prevent injury in a motor vehicle collision.
- **Infants and children should always ride in approved and properly installed safety seats.**
- Teenagers and others learning to drive should receive adequate training, such as in drivers' education courses.
- Always obey the rules of the road.
- Watch for pedestrians and cyclists in the road.
- Drive only when alert. Do not drive after drinking alcohol, taking drugs, or using medication with a sedative effect, or when feeling especially tired.

Figure 15–8 Safety clothing and/or equipment are required for some jobs.

- Be sure the vehicle is in safe condition, with brakes, tires, lights, and exhaust system all working properly.

Follow these guidelines for boats and recreational vehicles as well.

Safety at Play

In sports and other recreational activities, you can prevent injuries and stay safe by always following guidelines for the activity and wearing the right protective headgear (Figure 15–9).

- When bicycling, always wear a CSA-approved helmet. This guideline includes children who even ride on the sidewalk using training wheels. Keep off roads that are busy or have no shoulder. Wear reflective clothing, use bicycle lights, and have reflectors on your bike wheels if you ride at night.
- Boaters should take the Red Cross *On Board* accredited boating course or other boating safety courses to learn safe boating practices.
- With any activity in which eyes could be injured, such as racquetball, wear protective goggles. Proper shoes can also prevent injuries. For contact sports, wear properly fitted protective equipment. Above all, follow the rules of the sport.
- If you do not know how to swim, learn how. Always wear an approved personal flotation device while on a boat or around the water. Look before you dive. Always supervise children around any kind of water, including swimming pools and bathtubs. Two thirds of all drownings happen to people who never intended to be in the water at all.
- If you run, jog, or walk, plan your route carefully. Exercise only in well-lighted, well-populated areas. Keep off busy roads. If you must exercise outdoors at night, wear reflective clothing and move facing traffic.
- Whenever you do start a new activity, such as boating, skiing, or motorcycle riding, take

lessons to learn how to participate safely. Many injuries result from inexperience. Make sure your equipment is in good working order. Ski bindings, for instance, should be inspected, adjusted, and lubricated by professionals before each season.

Good Health for Special Groups

Sexually Active Individuals

Early chapters of this book describe how to prevent the transmission of HIV, the virus that causes AIDS, when giving first aid. HIV is most commonly transmitted via sexual activity through the exchange of body fluids. Sexually active individuals can protect themselves from HIV by practicing safe sex, such as by using a condom. Safe sex practices are important even if both partners believe they do not have the virus, because it can live in the body for many years after being transmitted without causing any symptoms. Safe sex practices can also help prevent the transmission of hepatitis B and many other sexually transmitted diseases.

Figure 15–9 Wear proper safety equipment during recreational activities.

Expectant Mothers

Good prenatal care starts even before your baby is conceived. Get your body in shape for pregnancy by attaining your ideal weight, getting plenty of rest, and making sure you have been immunized against diseases such as rubella (German measles). Rubella can cause devastating birth defects.

Before becoming pregnant, stop smoking, stop drinking alcohol, and take no medications unless advised by your doctor. You may be four to six weeks' pregnant by the time you know it, and these substances can be very harmful to the fetus.

Prepare for parenthood by learning infant care in advance. Doctors, hospitals, and community organizations offer classes. When you become pregnant, follow your obstetrician's or midwife's advice about nutrition, exercise, and other good health habits.

Older Adults

For older adults an active social life is a part of good health. Regular physical activity, such as daily walks, can add to both physical and psychological well-being (Figure 15–10). Some older people have special dietary needs. Because appetite often decreases with age, meals must be planned carefully for good nutrition.

Figure 15–10   Older adults can benefit from regular physical activity.

Adults over 40 need medical checkups at least once a year. Taking too many medications can be a problem, so patients or the family should frequently ask the doctor to review prescriptions. Adults over 65 should also receive an annual flu shot.

Falls are the leading cause of injuries among older adults. Good lighting, railings on staircases, and nonslip floors and rugs make for safer footing. Bathtubs and showers should have safety hand rails installed.

Personal Preparedness for Disasters

Disasters and personal emergencies can and do happen anywhere in Canada. House fires, severe storms, floods, earthquakes, industrial emergencies, and other natural disasters can strike without warning. Such emergencies may also include incidents such as large-scale hazardous material spills or fires, industrial fires or explosions, airplane crashes or multiple-vehicle highway pileups, power and utility outages, and so on. Such disasters can disrupt not only your personal life but also the entire community. This section helps you prepare for the possibility of an emergency so that you are better able to care for yourself and your loved ones.

The key to personal preparedness is first to identify the potential for disasters in your home, work place, or recreational area. Then anticipate what you need to do to survive the disaster and care for yourself and others if additional assistance is not immediately available. Take steps to have the right supplies ready, to be sure everyone has the right information and training, and to practice what you will do should disaster occur. First aid training is a key part of this personal preparedness.

What you do to prepare depends in part on the type of disaster that may occur. For example, you might need to have enough water and food for 3 days to be ready for surviving after an earthquake. However, in an isolated area prone to long-lasting blizzards, one might be snowed in and unable to renew food or water supplies for much longer than 3 days.

Consider Potential Disasters

Talk with your local Red Cross about what disasters can occur in your area. Then follow these guidelines:

- Ask how to prepare for each type of disaster.
- Ask how you would be warned in an emergency.
- Learn your community's evacuation routes.
- Ask about special assistance for elderly or people with disabilities.
- Ask at your work place about emergency plans.
- Learn the emergency plans at your children's school or day care centre.

Develop an Emergency Plan

- Meet with household members and talk about the dangers of fire, severe weather, and other emergencies possible in your area.
- Discuss how your household would respond to each type of disaster.
- Plan what to do in case of power outages or personal injuries.
- Draw a floor plan of your home and mark two escape routes from each room.
- Learn how to turn off the water, gas, and electricity at the main switches. After a disaster, these utilities should be reconnected only after they have been inspected by the respective utility company.
- Post emergency telephone numbers near telephones.

- Teach children how and when to call emergency numbers.
- Instruct household members to turn on the radio for emergency information.
- Pick one local and one distant friend or relative for family members to call if separated by disaster. Teach children how to call long distance.
- Pick two meeting places—one near the home in case of fire, one outside the neighborhood in case you cannot return home after a disaster.
- Take a first aid course.
- Keep family records in a waterproof and fireproof container.

Prepare an Emergency Supplies Kit

Have supplies ready for an emergency. Store them in a backpack or duffle bag so you can take them with you if you have to evacuate.

- A water supply of 4 litres per person per day. Use sealed, unbreakable containers. Date them and replace the supply every 6 months.
- Nonperishable packaged or canned food with can opener. Replace food once a year.
- A change of clothing, walking shoes, and rain gear.
- Blankets or sleeping bags.
- First aid kit and prescription medications.
- Toilet paper and other personal supplies.
- Extra pair of glasses.
- Battery-powered radio and flashlight, with extra batteries.
- Credit cards and cash.
- Extra set of car keys.
- List of family doctors.
- Important family information such as medical conditions and any medical devices used, such as pacemakers.
- Special items needed for infants, elderly, or disabled household members.

Prepare an Emergency Car Kit

- Battery-powered radio and flashlight, with extra batteries.
- Blanket.
- Booster (jumper) cables.
- Fire extinguisher.
- First aid kit and manual.
- Bottled water and nonperishable high-energy foods.
- Maps.
- Shovel.
- Flares.
- Tire repair kit and pump.
- Matches and a "survival" candle in a deep can.

Prepare the Home

Inspect the home for anything that might cause injury or damage in a disaster. Anything that can move, fall, break, or cause a fire is a potential hazard.

- Repair any defective wiring or leaky gas connections.
- Be sure shelves are secure.
- Put large heavy objects on lower shelves.
- Hang pictures and mirrors away from beds.
- Be sure overhead light fixtures are well braced.
- Strap the water heater to wall studs to secure it.
- Repair any cracks in walls, ceiling, or foundation.
- Store any poisonous or flammable substances away from heat sources.
- Clean and repair chimneys, flue pipes, vent connectors, and gas vents.
- To prevent fire, follow the guidelines given in Chapter 12.

After a Disaster

Preparedness also involves knowing what to do after a disaster occurs.

- Check for physical hazards resulting from the disaster. Use a flashlight to check for broken gas lines, downed wires or damage to the house electrical wires or structural damage that could result in dangerous conditions. Watch out for broken glass. Move people out of unsafe areas.
- Unless you need to call EMS, stay off the telephone, because telephone lines may be needed by others with emergencies.
- Listen to your local radio station on your battery-powered radio for instructions.
- Continue to monitor your surroundings and watch for developing unsafe conditions. Natural disasters can upset natural balances and lead to unusual problems, such as snakes entering dwellings after flooding.
- Register with the local Red Cross if you are separated from your family as a result of an emergency.
- Cooperate fully with disaster rescue workers. In large-scale disasters many EMS professionals, police, firefighters, Red Cross volunteers, and others will be involved in meeting the medical and other needs of those affected by the disaster. These people have been specially trained for such disasters, and your patience and cooperation help ensure that both you and others will get the assistance you need to cope with the situation.
- Check on your neighbours, especially the elderly or people with disabilities.
- If you have to evacuate, wear protective clothing and sturdy shoes. Take your emergency supplies kit. Lock your home when you leave, and use travel routes specified by local officials.

Summary

- You can achieve a healthier lifestyle by
  Eating healthy foods
  Exercising
  Controlling stress

- Break habits like smoking, over-eating, or drinking alcohol.

- Schedule regular, appropriate medical and dental care.

- Prevent injuries through safety practices at home, work, and play.

- Identify potential disasters and be prepared for them.

Appendix A:
First Aid Supplies

First Aid Kit

Keep a first aid kit readily available in your home, cottage, automobile, boat, work place, and recreation area (Figure A–1). Store it in a dry place and replace used and outdated contents regularly. A first aid kit should contain the following:

1. Emergency telephone numbers for EMS, the poison control centre, and personal physicians. Include the home and office phone numbers of family members, friends, or neighbours who can help.
2. Sterile gauze pads (dressings), in small and large squares to place over wounds.
3. Adhesive tape.
4. Roller and triangular bandages to hold dressings in place or to make an arm sling.
5. Adhesive bandages in assorted sizes.
6. Scissors.
7. Tweezers.
8. Safety pins.
9. Ice bag or chemical ice pack.
10. Disposable gloves such as surgical or examination gloves.
11. Flashlight, with extra batteries in a separate bag.

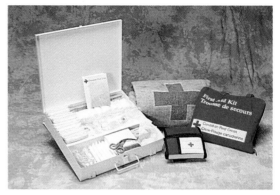

Figure A–1 Be prepared for emergencies with a well-stocked first aid kit.

12. Antiseptic wipes or soap.
13. Pencil and pad.
14. Emergency blanket.
15. Eye patches.
16. Thermometer.
17. Barrier devices (i.e., pocket mask or face shield and gloves).
18. Coins for pay phone.
19. Canadian Red Cross First Aid manual.

For more information on the different models of Canadian Red Cross First Aid kits available, please contact your local Red Cross office.

Appendix B: Sample Examination Questions

If you are registered in an Emergency First Aid course, you should answer questions *1 through 25 and* *51.* If you are registered in a Standard First Aid course you should answer all 51 questions.

---

1. What are the Fundamental Principles of the International Red Cross and Red Crescent Movement?
   1. Nonprofit, international, safety
   2. Relief, development, first aid
   3. Humanity, universality, unity, neutrality
   4. Impartiality, independence, voluntary service
      a. 1 and 2
      b. 1 and 3
      c. 2 and 4
      d. 3 and 4

2. The Red Cross is an international, nonprofit, humanitarian organization dedicated to helping people through response to emergencies and disasters, and educational programs.
   a. True
   b. False

3. Which of the following statements best describes the emergency medical services (EMS) system?
   a. The EMS system provides an ambulance to transport the casualty to the hospital.
   b. Personnel and equipment for removing casualties from dangerous locations are part of the EMS system.
   c. The EMS system consists of community resources organized to care for casualties of sudden illness or injury.
   d. The EMS system is organized to prevent the occurrence of injuries and sudden illness.

4. When calling EMS personnel for help, three things you tell the dispatcher are your name, the address, and the phone number from which you are calling.
   a. True
   b. False

5. Why is it necessary to complete a primary survey in every emergency situation?
   a. To check for minor injuries
   b. To determine if there are any life-threatening conditions that need immediate care
   c. To get consent from the casualty before providing care
   d. To ask for information about the cause of the illness or injury

6. In what order do you assess the three elements of a primary survey?
   a. Airway, circulation, breathing
   b. Breathing, airway, circulation
   c. Circulation, airway, breathing
   d. Airway, breathing, circulation

7. If a casualty's behaviour threatens your safety while you are attempting to provide first aid, what should you do?
   a. Try to restrain the casualty and prevent harm to yourself and others
   b. Attempt to calm the casualty by gently touching his or her arm and talking softly
   c. Try speaking forcefully and authoritatively to the casualty to gain cooperation
   d. Withdraw from the immediate area and wait for EMS personnel

8. A car has crashed into a power pole, and a live electrical wire is draped over its roof. The driver of the car is slumped against the steering wheel and appears to be bleeding heavily from a facial injury. What should be your immediate action in this situation?
   a. Approach the driver and determine if he is conscious and breathing
   b. Move the live wire off the car using rubber gloves and a dry branch or pole
   c. Stay back from the car and call EMS personnel to deal with the situation
   d. Instruct the driver to carefully open the door and jump clear of the car

9. You have decided to give rescue breathing to a casualty of respiratory arrest. Which technique should you use to keep the airway open when there is no suspected head or spinal injury?
   a. Chin lift
   b. Head tilt/neck lift
   c. Jaw thrust without head tilt
   d. Head tilt/chin lift

10. What should you do for a conscious adult casualty who is choking and cannot speak, cough, or breathe?
    a. Give abdominal thrusts
    b. Give two full breaths
    c. Do a finger sweep
    d. Lower the casualty to the floor and open the airway

11. A woman is choking on a piece of candy but is conscious and coughing forcefully. What should you do?
    a. Slap her on the back until she coughs up the object
    b. Give abdominal thrusts
    c. Encourage her to continue coughing
    d. Do a finger sweep

12. Trying to swallow large pieces of food is a common cause of choking.
    a. True
    b. False

13. For which condition should you give rescue breathing?
    a. Respiratory distress
    b. Acute angina
    c. Asthma
    d. Respiratory arrest

14. Air in the stomach rarely causes vomiting during rescue breathing.
    a. True
    b. False

15. When performing rescue breathing, what should you do after giving the first two full breaths?
    a. Adjust the head tilt to a neutral position and continue rescue breathing
    b. Check for signs of circulation; if present, continue rescue breathing
    c. Continue rescue breathing if the casualty has no heartbeat
    d. Call for help from EMS personnel

16. Which is one of the major functions of blood?
    a. Transporting nutrients and oxygen
    b. Carrying minerals to bones
    c. Maintaining pressure within blood vessels
    d. Preventing internal bleeding

17. Casualties of heart attack do not always experience chest pain.
    a. True
    b. False

18. In which position should you place a casualty who may be experiencing a heart attack?
    a. Lying on his or her left side
    b. Sitting or semi-sitting
    c. His or her most comfortable position
    d. Lying on his or her back with legs elevated

19. The ratio of compressions to ventilations in adult one-rescuer cardiopulmonary resuscitation is:
    a. 15 compressions to 1 ventilation
    b. 15 compressions to 2 ventilations
    c. 5 compressions to 1 ventilation
    d. 5 compressions to 2 ventilations

20. Cardiopulmonary resuscitation is needed
    a. When the casualty is not breathing
    b. When the casualty's heart stops beating
    c. For every heart attack casualty
    d. When the heart attack casualty loses consciousness

21. If chest compressions and rescue breathing are not started, how long after cardiac arrest will brain cells begin to die?
    a. Immediately
    b. 2 to 4 minutes
    c. 4 to 6 minutes
    d. 10 minutes or more

22. Which is the first step in managing external bleeding?
    a. Add bulky dressings to reinforce blood-soaked bandages
    b. Apply pressure at a pressure point
    c. Apply direct pressure with a clean or sterile pad
    d. Move the casualty away from danger

23. Two of the major concerns associated with open wounds are severe bleeding and infection.
    a. True
    b. False

24. The purpose of the secondary survey is to
    a. Find injuries or conditions that are not immediately life threatening.
    b. Determine if the casualty is bleeding severely.
    c. Survey the scene for hazardous conditions.
    d. Find out if the casualty has medical insurance.

25. Which steps should you include in the secondary survey?
    a. Interviewing the casualty and surveying the scene
    b. Sending a bystander to call EMS personnel and doing a head-to-toe examination
    c. Looking for hazards around the casualty and checking for changes in the casualty's breathing
    d. Doing a head-to-toe examination and interviewing bystanders

YOU HAVE COMPLETED THE EMERGENCY FIRST AID PORTION. PLEASE GO DIRECTLY TO QUESTION 51.

26. Five signs of internal bleeding are rapid, weak pulse; rapid breathing; nausea and vomiting; excessive thirst; and discolouration of skin in the injured area.
    a. True
    b. False

27. What should you do if you suspect serious internal bleeding?
    a. Call EMS personnel immediately
    b. Apply pressure at the closest pressure point
    c. Place an ice pack on the affected area
    d. Wrap a pressure bandage around the affected area

28. Which sign of shock results from a prolonged lack of oxygen?
    a. Excessive thirst
    b. Weakness
    c. Pale, moist skin
    d. Anxiety

29. Casualties of serious chest or abdominal injuries may develop the signals of shock resulting from
    a. Loss of blood into the chest or abdomen
    b. Breathing difficulty
    c. Severe pain from fractures and wounds
    d. All of the above

30. Which can cause a casualty to develop shock?
    a. Severe blood loss
    b. Extensive burns
    c. Injury to the spinal cord
    d. All of the above

31. Wait to give care to minimize shock until you have completed a secondary survey.
    a. True
    b. False

32. Which signals would make you suspect that a person has had a stroke?
    1. Numbness or weakness in one arm
    2. Sudden, severe headache
    3. Slurred speech
    4. Loss of bladder control
        a. 1, 2, and 4
        b. 2, 3, and 4
        c. All of the above

33. You should immediately call EMS personnel for burns resulting from an explosion or electricity.
    a. True
    b. False

34. When one body system is seriously injured, there is no effect on the other body systems.
    a. True
    b. False

35. If a person has sustained a severe head injury, you should care for him or her as a possible spinal injury casualty as well.
    a. True
    b. False

36. Which is the proper first aid care for an injured person showing blood or fluid discharge from the right ear?
    a. Place the casualty on his or her right side with the involved ear down
    b. Cover the ear lightly with a sterile dressing
    c. Control the discharge with direct pressure and gauze packing
    d. Leave the ear uncovered to drain and elevate the head

37. Nausea or vomiting is one of the signs of a head injury.
    a. True
    b. False

38. What should you not do to correctly splint a suspected fracture of the lower leg?
    a. Have a bystander help you straighten the leg before you apply a rigid splint
    b. Leave the leg unsplinted until the casualty can be moved to an ambulance
    c. Apply a rigid splint padded to fit the leg and secure with bandages
    d. Bandage the leg using bulky dressings to immobilize the fracture area

39. You have splinted a suspected closed fracture of the forearm and determined that the casualty has no other injuries. It would now be appropriate for you to arrange transport of the casualty to a medical facility.
    a. True
    b. False

40. Which should be included in your first aid care for a wound with minimal bleeding and superficial damage?
    a. Washing the wound with soap and water before controlling bleeding
    b. Stopping the bleeding
    c. Applying a sterile dressing over the wound and then a bandage
    d. All of the above

41. First aid care for a first-degree sunburn should include application of ointments.
    a. True
    b. False

42. In most cases, the proper position for a casualty of a nosebleed is sitting with the head tilted back.
    a. True
    b. False

43. The three conditions that can result from overexposure to heat are
    a. Heat cramps, heat stroke, and heat strain
    b. Heat stress, heat exhaustion, and heat strain
    c. Heat sensitivity, heat shock, and heat stroke
    d. Heat cramps, heat exhaustion, and heat stroke

44. A casualty of hypothermia will have a glassy stare and an increasingly aggressive attitude as the condition worsens.
    a. True
    b. False

45. Which signals would you see in a casualty of a diabetic emergency?
    a. Rapid pulse, slow breathing, changes in consciousness
    b. Rapid pulse, rapid breathing, changes in consciousness
    c. Normal pulse, rapid breathing, normal consciousness
    d. Slow pulse, normal breathing, normal consciousness

46. In caring for a casualty having a convulsion, you should
    a. Move any nearby objects that might cause injury
    b. Try to hold the casualty still
    c. Place something between the casualty's teeth
    d. Douse the casualty with water

47. Two of the signs and symptoms of hypothermia are
    a. Frostbite, shivering
    b. High fever, numbness
    c. Shivering, numbness
    d. All of the above

48. A casualty who has ingested poison is conscious. You should give him water to drink as soon as possible to dilute the poison and then you should call the poison centre for further instructions.
    a. True
    b. False

49. Which of the following poisons should not be eliminated by inducing vomiting?
    a. Poisonous foods, such as berries
    b. Corrosive compounds, such as drain cleaner
    c. Medications, such as sleeping pills
    d. Alcoholic beverages

50. To avoid an unintentional misuse or overdose of a prescription drug, you should know
    a. The effects of the drug.
    b. The potential side effects of the drug.
    c. The drugs with which it will interact.
    d. All of the above.

51. What will you do to prevent emergency situations and injuries after you leave this course?

    In your home? _____

    _____

    At your work place? _____

    _____

    In your community? _____

    _____

Appendix C: Sample Examination Answers

Note to the Instructor:

Question 51 is not to be graded. Instead, please encourage your learners to follow through on the actions they proposed in their personal answers. It is the Red Cross' hope that they will embrace injury prevention and healthy lifestyles in order to help reduce the number of preventable deaths occurring in Canada each year.

1. D	11. C	21. C	31. B	41. B
2. A	12. A	22. C	32. C	42. B
3. C	13. D	23. A	33. A	43. D
4. A	14. B	24. A	34. B	44. B
5. B	15. B	25. D	35. A	45. B
6. D	16. A	26. A	36. B	46. A
7. D	17. A	27. A	37. A	47. C
8. C	18. C	28. C	38. A	48. B
9. D	19. B	29. D	39. A	49. B
10. A	20. B	30. D	40. D	50. D

Index